The Unofficial

PATRICIA
CORNWELL
COMPANION

Also by George Beahm

The Vaughn Bode Index
Kirk's Works
How to Buy a Woodstove—and Not Get Burned!
The Stephen King Companion
The Stephen King Story
War of Words: The Censorship Debate
Michael Jordan: A Shooting Star
The Stephen King Companion (revised edition)
The Unauthorized Anne Rice Companion
Stephen King: America's Best-Loved Boogeyman
Stephen King from A to Z
Stephen King Collectibles: An Annotated Price Guide
Straight Talk for Tough Times

The Unofficial

PATRICIA CORNWELL COMPANION

GEORGE BEAHM

St. Martin's Minotaur New York

www.minotaurbooks.com

"Author Had Long Struggle with Book," by Dannye Romine. This newspaper article originally in the *Charlotte Observer* (Charlotte, N.C.) and is reprinted with permission.

"Forensic Institute a Reality," by Michael Hardy. This newspaper article originally appeared in the *Richmond Times-Dispatch* (Richmond, Va.). The article is © *Richmond Times-Dispatch*. Used with permission.

Cornwell interviewed by Paul Duncan, for *Deadly Women*. The interview is © 1997 Paul Duncan, reprinted with the author's permission. This is a shortened version of the interview in *The Third Degree: Crime Writers in Conversation*, edited by Paul Duncan.

"A Book Signing in Boston," by Kevin Quigley. This article is © 2001 by Kevin Quigley and was written especially for this book.

"So You Want to Be a Medical Detective." This originally appeared as text for a brochure published in 1993 by the National Association of Medical Examiners and is reprinted with the permission of its executive director, Denise Settlemoir.

Abbreviations in the Scarpetta novels, compiled by Birger Nielsen. This originally appeared on Nielsen's Web site and is reprinted with the permission of the author.

Cornwell interviewed by *Publishers Weekly*. This article originally appeared in *Publishers Weekly* and is reprinted with permission.

The excerpted book reviews from *Publishers Weekly* are reprinted with the permission of the magazine.

The excerpted book reviews from *Kirkus Reviews* are reprinted with the permission of the magazine.

The excerpted book reviews from *Library Journal* are published with the permission of *Library Journal,* a publication of Cahners Business Information, a division of Reed Elsevier. These include: *The Body Farm* (Sept. 1, 1994, issue), *Point of Origin* (April 15, 1999, issue), and *The Last Precinct* (October 15, 2000, issue).

Library of Congress Cataloging-in-Publication Data

Beahm, George W.
    The unofficial Patricia Cornwell companion / by George Beahm.—1st ed.
      p. cm.
    ISBN 0-312-30732-2
    1. Cornwell, Patricia Daniels—Characters Kay Scarpetta—Handbooks, manuals, etc. 2. Detective and mystery stories, American—Handbooks, manuals, etc. 3. Scarpetta, Kay (Fictitious character)—Handbooks, manuals, etc. 4. Richmond, (Va.)—In literature—Handbooks, manuals, etc. 5. Medical fiction, American—Handbooks, manuals, etc. I. Title.

PS3553.O692 Z53 2002
813'.54—dc21

2002069834

First Edition: October 2002

10 9 8 7 6 5 4 3 2 1

Semper Fidelis

To Ronald and Richard Doran,
two stars in a field of blue

CONTENTS

ACKNOWLEDGMENTS

Rounding Up the Usual Suspects

Writing a book is a solitary act, but publishing it requires a team effort.

I'd like to publicly acknowledge the following fine folks who were instrumental on this project:

- The fine folks at the *Richmond Times-Dispatch,* who provided me with much-needed resources—photos, faxes of key pieces, and photocopies from the paper's library, appropriately termed the Morgue.
- *Jan Blodgett,* college archivist and records management coordinator at the library of Davidson College (Charlotte, North Carolina), for research assistance, photocopying of much-needed files, and coordination.
- *Otto Penzler,* who took the time to give me an interview and proofread it afterward for corrections.
- *Kathy Reichs,* who took time from her too busy schedule to give me an interview, suggest additional resources, and coordinate efforts with her publisher to send me material.

- *Kevin Quigley,* a talented writer who, as usual, stopped everything he was doing to help with this project.
- *Gary Ink* at *Publishers Weekly,* who has, over the years, always gotten back to me quickly whenever I've asked for permission to reprint, for several book projects.
- *Arthur Morey,* the managing editor at Renaissance Press, who took the time to write a lengthy letter suggesting much-needed editorial advice that improved the manuscript immeasurably.
- *Amanda Pisani,* my former editor at Renaissance Press, who helped whip this book into shape. She is, as Morey explained to me, "very bright, also experienced and brings a fresh set of eyes to the project." She's all of that . . . and more.
- *Ben Sevier,* my editor at St. Martin's Press, who editorially took the book to the finish line.
- *Heather Florence,* who painstakingly read the manuscript to insure it was vetted for legal concerns.
- *Colleen Doran,* a fellow creator, a treasured friend who always know when I could use a much-needed coffee break. (This book is dedicated to her father, Ronald, and brother, Richard.)
- My wife, *Mary,* before whom I am at a loss for words.

Finally, I wish to thank Patricia Cornwell, for her books and many hours of pleasurable reading.

If I've left anyone out, I apologize.

Thank you, one and all.

I'd say she and I both have lives consumed by what we do and what we believe. It's that I express mine in a different way than she does. She actually works the cases and I tell the story of the cases. I have said many times that what I really consider myself to be is a scribe to the people out there doing the real work, whether it is the forensic pathologists, the FBI agents, the police, the scientists, the prosecutors. Someone needs to tell their stories, go in their labs and find out exactly what they're doing today. . . . They need someone like me to do that, and that's really what I consider my job.

For one to say that Scarpetta is obsessive or driven is like saying that a priest is. It's like a calling. She has taken on the mantle to help people who have no power. She's like a missionary or a minister or priest to the people who can no longer speak in a language that other people can understand. That's the way I regard what I do, too.

—ON HERSELF AND SCARPETTA: PATRICIA CORNWELL
INTERVIEWED BY PAUL DUNCAN

INTRODUCTION

If somebody translated your life for you, it would be very unnerv-
ing, wouldn't it?
— PATRICIA CORNWELL, QUOTED BY DANNY ROMINE,
THE *Charlotte Observer*

I focused on my goal—to shoot Patricia Cornwell—and realized
the best opportunity would present itself at her upcoming Barnes
& Noble book signing in Richmond, where she would fly in on
her personal helicopter. She would be signing her latest Kay Scarpetta novel, *Cause of Death*.

On the day of the signing, I arrived late. It'd be easier to blend
in. I immediately headed inside, making straight for the rear of
the bookstore where Cornwell was seated behind a table, flanked
by Richmond police. She is dressed casually, in T-shirt and jeans,
and chats briefly with each customer who has stood in line for
hours to get her name scrawled in bold script on the title page of
Cause of Death with a black Sharpie pen.

I thought I was unobtrusive, since she never gave me any indication that she noticed me, so I began firing away . . . with my
Nikon camera.

After four companion-style books—on Michael Jordan, Stephen
King, Anne Rice, and censorship—I wanted to write a fifth, and
my last, before moving on to new fields.

As with Jordan, King, and Rice, the figure would have to be someone I felt had led an instructive life, someone who hadn't been written about previously in a companion book—this time, someone who lived in Virginia.

The list quickly narrowed down to one writer: Patricia Daniels Cornwell.

Unlike King and Rice, who had been covered exhaustively in the media at large and in books studying their work, Cornwell has kept a low profile: no book-length works had been published about her or her work, and because she zealously guards her time and personal access, especially with the media, only a handful of profile pieces had been published to date, few of them flattering.

Understanding Cornwell

Rather appropriately, given the kind of book she writes, Cornwell as a private figure is shrouded in mystery. Despite being in the public eye since the publication of *Postmortem* in 1990, Cornwell prefers to concentrate on writing books, tending to business, overseeing her staff on both coasts, and spending as little time as possible with the media. In other words, Cornwell is one of those rare celebrities who prefers to mind her own business and would prefer that other people let her live life on her own terms.

As Cornwell has found out over the years, the books aren't enough to satisfy her fans, who want to know more about Kay Scarpetta and about Cornwell herself. To satisfy them, Cornwell has posted an official Web site currently under construction, which answers most (if not all) of the questions her fans have posed over the years, and also provides photos, news stories, notifications of upcoming personal appearances, and a mixture of need-to-know information and trivia.

Of the forty-eight frequently asked questions she answers, most have to do with publication of her books, the writer's life, and the inevitable requests for information on her favorite restaurants, wines, desserts, color, actors, food—take your pick. Cornwell's readers, it seems, are consumed not only by Scarpetta's world but by Cornwell's world, as well.

The bedrock of Patricia Cornwell—the solid foundation on which she has built her life and the fictional life of Kay Scarpetta—is her personal credo, simply stated on her Web site: "Enlightenment. Justice. Do no harm. Fight the fight. Leave the world better than you found it."

Cornwell's crest, emblazoned on her personal stationery, her clothing, and of course her helicopter, is a visual representation of her credo, her philosophy of life that finds expression professionally and personally.

Cornwell's crest can be found on caps and shirts for sale, with all the proceeds going toward charitable causes. In addition, Cornwell has been a major benefactor to many worthy causes, making her one of the city's most prominent philanthropists. When she opens up her heart, she inevitably opens up her wallet as well, generously giving back to the local community. I suspect she's donated a lot more than she'd care to admit, which makes her the target for every organization that wants to hit on her.

Dr. Kay Scarpetta

Ever since the publication of *Postmortem,* Cornwell fans have wondered how much of Cornwell (and, to some extent, Dr. Marcella Fierro) can be found in the fictional character of Dr. Kay Scarpetta.

Cornwell is quick to point out that making a fictional character real is not simply a matter of personality transposition: Scarpetta is not merely a thinly disguised Patricia Cornwell or, for that matter,

Dr. Fierro. Well-rounded fictional characters have a life of their own, as Cornwell found out when the eleventh Scarpetta novel stubbornly resisted writing. (As it turned out, Scarpetta has a mind of her own and refused to play a role in the plot that Cornwell had written—a plot that was reworked into that of the third Judy Hammer novel, *Isle of Dogs,* published in 2001. A good cook, after all, lets nothing go to waste.)

Who knows what evil lurks in the hearts of men? Dr. Kay Scarpetta knows, for she has often seen the results of their evil handiwork: the victims and their relatives who come to her office to look for answers, to seek empathy, to achieve closure.

Scarpetta fights the good fight. Scarpetta clearly subscribes to a major tenet of Cornwell: Leave the world a better place than you found it. Be a force for good. Know that you don't win every battle; but if you win enough of them, then perhaps you'll win the war. At least you don't go down without a fight. It's this philosophy that has no doubt earned Scarpetta and Cornwell their legions of fans.

Cornwell, who has stated that she writes about the world she lives in, understandably finds little rhyme or reason as to why bad things happen to good people. She does, however, realize that it's a never-ending war, and that Scarpetta cannot simply look the other way: The damning evidence, in the form of a homicide victim, attests to the enduring nature of evil.

In her life and in her fiction, Patricia Cornwell hasn't merely adopted a lofty sounding credo—she *lives* it.

The virtue of writing an unauthorized book is that it gives the author tremendous freedom. Authorized books, by their very nature, are more or less beholden to their subjects—it is the unspoken price of access if you want the stamp of official approval.

When I began this book, I had heard all the usual criticisms leveled against Cornwell—criticisms that you'll find discussed by various people who contributed to this book—and, on the whole, I've dismissed them. Personal and professional jealousies exact a toll; being famous and rich exacts another toll; and perhaps the highest toll of all—attacks from the press, for which there are no adequate rebuttals—comes with the territory.

After studying Cornwell's life and work, insofar as I'm concerned, my verdict is in: Patricia Cornwell has battled personal and professional demons to become one of the most popular and successful writers in our time, regardless of what her detractors say. She richly deserves her success; she's also entitled to a measure of privacy in her personal life. Case closed.

Much of what is in this book is common knowledge, collected for the first time under one set of covers. Drawing from public sources, this book strikes a balance between what her readers would like to know and the privacy to which Cornwell is entitled.

I do agree with the statement expressed on Cornwell's Web site that her life would make a fascinating story in itself. My hope would be that she finds an official biographer whom she can trust, just as Ruth Bell Graham entrusted Cornwell to write her life story; the alternative would be a short memoir, a mixture of personal reminiscences and "how to" information about the field of criminology, and some advice on writing, similar to what Stephen King did in *On Writing* (Scribner, 2000).

No matter what form Cornwell decides her official story should take, the story of her life will make for fascinating reading. In the meantime, Cornwell fans will find plenty on their plate: In addition to the two unpublished, previously signed Scarpetta novels, she has signed a new contract for two more, ensuring readers that Scarpetta will be around for many years to come.

SECTION I

THE FACTS: A LOOK AT THE LIFE OF PATRICIA CORNWELL

CHRONOLOGY

Note: The chronology that follows is abbreviated, focusing on key personal moments and professional publications. For more information, consult Cornwell's official Web site.

1956
- Born June 9, in Miami, Florida; daughter of Sam and Marilyn Daniels.

1963
- Moves with family to Montreat, North Carolina.

1965
- With her two brothers, she comes under the care of Ruth and Billy Graham, who place them with nearby missionaries who raise them after Marilyn Daniels is hospitalized.

1979
- Graduates from Davidson College, earning a B.A. degree.
- Works at the *Charlotte Observer* (Charlotte, North Carolina) until 1981.

1980
- Marries Charles Cornwell, June 14.

- Receives Investigative Reporting Award for a series on prostitution from the North Carolina Press Association.

1981

- Moves to Richmond, Virginia, with her husband, who enrolls in the Union Theological Seminary.
- Begins work on a biography of Ruth Bell Graham (wife of evangelist Billy Graham).

1983

- Publishes *A Time for Remembering: The Ruth Bell Graham Story.*

1984

- Begins work on her first novel, about a male detective.
- Meets Dr. Marcella Fierro, a medical examiner in Richmond, who is generally considered the inspiration for Dr. Kay Scarpetta.

1985

- Works in the office of the Chief Medical Examiner (Richmond, Virginia).
- Receives the Gold Medallion Book Award from the Evangelical Christian Publishers Association for her biography of Ruth Bell Graham.

1987

- Real-life inspiration for *Postmortem:* a series of stranglings in Richmond in the summer.

1988

- *Postmortem* is submitted to publishers via Michael Congdon, her first literary agent.

1989

- Scribner buys *Postmortem.* The beginning of Cornwell's relationship with Susanne Kirk (a Scribner editor).
- Divorces Charles Cornwell.

1990

- Publishes her first novel, *Postmortem.*
- Receives numerous awards for *Postmortem,* including:

  John Creasey Award (British Crime Writers Association)
  Edgar Award (Mystery Writers of America)
  Anthony Award (Bouchercon, World Mystery Convention)
  Macavity Award (Mystery Readers International)

- Buys home in Windsor Farms, in Richmond.

1991

- Receives French Prix du Roman d'Adventure, for *Postmortem.*
- Publishes *Body of Evidence,* the second Scarpetta novel.

1992

- Publishes *All That Remains,* the third Scarpetta novel (August).

1993

- Publishes *Cruel and Unusual,* the fourth Scarpetta novel.
- Receives Gold Dagger Award for *Cruel and Unusual.*

1994

- Changes literary agents; retains Esther Newberg of ICM.
- Publishes *The Body Farm,* the fifth Scarpetta novel (August).

1995

- Publishes *From Potter's Field,* the sixth Scarpetta novel (August).

1996

- Changes publishing houses; moves to G.P. Putnam.
- Publishes *Cause of Death,* the seventh Scarpetta novel (July).
- Publishes *An Uncommon Friend: The Authorized Biography of Ruth Bell Graham,* a reprinting of her first book under a new title.

1997

- Publishes *Ruth, a Portrait: The Story of Ruth Bell Graham,* reprinting the previous biography, adding a new introduction and epilogue (September).
- Publishes *Hornet's Nest* (January), establishing a new series.
- Publishes *Unnatural Exposure,* the eighth Scarpetta novel (August).
- Publishes *Point of Origin,* the ninth Scarpetta novel (July).
- Publishes *Scarpetta's Winter Table* (October); a novella in hardcover.

1999

- Publishes *Southern Cross* (January).
- Publishes *Black Notice,* the tenth Scarpetta novel (August).
- Publishes *Life's Little Fable* (May).

2000

- Cornwell attends birthday party to celebrate Ruth Bell Graham's eightieth birthday.
- Publishes the eleventh Scarpetta novel, *The Last Precinct* (November).

2001

- Publishes *Isle of Dogs,* the third Judy Hammer/Andy Brazil novel.
- Publishes *Food to Die For: Secrets from Kay Scarpetta's Kitchen,* with Marlene Brown.

2002

- Publishes *Jack the Ripper, Case Closed,* a nonfiction book.

2003

- Tentative publication of the twelfth Kay Scarpetta novel. (*Note*: This will be the first of four Scarpetta novels currently under contract).

PATRICIA CORNWELL:
LIFE BEFORE *POSTMORTEM*

The best biography of Patricia remains unwritten, and any great one would run for pages.
—FROM THE OFFICIAL PATRICIA CORNWELL WEB SITE

It's an unseasonably warm Saturday afternoon in Richmond, Virginia, where a line of several hundred people wait patiently for the arrival of Patricia Cornwell, scheduled for a book signing at the newly renovated Science Museum located downtown.

Mostly adults, evenly mixed between men and women, almost all are holding a copy of her eleventh Kay Scarpetta novel, *The Last Precinct,* published earlier in the month.

Since Cornwell lives in Richmond, it seems logical that she'd arrive by car, perhaps driving her own Mercedes, with a designated parking place to be held for her. But Cornwell knows the impact of a Grand Entrance, which she makes, not by car, but by helicopter—her own, in fact, a Bell JetRanger that slowly ascends as hundreds of fans look upward, shielding their eyes from the noon sun.

Patricia Daniels Cornwell, whose first Scarpetta novel sold for six thousand dollars and who now commands millions for each new book, is soon seated behind a table inside the museum and basks in the attention of her fans, some of whom have traveled a considerable distance just to get a book signed.

Cornwell is justifiably enjoying her day in the limelight. You can't buy the loyalty of fans like this, as she knows; instead, you must *earn* it, book by book, slowly building up a body of work that keeps the fans coming back for more.

The challenge, as Cornwell knows, is not to simply write formulaic fiction, which will turn even the most ardent fan into a nonbeliever, but to up the ante with each new book, as she has done with *The Last Precinct,* which clearly shows us more about Kay Scarpetta herself than any other book Cornwell has written.

The fans always want to know more about Scarpetta, Cornwell says in a television interview with Katie Couric on *Good Morning America* (November 2000), and who is she to disappoint her loyal fans?

Patricia Daniels Cornwell—whose own life is as colorful as one of her books—is *exactly* where she wants to be in her life: a bestselling author who has the luxury of writing the books she wants to write; a respected and powerful figure, with many friends in high places; an advocate for crime victims, donating time and money to worthy causes; and a major philanthropist who has given to numerous charities, many in the Richmond community she lived in for many years.

Predictably, all of this has made her a convenient target for all comers. Former friends paint a dark picture of her as someone afflicted by rampant paranoia, obsessed with personal security; disgruntled former employees bitch about the boss; literary critics pay more attention to the details of her book contracts than to the books themselves; and the press has a field day when anything scandalous in her life comes to surface.

Perhaps this is a good thing; John Lennon, Rebecca Shaffer, and Selena might still be alive if they'd understood the nature of the abuse of power—the theme that dominates Cornwell's work—and the dark nature of fan worship and obsession.

The general facts about Cornwell's life are well-known, thoroughly documented, and oft repeated. The specifics are largely unknown because Cornwell—unlike many of her contemporaries—feels adamantly that her personal life is her own business and shares little (if anything) about her family.

Consequently, we know very little about her father and mother. We know nothing about her two brothers, just as we know virtually nothing about her former husband, with whom she's remained on good terms.

The Early Years

Born in Miami, Florida, on June 9, 1956, Patricia Daniels was the second of three children of the late Sam Daniels, an attorney, and Marilyn Zenner. Patricia, however, was the only daughter.

We know little of what life was like in the Daniels family, although Cornwell makes occasional references to her childhood in the rare interviews she grants. Many of those references—perhaps magnified through a child's eyes—point to an acrimonious relationship between her parents.

The marriage was clearly headed toward rocky shores by the time Patricia Daniels was five; two short years later, Marilyn Daniels left with her three children in tow and headed to Montreat, North Carolina.

Faced with the twin devils of having to raise the children on her own and dealing with her own illnesses, she found herself turning not to God but to one of his most famous servants—the world-famous evangelist, Billy Graham—for succor.

Ruth Bell Graham took the wayward family in, fed them lunch, and soon arranged for the Daniels children to be raised not by them but by missionaries, Manfred and Lenore Saunders, who had recently returned from Africa. Marilyn Daniels, suffering from severe depression, was hospitalized.

What could have been going through Patricia Daniels's mind at the time? Having lost her father through divorce and her mother through illness, Patricia Daniels understandably turned to Ruth Bell Graham as an authority figure who would prove then, and for the years to come, a pivotal figure in her life.

In *Ruth, a Portrait: The Story of Ruth Bell Graham,* Patricia Cornwell tells the fascinating story of how she and Ruth Bell Graham bonded. Perhaps the best way to summarize how Cornwell felt about Graham is to simply quote the dedication to the book, with its understated admiration: "To the wise old woman."

A bright student, a pretty young woman, and a determined athlete on the tennis court, Patricia Daniels graduated from high school and briefly attended King College in Tennessee. She soon transferred to Davidson College (Charlotte, North Carolina) on a tennis scholarship, which she later rejected when it became clear to her that although she was good, there were others who were naturally better, more gifted athletically, and perhaps her real talents lay elsewhere. Highly competitive and determined, Patricia Daniels was not interested in being second best.

Patricia Daniels's considerable talents, as it turned out, were creative in nature. A capable cartoonist, her real talent lay in writing—a talent noticed by her mentor, Ruth Bell Graham, who encouraged her literary efforts.

Patricia Daniels's contributions to the school yearbook—notably a lengthy travelogue—made it clear that she would make her mark, so to speak, not on athletic fields but on paper: A born storyteller—gifted with a rich imagination and intelligence—Patricia Daniels, an English major, graduated from college in 1979 with a B.A. degree.

Known for her determination, Patricia Daniels surprised no one with her academic excellence; she likely surprised many, though, when as an undergraduate she pursued one of her professors, Charles Cornwell, whom she would later marry.

For the next two years, Patricia Daniels put her writing skills to work at the local newspaper, the *Charlotte Observer,* where she started at the bottom: editing television listings, then working in features, and finally becoming a reporter, where she got her first real taste of what would prove irresistible and addictive: the world of law enforcement.

This, she knew, was something she could sink her teeth into, so to speak. The real world where, as cops put it, the rubber meets the road, a world in which the good guys went out to do battle with the bad guys; and Patricia Daniels found it a heady experience. This would prove to be, as she would find out, her milieu.

As a journalist, you are judged by your peers and your superiors by the kind of journalism you do. Covering a Little League baseball game is not the kind of story that builds careers or reputations. The *real* journalists went out and carved a niche, made a name for themselves, as Patricia Daniels did in a series on prostitution. It earned her an Investigative Reporting Award from the North Carolina Press Association and marked her as a journalist to watch, someone on the fast track.

On June 14, 1980, Patricia Daniels married her former college professor, Charles Cornwell, and took his name. But marriage also meant compromise, sacrifice, and decisions to make—notably, what to do with her promising career as a journalist when her husband decided to put the world of academe behind him and seek a divinity degree at the Union Theological Seminary in Richmond, Virginia.

Because Patricia Cornwell has revealed nothing about her marriage to Charles Cornwell, we can only speculate as to the nature and extent of their discussions as Patricia wrestled with the prospects of moving and leaving her promising career as a journalist behind to begin life anew in a strange city.

Patricia Cornwell, torn in her decision, confided in and consulted with the one person whom she knew she could trust, Ruth Bell Graham, who was likely more sympathetic to Patricia's plight than Charles, though Graham (of all people) knew firsthand the dynamics that lay behind a decision to attend the seminary.

From a purely practical view, instead of two steady paychecks—Charles's salary as a professor, Patricia's as a journalist—there would soon be one, and only if Patricia found employment immediately upon moving. There was, after all, no guarantee that Patricia Cornwell would find a job with the local paper, the *Richmond Times-Dispatch,* if indeed that was her intent. Having tasted the fruit of publication and peer recognition, Patricia Cornwell clearly didn't want to let her writing skills go fallow.

Becoming a Writer

Patricia Cornwell was only twenty-four when she made up her mind to write an authorized biography of Ruth Bell Graham, which she pursued with dogged determination. As Cornwell put it (in an introduction to *Ruth, a Portrait,* the revised version of the biography published in 1997), "[Ruth Graham] could not see what good would come of my writing her biography. It was difficult convincing her."

In the end, Patricia Cornwell prevailed, winning Ruth Bell Graham over.

Throughout 1981 and 1982, Patricia Cornwell worked on the biography as her husband—the former professor turned student—pursued his new studies. *A Time for Remembering: The Ruth Bell Graham Story* was published in 1983. It received good reviews and its success ensured that if Cornwell wanted to pursue a career writing biographies of major religious figures, there were many others yet to be written.

The success of the book, though, came with a hidden cost: According to Patricia Cornwell (in *Ruth, a Portrait*), her friendship with Ruth Graham suffered a major blow—they weren't on speaking terms for eight years following the book's publication.

It was time for a change. Though her publisher probably encouraged her to repeat herself with another book-length biography on a
major religious figure, Patricia Cornwell may have had misgivings:
First, would a new book create the same personal rift between interviewer and subject? And, second, was this *really* what she wanted to
write? Moreover, she may have been concerned about being typecast
as a nonfiction writer specializing in religious biographies.

Though Cornwell could clearly write such books, she made a
major decision and, drawing on her first love, began writing her
first novel in 1984, which featured a male detective named Joe
Constable—hardly original fare. Cornwell's problem was that
while she had *observed* crime on the streets, she never knew what
went on behind the scenes after the crime was committed.

As *Publishers Weekly* put it, in Cornwell's first major profile:
". . . a physician friend in Richmond suggested she talk with a
medical examiner to get an insider's view of the morgue and the
working of the examiner's office . . . ."

Cornwell followed that advice, called the deputy medical examiner in Richmond, Dr. Marcella Fierro, and during the course of a
subsequent interview Cornwell discovered, to her horror, that she
didn't know enough about the subject to write convincingly. Dead
men, she likely realized, *did* tell tales . . . *if* you knew what to look
for, *if* you could see the clues that told the story behind their
untimely deaths. They would speak volumes if you knew how to
listen.

As Cornwell told *Publishers Weekly,* she soon realized that not only
was she fascinated by the procedural work performed in the morgue
but that she was out of her league: She realized the depths of her
ignorance in a complex, demanding, and ever-changing field.

Cornwell became a frequent visitor to the medical examiner's
office, witnessing autopsies, asking questions, and showing a keen
interest in the workings of forensics.

Hired as a part-time scribe, recording what Fierro saw during the autopsies, Cornwell routinely witnessed the ultimate abuse of power—the taking of human life. After a day's work at the morgue, she'd return home, take off the white lab coat, and put on the blue uniform of a volunteer police officer for the city of Richmond. This experience would prove invaluable later, as would the time she spent with homicide detectives, giving her an insight as to how crimes were solved.

Now she had the background to write convincing fiction, but her focus was wrong: Joe Constable never rang true with the editors who had seen her first three novels, which is why those novels had been rejected. Frustrated, Cornwell asked for advice from Mysterious Press's Sara Ann Fried, who suggested that a secondary character might be fleshed out—Dr. Kay Scarpetta—because the primary character, Det. Joe Constable, wasn't working.

Patricia Cornwell took Fried's advice and, drawing on a string of murders in Richmond, in the summer of 1987, she shifted gears and began seeing the world through Dr. Kay Scarpetta's eyes.

Going through two rewrites, hoping to sell the book to The Mysterious Press, Cornwell finally decided—as she later told its publisher—that she didn't want to suffer rejection a third time at their hands and so submitted it elsewhere, to Scribner.

Patricia Cornwell's professional future looked promising, but on the personal side, her life had become increasingly problematic. When her husband received a job offer as a pastor for a church in Texas, Patricia Cornwell once again had to make a decision to follow her husband's career path . . . or her own. This time, she chose the road less traveled, and in late 1988, she and Charles Cornwell agreed to an amicable separation.

In 1989, Patricia and Charles Cornwell divorced. Patricia Cornwell, faced with using her maiden name for *Postmortem* or retaining her married name, chose the latter because of its brand-name identification with her book on Ruth Graham Bell; it won the Gold Medallion Book Award in 1986 from the Evangelical Christian Publishers Association.

In 1990, *Postmortem,* subtitled *A Kay Scarpetta Mystery,* was published. Cornwell's reign as the mistress of mayhem had begun.

Cornwell's Journal

In the biography section of the initial official Cornwell Web site, page eight shows a photograph of a red, leather-bound journal with a locked clasp. According to Cornwell, in an essay titled "The Last Precinct: A Philosophy," Ruth Graham had bought it for herself but decided to give this one to Patricia Cornwell, who recalled that "it was the most beautiful book I had ever seen, rich soft leather and pages edged in gold. She had bought it in Switzerland for herself because, as I would find out many years later when I became her biographer, she kept extensive journals."

The gift touched the aspiring writer, and to this day, Cornwell reportedly travels with a leather-bound journal on hand to jot down random thoughts, notes, and perhaps a cartoon, as well. So enamored of the gift was Cornwell that she would later give a similar journal to the man she was courting, Prof. Charles Cornwell.

Cornwell on Writing and Publishing Her First Book

If you ask any professional writer which book was the most difficult one to get published, the answer is almost always the first book. First books are not always the blockbusters, either. Can you remember the name of Dean Koontz's first book? Neither can I. Or what about the sales of John Grisham's first book, *A Time to Kill*? Published by a small New York house, Grisham wound up selling copies out of his car trunk to booksellers in the South.

In Cornwell's case, how many readers could identify Cornwell's first book? Most people would cite, in error, *Postmortem*.

Contrary to what you may think, Cornwell's first book had encountered several hurdles, thrown up by Ruth Graham herself, as well as Cornwell's publisher. And therein lies the story behind the book that launched her career, illustrated in this feature article written at the time.

AUTHOR HAD LONG STRUGGLE WITH BOOK
by Dannye Romine

Patricia Daniels Cornwell says Bill Graham's wife had the flu and was "soft in the head" when she agreed to let Cornwell, a 24-year-old police reporter, write about her.

The result is *A Time for Remembering: The Ruth Bell Graham Story* (Harper & Row, $13.95), which will be on the bookstands in November. Excerpts from the book start today in *The Observer* and will run through Thursday.

Cornwell, now 27, says she wonders who she thought she was to be writing a biography about the wife of the world-famous evangelist.

"I'd been writing about prostitutes on West Trade Street!" she says.

During her two-year stint at *The Observer*, June 1979 to May 1981, Cornwell also wrote about the gory tragedies of shootouts, crashes, murders, fires and robberies.

A 1979 Davidson graduate, she had had a long-standing desire to write a biography of Ruth Graham, a woman Cornwell had admired since she was a child in Montreat. That desire surfaced when Cornwell's husband, Charles Cornwell, decided to leave his teaching post in Davidson's English department and enter Union Theological Seminary in Richmond. The move provided a break in Cornwell's newspaper career and an opportunity for a new venture.

"I had had very vivid memories of Ruth ever since I was a little girl," says Cornwell. "I had this feeling there was something about her that was going to affect me someday."

But Cornwell says she would never have been able to "sneak into the [Grahams'] kingdom if not for her friendship with Ruth.

That friendship, which Cornwell describes poignantly in the book's preface, began in Montreat when Cornwell was 7 and Ruth was 43.

Lonesome for her grandparents in Miami, saddened by her parents' divorce, Patsy frequently visited Ruth Graham's parents, Virginia and Nelson Bell. She spent hours playing Scrabble and Rook with Virginia Bell, and she loved the woman's homemade custards.

"I think Ruth was touched that I paid attention to her parents. I think maybe that made me a little special to her," says Cornwell today.

Cornwell drove to Montreat on a bitter January morning in 1981 to get Ruth's permission to write a book about her.

In the bedroom, logs smoldered in the fireplace. Ruth Graham was sick with the flu, propped up in her hand-built bed. In the preface, Cornwell says Graham's "bones ached and her eyes were glazed with fever."

"I want to write a book about you," Cornwell told Graham.

"You want to do what, honey?" Graham asked.

"You know, I want to write your biography," Cornwell said.

"Well, sure. That's fine," Ruth said. "But I don't think it would be very interesting."

A month later, Graham called Cornwell at *The Observer.*

"Patsy," she said. "*No way* you're going to write a book about me."

Cornwell persisted. Finally, she talked Graham into a compromise.

Cornwell would write a profile of Ruth Graham for *The Observer.* If Ruth liked the profile, then Cornwell would proceed with the biography.

The profile appeared in May, 1981, and Cornwell met Graham for coffee in Charlotte and watched as Ruth read the story.

"I thought, 'Oh, she's just going to love it,'" says Cornwell today. "But I saw she was reading it with this frozen smile on her face and she wasn't saying much at all."

"Ruth," Cornwell said, "I haven't changed my mind about the biography."

Graham looked dejected, but she told Cornwell she would let Bill read the profile. "Then we'll pray over it," she said.

Billy Graham's reaction, according to Cornwell, was to advise his wife to get an experienced biographer—not a 24-year-old girl who used to live down the street.

Cornwell says Ruth told her husband: "What Patsy needs is practice, and I'm just going to let her practice on me."

Setting Up Camp

For three and four days at a time, Cornwell would set up camp in an upstairs bedroom in the Grahams' Montreat home. She would batter Graham with questions far into the night.

"I would try to get her to remember what color shoes she had on during a certain crusade in a certain year, and she would start raking her fingers through her hair," Cornwell recalls. "I exhausted her.

"She'd be in her bed with a microphone attached to her nightgown, and a lot of times she'd get out of the bed and shoo me upstairs."

Cornwell also worked from 2,000 pages of Ruth Graham's letters and journals, as well as some 1,300 letters written by Ruth's father, Nelson Bell, when he was a medical missionary in China.

She interviewed the Graham children and such celebrities as William Buckley Jr., June Carter Cash, Julie Nixon Eisenhower, Paul Harvey, William Randolph Hearst Jr., Sen. Jesse Helms, Lady Bird Johnson, Dan Rather and Billy Graham.

When Cornwell finished her first draft in November 1982— 460 pages on computer print-out paper—she sent it to Ruth Graham in New York.

"I was sitting in Richmond on pins and needles. I was so excited, and I had all these visions of her calling me and telling me what a genius I was. I waited six days and nothing happened. I was so depressed," says Cornwell.

"When she got back to Montreat, I called her, and I said, 'How did you like it?' and she said, 'We need to talk about it.' Later the secretary calls and says to get up here right away."

Ruth Graham thought Cornwell wrote like a reporter. She objected to her referring to people by their last names only. Even more strenuously, she objected to Cornwell's throwing in willy-nilly people's crime records, as if she were still on the police beat.

"Why did I ever let you do this?" an exasperated Graham would ask Cornwell.

By December 1982, Cornwell had finished another draft, and once again the secretary summoned Cornwell to Montreat.

"It was like going to the principal's office," says Cornwell.

Again Ruth Graham objected. There was still too much blood on the linoleum to suit her, according to Cornwell.

At this point, Ruth Graham called Harper & Row and asked for a six month's extension on the deadline for the manuscript.

According to a contract between Ruth Graham and Cornwell, Graham had the right to approve the final manuscript. At that point, she felt the manuscript needed to be completely rewritten.

Cornwell says she now believes Ruth's instincts were right.

But at the time, "I got so mad at her! We called each other names. She called me retarded. I called her a dodo. She'd say, 'Don't antagonize me.'"

Four months later, in March 1883, Ruth Graham read the third draft in San Francisco. When she finished the first 40 pages, Ruth Graham sent Patsy a big basket of flowers and a check for $100 for the Cornwells to have dinner out.

"Then something happened," says Cornwell. "The wagon left the road."

Ruth Graham had 30 days to approve or disapprove the manuscript. She made some changes, but Cornwell believes Graham still had some qualms and that as the deadline approached she became more and more apprehensive. The 30 days came and went, and Ruth Graham was still not ready to give her final approval.

In May 1983, two people met with Ruth to go over the manuscript at her Montreat home: Roy Carlisle, a Harper & Row editor, and Ruth's daughter, Bunny Dienert of Argyle, Tex.

"A lot of people were giving Ruth a lot of grief," says Cornwell. "They thought I was taking advantage of her. They would say, 'You better not let her [Cornwell] do this and that.' Finally," says Cornwell, "she threw up her hands in despair and bowed out of the project. She couldn't take it anymore, and her daughter, Bunny, told me not to talk to her about it anymore."

Rights Transferred

Rights of approval for the manuscript were transferred to Dienert, who worked with Cornwell throughout the fourth and final draft.

But Cornwell says a lot of stylistic changes were made at that May meeting, none of them with her approval.

When the galley proofs came in June, she realized she was no longer the sole, original author and she knew she could not allow Harper & Row to publish the book with her name on it.

"None of the changes had been made out of malice," says Cornwell. "But somebody would remember anecdotes and insert them in their own words. And somebody else would not like the way I expressed myself, and rewrite what I had written. And somebody else would make grammatical changes, which were incorrect. A lot of people thought they were helping me. They thought they were teaching me how to write, and it just wasn't my book anymore."

In June 1983, Cornwell found a Richmond lawyer, Joseph Carter Jr., who called Harper & Row in July and negotiated a new contract for the book.

Cornwell finished her fourth and final draft in August, and the new set of galley proofs arrived in September. Both she and Dienert were pleased with the final draft.

Official publication date for the $13.95 book is Nov. 24.

Cornwell says bookstores will probably receive the books by the first of November.

The first printing of the book is 65,000 copies. The Grason Co., a mail-order division of the Billy Graham Evangelist Association, has purchased 25,000 copies.

None of the proceeds goes to the Grahams, but Ruth Graham has the right to approve or disapprove movie rights to the book.

Cornwell says she believes that some of the frustration about the book resulted from Ruth Graham's belief that Cornwell was going to write "a sweet book about our friendship, and she didn't think I was going to do a real biography.

"I wanted this to be my gift to her," says Cornwell. "I was heartbroken when she didn't like it. But who likes their own photographs? If somebody translated your life for you, it would be very unnerving, wouldn't it?"

Ruth Graham's response to the book was relayed through her secretary in a prepared statement: "Patsy is a gifted writer, and I was amazed at how well she crammed 63 years into 263 pages."

Cornwell says that "there's a depth in Ruth you don't find in the crusade mentality."

"You can't label her evangelically. The minute you try to label her, she surprises you with something. I don't want to knock the evangelicals," says Cornwell. "But she is not fossilized. She's very fluid.

"She changes like the clouds," says Cornwell. "She's not the same person now I wrote the book about. She keeps changing and growing."

Cornwell remembers that when she was about 12, Ruth Graham would read Cornwell's poetry and marvel over it.

Later, Cornwell asked her: "how do you have it in you to spot the good and seize it? Where do you get the energy?"

Said Graham: "You can't imagine what a wonderful thing it is to see a little bit of fire in someone and fan it into a bigger one."

Cornwell believes that's why Graham let her write this book. "That's about the most visible way I can think of of giving your life to someone else," says Cornwell. "To allow you to write about them."

How to Get a Signed Copy of Ruth, a Portrait

The best source may be Patricia Cornwell herself. On her official Web site, she used to offer signed copies of the British hardback edition of *Ruth, a Portrait* for thirty dollars. Though the Web site is currently "under construction," when erected, it will surely offer memorabilia and some signed books as well.

CORNWELL AT DAVIDSON COLLEGE

Davidson taught me to think creatively and waste nothing. . . . My college years taught me that the world is my laboratory. . . . There are no limitations, just as there are no excuses. . . . To learn is to feel alive while relentlessly seeking truth, and that is why Davidson was not my education. It was my induction into who I am today.
—PATRICIA CORNWELL (CLASS OF '79), IN THE
Davidson College Alumni MAGAZINE

Serendipity has played an important role in Patricia Cornwell's life. What, one wonders, might her life have been like if she had not met Ruth and Billy Graham? Or if her then-husband had not uprooted them from North Carolina to move to Richmond, what effect would that have had on her writing career?

Cornwell's college days began not at Davidson College but at King College in Tennessee. King College, however, was not a good fit for her; and as she searched for answers, she had a chance meeting at a tennis court with Ed White, the admissions director for Davidson College, who suggested she apply to his school. Cornwell applied and was accepted a month later.

In looking back at Cornwell's college career, it's fascinating to see the directions in which her creativity flowed. She contributed cartoons, wrote nonfiction, and was the graphics editor for the school newspaper, the *Davidsonian*. For *Miscellany*, the school's literary magazine, she contributed poetry and also became a coeditor. She was a Leopold Schepp Scholar and also won the Vereen Bell Award.

Among her college work, it's fair to say that she's more a doodler than a professional cartoonist and a poet of promise, but she shined in her nonfiction for her college newspaper, the *Davidsonian*.

In the May 7, 1979, issue of the *Davidsonian,* she wrote a well-reasoned opinion piece, "The Definition of Art or What True Art Is Not," that showed her abilities as an essayist. Later, in the April 20, 1979, issue, she contributed a well-written travelogue that showed her eye for detail, "St. Anne's: Advice from Someone Who's Been."

Breaking from tradition, Cornwell did not become a junior editor at a magazine or book publisher but instead became a journalist at the local newspaper.

From classroom to newsroom, Patricia Cornwell had taken the first step toward discovering her calling as a writer.

A SCRIBE AT THE *CHARLOTTE OBSERVER*

I am grateful to my old friends at the *Charlotte Observer* who gave me access to the paper's library. I will never forget that it was editors there who gave me my first job in journalism.

—PATRICIA CORNWELL, IN "CREDITS"
FROM *Ruth, A Portrait*

To most people who don't know the newspaper industry, who know of it only through the movie *All the President's Men,* in which two *Washington Post* reporters bring down the Nixon presidency, there's an aura of glamour about the trade that is more romantic fantasy than reality.

Investigative reporting is where the action is, but in order to put together a newspaper, it takes a score of reporters who will cover what doesn't make the front page news, the everyday happenings that comprise the daily lives of any community. In other words, the Woodwards and Bernsteins are the exception. For most print journalists, it means a long apprenticeship even before you are assigned to write the "hard" news stories. For most, it means writing about the world of the ordinary, the bean suppers, the dedications of new roads, the obits, local sports. Not exactly the kind of stuff that sets the world on fire.

Most papers prefer, if not require, a degree in journalism, since news stories are written in a standard formula of the five Ws: Who, What, Where, When, and Why. It's a writing format designed to get across the facts in the order of descending importance, with the reporter as objective observer. In other words, it's a far cry from

what liberal arts majors like Cornwell have been taught to write—
subjective pieces like essays or fiction.

To her credit, Cornwell's drive to succeed—the same laserlike
focus that characterizes a semipro tennis player or aspiring college
writer—served her in good stead when she turned her attention to
her first full-time job.

In the summer of 1979, Patricia Cornwell began work at the
Charlotte Observer, where she started out at the bottom rung of the
ladder, editing television listings in the features department. By
dint of her hard work and persistence, she began taking on more
challenging assignments, writing features, and earning her own
byline as a staff writer; from there, she specialized in crime reporting, which culminated in an investigative story on prostitution in
downtown Charlotte that drew considerable attention and won
her a major press award.

No question, Patricia Cornwell could have made a name for
herself as a journalist, but like Carl Hiassen—a Florida journalist
who went on to become a bestselling popular novelist—Cornwell's real talent in writing, as a novelist, had not yet emerged.

In the voluminous files of the *Observer*'s library, called the
"morgue," under the byline "Patsy Daniels" (an *Observer* staff
writer), you will find thick packets of newspaper clippings, piles of
yellowed pulp paper that bear her byline.

Her first story appeared on June 29, 1979. Titled "Take Your
Pick of 4th of July Celebrations in Charlotte," the piece begins:
"You say you decided not to leave Charlotte this Fourth of July
because you were worried about finding gas? You made the right
decision. This Fourth of July, you'll have a choice of two celebrations in the Charlotte area."

The clippings, dated from June 29, 1989, to April 1981, show Patricia Cornwell's skills as a nonfiction writer, recording with a clinical detachment what she saw through her lens as a journalist.

Cornwell would also write a major profile for the *Observer* on Ruth Bell Graham, a trial run for the book she intended to write. Here's a sampling of the stories she published for the paper:

- "37 Officers Collar 3 Men Who Stole $1 Bill."
- "Policeman Who Took Lennon to Hospital Recognizes Ex-Beatle."
- "70-Year-Old Woman Is Robbed, Kidnapped."
- "Shot Hits Patrol Car's Bumper."
- "12 Arrested in Charlotte Drug Probe."
- "2 Boys Force 5-Year-Old Girl into Pond."
- "Next Police Chief Likes What He Sees Here."
- "Bank's Film of Robbery Leads to Suspect's Arrest."
- "10-Year-Old Girl Critically Wounded When Shot in Head."
- "Woman Jumps to Her Death from Hotel Window."
- "Charlotte Man Shot to Death—Woman Charges He Raped Her."
- "Man Charged in Fuel Theft."
- "When Charlotteans Go to Church, Thieves Go to Their Cars, Homes."
- " 'Downtown Flasher' May Have Left City."
- "Security Guard Raped, Stabbed Outside Her 4th Ward Apartment."
- " 'Ancient' Skull Leads Officials to Skeleton."
- "Man Charged with Raping Woman, 62."

- "Skull Leads Authorities to Skeleton."
- "Suspect Arrested in Death."
- "Man Is Found Shot to Death in N. Charlotte."
- "Woman Is Kidnapped, Raped."
- "'Suspicious' Fire Burns Charlotte Restaurant."
- "Mecklenburg Residents Can Get Free Tests for Auto Pollution."
- "40 Percent of Cars Fail Pollution Test."
- "It Might as Well Be Spring—Warm Weather Gives Charlotteans a Taste of Things to Come."

PATRICIA CORNWELL FROM A TO Z

This list is a mixture of actual people, places, and things and creations from Cornwell's books. This list covers some of the high points in Cornwell's life. The Scarpetta fan will obviously see the overlap where the fiction and real worlds intersect, and read the section on Cornwell's body of work to see how her life has influenced her novels. Note: All references herein to the *Times-Dispatch* refer to the Richmond, Virginia, newspaper.

$20 million deal. This three-book deal, reported the *Times-Dispatch* (March 6, 1996), places Patricia Cornwell as one of the most highly paid (if not *the* most highly paid) female writers in our time. An unnamed, close source to Cornwell told the paper: "We believe it's the largest deal ever signed by a woman crime writer." The motto of the Mystery Writers of America is "Crime doesn't pay . . . enough." But writing about crime *does* pay enough *if* your name is Patricia Cornwell.

48 Hours. Cornwell's first national television appearance was on this news program on CBS-TV. Although the final footage, focusing on Cornwell's use of forensics in her work, aired for only seven minutes, the camera crew dogged her. "These people are following you around for 2½ days. They've got a tape recorder running the entire time. They've got you wired. You just don't know what they're going to use." (*Times-Dispatch,* September 26, 1991.)

Algonquin Hotel. In New York City on West Forty-fourth Street, best known for being a watering hole for the literati and glitterati of the book world. After signing her first book contract, Cornwell and her agent ate a celebratory lunch at this restaurant. (*Times-Dispatch,* April 28, 1992.)

Armani. Dressed to kill, especially for book jacket photos, television interviews, and bookstore signings, Patricia Cornwell has a taste for the good stuff, notably from the Armani line. (*Fact:* Jodie Foster, whom Cornwell admires, also prefers wearing Armani, though usually in a more casual manner—an Armani jacket over jeans.)

ATF: The Movie. A made-for-television movie that aired on ABC-TV on September 6, 1999, with the Bureau of Alcohol, Tobacco and Firearms (ATF) and the Waco raid as the focal points. Produced by Michelle Ashford and cowritten with Cornwell, this movie starred Amy Brenneman and Kathy Baker. On *Good Morning America* (September 6, 1999), Cornwell remarked: "I spent about three months living in Washington when I was doing the research, and I talked to about half a dozen ATF agents who actually were on that raid at Waco. And in fact, it's the only time in my life when I've done research where the information was so painful I didn't take any notes."

Authenticity. "The [Scarpetta] novels are praised for their accurate detail based upon research Cornwell did in the Virginia Medical Examiner's Officer, witnessing scores of autopsies." (*Contemporary Authors,* New Revision Series, Volume 53.)

Autographs, obtaining one. "The best way to get an autographed book is either off the Web site, or check the Web site for book signings. We can't really have people sending books in, because there would just be too many." (*Court TV* transcript, with Catherine Crier.)

Bailor, Chris. A former law-enforcement officer, Bailor has an impressive resume. The *Times-Dispatch* (January 7, 1994) reported that as a woman she scored several "firsts"—first to be named Rookie of the Year, first to be a police lieutenant, first to command a division, and first to command a precinct. Leaving behind 17.5 years of service as an officer, Bailor was hired by Cornwell in 1994 to be the vice president and chief of staff of her company. Bailor later became Cornwell's chief research assistant and head of security.

Bass, Dr. William, forensic anthropologist. Generally considered to be the inspiration for Dr. Katz in *The Body Farm*. His name also crops up in *Isle of Dogs*.

Bell 407 helicopter. When she's not chartering a private jet, Patricia Cornwell owns, and flies, her own helicopter, a Bell 407 JetRanger.

Bell Vision Visual Communications. Patricia Cornwell's in-house art studio for film production and graphic design. (They've designed, among other things, print ads for Virginia Blood Services of Richmond and her book covers.)

Bennett, Eugene A. A former FBI agent currently serving time in prison for a failed murder plot against his ex-wife, Marguerite "Margo" Bennett, herself a former FBI agent. Unfortunately, this American tragedy included Patricia Cornwell, whose connection to Marguerite was, as the world press reported, something straight from the pages of one of her crime novels.

Bennett, Marguerite. A former FBI agent whose relationship with Patricia Cornwell became a focal point in the trial of Marguerite's former husband, Eugene Bennett. As the *Times-Dispatch* (January 30, 1997) reported, Marguerite Bennett testified that under cross-examination she said, "I admit I had two encounters with Patricia Cornwell."

Black Notice. "It's a story of triumphing over the evil that perches outside our door and in our hearts. Scarpetta faces a very real monster and her odyssey takes her to Interpol and the Paris morgue." (Bookpage.com, August 1999.)

Champlin, Charles (*Los Angeles Times Book Review*). Reviewed *Postmortem,* saying that "these passages have the ring of truth as experienced, and so does the portrait of an investigative reporter who abets the solving."

Charlotte Observer. Major daily newspaper published in Charlotte, North Carolina. After college Cornwell began work for the paper, starting at the bottom: editing television listings. Working her way up the ladder, she became a crime reporter and won an investigative writing award in 1980 from the North Carolina Press Association for a series she wrote about prostitution. When her then-husband wanted to move to Richmond, Cornwell observed, "I did not want to give up the *Observer.* It was a very bad time for me." (*People* magazine; Joe Treen, interviewer.)

Congdon, Michael. Patricia Cornwell's first agent who also edited her first four Scarpetta books.

Connecticut. Cornwell moved to Greenwich, Connecticut, in late 2001. She is a frequent visitor to New York City, where she has friends and where her publisher is located. She now lives less than a half hour away from the city.

Cops. When asked, "What's the most surprising thing you've learned over the many years you've been writing about cops," she responded, "I think it's how absolutely fragile they are. They live with a lot of fear, and the way they deal with their sensitivity and the horror of their work is that they laugh at things sometimes I thought they shouldn't laugh at. . . . It's because they can't cope. I think it's a job where you suffer from enormous depression. How can you go out and see someone's tragedy every day and not be affected by it?" (*Times-Dispatch,* March 7, 1999.)

Cornwell, Charles. Former husband of Patricia Cornwell. Both value their privacy and have never discussed their marriage with the media. A former professor at Davidson College, Charles Cornwell earned his doctorate in English from the University of Virginia. After his stint at Davidson College, he received a degree from Union Theological Seminary in Richmond.

Cornwell's autobiography. In the wake of the Bennett brouhaha: "I've told people that *Unnatural Exposure* should be the title of my autobiography. I sort of expect at least one unfortunate thing every year now because that's the way it's been the last couple of years. I try to take it all in stride." (*Times-Dispatch,* April 9, 1997.)

Crime stoppers program. In 1993, Cornwell donated twenty-six hundred dollars from book sales at a Richmond signing of *Cruel and Unusual* to this program. In the memo section she wrote: "This is the beginning." (*Times-Dispatch,* June 18, 1993.)

Davidson College. A liberal arts college located in North Carolina from which Patricia Cornwell graduated with an English degree in 1979. While there, she dated one of her professors, Charles Cornwell, whom she married in 1980 but subsequently divorced.

Day job, Cornwell's. Even though *Postmortem* was a success, Cornwell still put in time at the office, her day job. "Now I'm a programmer in a morgue," she told the local paper. "I consider this my job. My writing is my passion, but this is my profession." (*Times-Dispatch,* December 6, 1987.)

Douglas, John E. A twenty-five-year veteran of the FBI, Special Agent Douglas is "a legendary figure in law enforcement and the model from which Jack Crawford was drawn for Thomas Harris's thriller, *Silence of the Lambs.* As chief of the Investigative Support Unit that tackles the most baffling and senseless of unsolved violent crimes, John Douglas is the man who ushered in a new age in behavioral science and criminal profiling." The author of several books in the field, Douglas cowrote with Mark Olshaker *Mindhunter: Inside the FBI's Elite Serial Crime Unit* (Scribner, 1995). The publisher used the following quotation from Cornwell on the book jacket: "John Douglas is the FBI's pioneer and master of investigative profiling, and one of the most exciting figures in law enforcement I've had the privilege of knowing. At last, in this chronicle of his remarkable and chilling career, he allows all of us to accompany him into unthinkably dark places where we find the bloody tracks of the Ted Bundys, John Hinckley, Jrs., and Charles Mansons. With Mr. Douglas we explore why there are monsters." In the Scarpetta novels, Special Agent Benton Wesley is the FBI's profiler. Douglas is not, however, the model for Wesley. Of Cornwell, Douglas has said: "She's very knowledgeable. Her books are very authentic. She really does her homework." (*Los Angeles Times,* July 11, 1996.)

Downside of fame. The negative side includes strangers driving slowly by her house, others leaving notes on her doorstep, and still others attempting alleged blackmail. She offered no details on the latter other than to say there were people "trying to ruin my reputation." (*Times-Dispatch,* 1994.)

Dreams/nightmares. "I used to have nice dreams. Now my dreams are so bad I don't even want to remember them. Usually I don't, and I'm thankful for that, because they're always, always awful. Because I've seen what some of these murders look like, my dreams are always anatomically correct ones." (*Atlanta Journal-Constitution,* August 8, 1998.)

Edgar Allan Poe Museum's seventy-fifth anniversary. In October 1997, Cornwell hosted the largest private showing of Poe material—seventy items, including books, manuscripts, his walking stick, and even a lock of his hair; most of the items came from a private collector in New York, Susan Jaffe Tane. The cost for admission was seventy-five dollars. (*Times-Dispatch,* October 3, 1997.)

Edgar Award. Given by the Mystery Writers of America. *Postmortem* won this award for 1991. Commented Cornwell, "I've had so much adrenaline flowing the last twenty-four hours. I was hopeful, but I really didn't expect to get it. After Great Britain [where she won the John Creasey Award from the British Crime Writers Association], I felt I'd gotten my award. . . . I'm almost speechless sometimes. I just think it can't keep going on like this. It seems like a dream sometimes, when you think how *Postmortem* started in the beginning, particularly. I think Richmonders can take a certain pleasure in it because it's our series, and it's getting recognition all over the world now." (*Times-Dispatch,* April 26, 1991.)

Fame. "Mystery master Patricia Cornwell is a rock star among writers." (*Advocate,* September 20, 1999.)

Fans at book signings. According to local estimates by the media and in-store staffers, Cornwell's appearance at a Richmond bookstore will draw up to twenty-five hundred fans. Cornwell, who has a flair for the dramatic entrance, has shown up for signings in her Bell helicopter. Because of the long lines, Cornwell is polite but professional; books are opened for her to sign with a supply of black Sharpie pens on hand; she signs the book in her bold script and thanks the fan for coming. As you'd expect, off-duty Richmond police provide tight security. At a book signing I attended, a policeman was at her side, several more were posted around the store, and her table was in a corner, making it impossible for someone to be behind her.

Fierro, Marcella, Dr. A medical examiner for the Commonwealth of Virginia who, in part, was an inspiration for Cornwell's fictional protagonist, Dr. Kay Scarpetta. On the recommendation of a friend, Patricia Cornwell went to see Fierro to glean information for research purposes. Fierro took the time to show Cornwell the ropes, so to speak, and it was the start of an enduring friendship. Of that first meeting, Cornwell observed, "I was shocked by two things. One, by how fascinating it was, and two, by how absolutely little I knew about it." (*Publishers Weekly,* February 15, 1991; interviewed by Joanne Tagorra.) Said Cornwell, "Marcella is my hero. And I *think* she's still my friend after reading [*Postmortem*]." (*Times-Dispatch,* November 11, 1989.)

Film concerns. "What they're really getting their hands on is Scarpetta. What I'm really saying is, 'Yes, you can come in the room with her.' I had to have the right suitor!" (*Times-Dispatch,* March 17, 1995.)

Films glorifying evil. "A lot of places would take my serial killer and make him the hero. They keep saying, 'Look, we'd like to see your killer a little bit more on screen. And I said, 'No. I don't want to see him at all. I will show him only as much as I have to.' You don't celebrate evil; you condemn it. And I do that through my good characters." (*Times-Dispatch,* November 13, 1995.)

Foster, Jodie. Through her agent at ICM, Cornwell arranged a meeting with Foster to discuss a film project, most likely a Scarpetta book. Foster's office, characteristically laconic, merely said the two had met "on a specific project that did not work out," and left it at that. In a way, that's unfortunate, because many fans believe Foster, who was brilliant as Clarice Starling in *Silence of the Lambs,* would have fit the role of Dr. Kay Scarpetta perfectly.

Fried, Sara Ann. An editor at The Mysterious Press whom Cornwell solicited for feedback on why her early novels were not selling. Cornwell said, "She said that I should write about what I knew. . . . And she advised me to make Scarpetta the main character. The male detective [in the early novels] just wasn't believable." (*Publishers Weekly,* February 15, 1991.)

Gaillard, Frye. An author who had worked with Cornwell at the *Charlotte Observer:* "She had an incredible drive, and she was very focused. She worked hard at what she did. To me, that's been the key to her success as a mystery writer." (*Atlanta Journal-Constitution,* August 8, 1998.)

Gaudet, Jim. When Patricia Cornwell was a volunteer police-woman, she rode with Gaudet.

Gault, Temple. Fictional nemesis in the Scarpetta novels who, as Elise O'Shaughnessy wrote in the *New York Times Book Review:* "With his pale blue eyes and his ability to anticipate the best minds of law enforcement, Gaunt is a 'malignant genius' in the tradition of Hannibal Lecter. Like Lecter's bond with Clarice Starling, Gault's relationship with Scarpetta is *personal.*"

Genre. "There are a lot of red herrings—every man in the book is seen as the possible murderer—but this is not a traditional who-dunit. Ms. Cornwell is from the new school of scientifically detailed fiction; her story is pure procedure, even if it eventually tells us absolutely nothing about the fiend. It's far removed from a mystery-loving Agatha Christie, and more attuned to unexplained scientific acronyms and gruesome bodily details. . . . This is a mystery that also is a lecture on the forensic sciences." (Robert Merritt, staff writer, *Times-Dispatch,* on *Postmortem,* December 10, 1989.)

Gifts for the Richmond Police Department. According to the *Times-Dispatch* (October 9, 1999), Patricia Cornwell has donated bullet-proof vests for the city's K-9 division, camcorders, 35-mm cameras with telephoto lenses, and computers.

Gilmore, James; former governor of Virginia. To support his election bid, Patricia Cornwell donated one hundred thousand dollars to his New Majority project PAC.

Giving tree ball. In December 1992, Cornwell was the guest of honor at the Cystic Fibrosis Foundation's seventh annual charity event at which a silent auction was held. (*Times-Dispatch*, December 3, 1992.)

Gold Dagger Award. Presented to Patricia Cornwell for *Cruel and Unusual*.

Graham, Ruth Bell. The wife of world-famous evangelist Billy Graham; a major inspirational figure in Patricia Cornwell's life; the subject of Cornwell's first book, a biography, *A Time for Remembering: The Ruth Bell Graham Story*.

Graham, Ruth Bell, on encouraging Patricia Cornwell's writing talent. "I felt she had real ability. I've kept every note I ever got from her." (*People* magazine; Joe Treen, interviewer.)

Grann, Phyllis. Highly respected in the publishing industry, Grann acquired Cornwell in an atypical fashion: Cornwell called her, reportedly at home, to discuss changing publishing houses. In December 2001, Grann left her longtime post as Putnam publisher to accept the position of vice chairman at Random House. Speculation that she would take Cornwell with her to Random proved unfounded; Cornwell stayed with Putnam. Note: *Isle of Dogs* is dedicated "to Friend and Publisher, Phyllis Grann."

Growth as a writer. "I try to become a better writer with each book. . . . It's about becoming a better storyteller and a better artist." (*Court TV* transcript, with Catherine Crier.)

Hacked chicken. *Entertainment Weekly* (online, 1992) reported that in her early years, when she was a scribe at the morgue, Cornwell would take care of business and, afterward, go to a Chinese restaurant to dine on this dish.

Hannibal. The third Hannibal Lecter novel by Thomas Harris. According to book industry insiders, Cornwell's *Black Notice* (1999) was originally scheduled to be released in July, which would have put it up against *Hannibal*'s release date. Cornwell's book was then moved to August. The problem, of course, is that having two bestselling books in the same genre out simultaneously creates havoc on the bestseller lists. Remarked Cornwell, "I will be honest—I don't think anyone wanted to come out the same time as that book." (*New York Post,* July 4, 1999.) Cornwell later noted that preorders for *Black Notice* exceeded those for *Hannibal,* perhaps showing which book is in better taste . . . even without a bottle of chilled Chianti and a plate of fava beans on the side.

Hard times. After Patricia divorced her husband Charles Cornwell, she recalled, "Success was nowhere near. I was penniless and in debt. Three of my books had been rejected, and when I finally finished *Postmortem,* it was rejected, too." (*Costco Connection,* January 1999.)

Hatch, Orrin Grant; Utah senator. *The Body Farm* is dedicated to him "for his tireless fight against crime." According to the *Atlanta Journal-Constitution* (August 2, 1998), they met at a hotel gym in California where she was exercising next to him; Cornwell thought she recognized him, introduced herself, and later gave him three of her novels. It was the start of a beautiful friendship. Cornwell later stopped by his office in D.C. to lobby on behalf of additional funding for the FBI academy, which he secured; he noted that she had done her homework before approaching him.

Hollywood. "Hollywood is all an illusion, really. Los Angeles is one of the strangest, most dramatic places I've ever been." (*Times-Dispatch,* February 22, 1994.)

Hughes, Jr., Melvin R.; Richmond circuit judge. In December 1998, he dismissed a lawsuit that alleged Cornwell had invaded the privacy of the parents of two young adults who were murdered at a rest stop off Interstate 64 in Virginia. *All That Remains* was the book at the center of the storm. According to the *Times-Dispatch,* such a suit is permitted "only when the name or likeness of a person is used without permission 'for advertising purposes or for the purposes of trade.' "

Jackson, Dot. Characterized as "Cornwell's best friend for years" (*Atlanta Journal-Constitution,* August 8, 1998), Jackson had worked at the *Charlotte Observer* with Cornwell. The friendship has run its course, with Jackson citing a professional disagreement over a screenplay written at Cornwell's behest. Cornwell, quoted in a profile for *Vanity Fair,* sees things differently: "To this day I don't know why she turned against me."

Jack the Ripper. The subject of a nonfiction book by Cornwell, to be published in 2002. Conducting extensive field research and spending an estimated $3 to 4 million in the process, Cornwell has become convinced that an Impressionist painter named Walter Sickert was the infamous prostitute killer who haunted London in 1888. Predictably, however, Cornwell's conviction is not universally shared. The general consensus is that the true identity of Jack the Ripper will never conclusively be determined.

Jamestown Rediscovery archeological project. Located in Jamestown near the James River. Patricia Cornwell literally digs this place. She's been there several times, most recently for a Thanksgiving dinner in 2000 with actor Dan Akyroyd and his wife, Donna Dixon. Although Cornwell had planned to use it as a major plot component in *The Last Precinct,* the material stubbornly resisted inclusion: Scarpetta, according to Cornwell, didn't want to follow the path the author had planned. The material was recycled for inclusion in the third Judy Hammer/Andy Brazil novel, *Isle of Dogs.*

K-9 Corps. After Patricia Cornwell read a newspaper report of the death of a police dog named Solo, she donated ten thousand dollars to buy bulletproof vests for Richmond's K-9 Corps. Observed Cornwell, "If I was out there with a K-9, I would hope I had some protection for my dog. Bad people will attack them, too." (*Times-Dispatch,* October 9, 1999.)

Kaliber whodunit mystery contest. A contest sponsored by Novel Futures Bookstore in Richmond and Kaliber nonalcoholic brew, the focus of this first contest was a "thumbnail mystery" written by Cornwell. Prizes include a weekend for two at The Homestead (a famous resort in West Virginia), dinner for four at a Richmond restaurant, and autographed copies of *Body of Evidence*. (*Times-Dispatch,* October 31, 1991.)

Kent, Bill (*New York Times Book Review*). "The follow-up novel, *Body of Evidence,* proved that Ms. Cornwell's success wasn't mere beginner's luck."

Kirk, Suzanne. The executive editor at Scribner who edited Cornwell's books. Cornwell dedicated *Cause of Death* to Kirk, calling her a "visionary editor and friend."

Life's Little Fable. Cornwell's first children's book. She read the book to hundreds of kids at the William Fox Elementary School. Said Cornwell, "I was a little bit nervous. Kids will be honest with you. If they don't like something they will let you know. . . . This book is my gift to children. I'm trying to give something back." (*Times-Dispatch,* June 2, 1999.)

Lockgreen subdivision in Richmond. Located off Cary Street, this was where Cornwell lived (*Times-Dispatch,* March 6, 1996). Purchased in 1994, the house is valued at $620,000 and the three acres of contiguous land are valued at $530,000. The house has alarm systems and twenty-four guards. (*Times-Dispatch,* March 1, 1996). Cornwell, who until recently owned two homes in Richmond, sold one and has leased the other out after moving to Greenwich, Connecticut.

Moore, Demi. Actress tapped by Cornwell to portray Scarpetta in the film version of *Cruel and Unusual.* Cornwell showed her a good time, taking her to the morgue, to Quantico for firing small arms, and having a private dinner at her Richmond home at which "Scarpetta's chili" was served. Nicknamed "Dead-eye Demi" for her firing accuracy on the range. Cornwell remarked later that she and Moore had bonded, smoking cigars in a hot tub. (*Times-Dispatch,* November 24, 1992.)

Morale in the police force. "If you went to work every day and were under-appreciated, and people only glared at you, and they didn't give you what you needed to do your job, what do you think your morale would be? You're going to have a percentage of people that are going to find it easy to make the wrong choices. They're going to be bitter and cynical and angry." (*Times-Dispatch*, November 13, 1995.)

Narrative drive. "I think when readers feel the surprise and freneticism in the books, that's because I feel it, too. By the end, I'm writing faster than I can type." (*Entertainment Weekly* online, 1992.)

Newberg, Esther. Agent at ICM who handles Patricia Cornwell's book deals. According to Deirdre Donahue reporting in *USA Today*, after Cornwell's three-book, $24 million deal, "Danielle Steel is believed to earn more per book. Tom Clancy and John Grisham are also believed to earn more than $8 million per book."

Notoriety. After the Bennett incident, Cornwell told the *Atlanta Journal-Constitution* (August 8, 1998) that "I would try to sneak out of my house and get the newspaper without my neighbors staring out the window and saying something awful. But you know what? People don't really care. They only care if you don't write another good book."

O Positive. Patricia Cornwell's blood type. (*Times-Dispatch*, March 1, 1996.)

Overnight success. "I was not the overnight success some people are nice enough to say I am." (*Court TV* transcript, with Catherine Crier.)

Personal handguns. Cornwell owns a .357 Colt Python, .380 Walther semiautomatic, and a .38 Smith & Wesson. Scarpetta carries a GLOCK 9-mm. (*Atlanta Journal-Constitution*, August 8, 1998.)

Personal holdings. According to the *Times-Dispatch* (April 9, 1997), Cornwell's holdings are considerable: an extensive stock portfolio, real estate (commercial and residential) in Virginia, and condos in the Cayman Islands and Hilton Head, South Carolina. Since then, Cornwell has relocated, personally and professionally, to Greenwich, Connecticut, put her office building in Richmond up for sale, and sold or leased her homes in Richmond.

Poggioshockoe. An Italian restaurant in Richmond at 12 North Eighth Street that, in October 1992, named its fall menu the "Dr. Kay Scarpetta Menu." Items on the menu included, among other mouth-watering delicacies, a "rib rack of free-range Virginia veal with cured ham and sage." No mention as to whether liver or raw meat was on the menu. (*Times-Dispatch,* October 1, 1992.)

Postmortem. The first Kay Scarpetta novel, purchased for an advance of six thousand dollars, published by Scribner in 1990, after being rejected by seven publishers. The second published book by Cornwell—her first was *A Time for Remembering: The Ruth Bell Graham Story* in 1983—a copy with dust jacket in fine condition, inscribed, can command up to $1,250 on the secondary market (the asking price of the Mysterious Bookshop for a copy listed on its Web site in July 2000). The novel won five awards: the John Creasey Award (British Crime Writers Association), Edgar Award (Mystery Writers of America), Anthony Award (Bouchercon, World Mystery Convention), Macavity Award (Mystery Readers International), and the Prix du Roman d'Adventure (French).

Princess Margaret. In December 1990, she presented the John Creasey Award from the British Crime Writers Association to Patricia Cornwell. This was the first time a woman had won both the Edgar and Creasey Awards for best first mystery novel.

Privacy. In the wake of the attempted murder trial of Eugene Bennett, Patricia Cornwell, hammered by the press, steadfastly held her ground when asked about her personal life. When asked about her marriage to Charles Cornwell, Patricia Cornwell stated, "I didn't talk about it when I was married, and I haven't talked about it since I was divorced." On the publicity that surrounded the disclosure of her friendship/relationship with Marguerite Bennett: "It hurts people around me, but I go on with my life. I know I'm a decent person. . . . I'm always comfortable telling the truth." (*Times-Dispatch,* April 9, 1997.)

Reading is fundamental. Patricia Cornwell has donated fifty thousand dollars to this charity.

Reality in her writing. "I have to live in the world I write about. . . . I try to use experience from my own life to give [Scarpetta], and the books, greater authenticity." (*Publishers Weekly,* February 15, 1991.)

Real-world locations in the Scarpetta novels. Cornwell sets her stories in the real world, which gives them verisimilitude. Regarding location, Mary B. W. Tabor (the *New York Times*) noted: "There is something especially savory about novels set in real places, with real street names, real shops, real sights and smells that ring true for those who know the territory."

Richmond police on Cornwell. "I think the Richmond Police Department and the entire Richmond community are extremely fortunate to have a fine friend like Patricia Cornwell. She continues to contribute to the community in more ways than can be counted," said Deputy Richmond Police Chief Fred Russell. (*Times-Dispatch,* June 13, 1999.)

Roses. In a gesture of ongoing thanks to her agent, Patricia Cornwell gives Esther Newberg at ICM a dozen roses for every million dollars in book contracts. Reports the *Times-Dispatch* (March 8, 1996): "So, in the past few years, Newberg has seen deliveries of 4.5 dozen, 12 dozen and, on Monday, 24 dozen roses. The latest delivery to Newberg's seventeenth-floor office included a note from the famous author: 'Esther, this is getting to be too much.'"

Sachs, Leslie Raymond. Richmond writer who published his own novel, *The Virginia Ghost Murders,* in 1998, with stickers on the front linking the book to Cornwell's eleventh Scarpetta novel, *The Last Precinct*. In response, Cornwell filed a $1.35 million lawsuit "demanding he stop the allegations and stop using her name," according to the *Times-Dispatch* (May 17, 2000). Said Cornwell in court when asked if she used ideas from his novel for her own novel: "The first time I've ever seen his book was when it was brought out in evidence in this courtroom." Sachs has since shut down his Web site promoting the book and said he's closed up shop.

Scarpetta, Dr. Kay. As the chief medical examiner for the Commonwealth of Virginia, she is the fictional protagonist in eleven novels, one novella, and one cookbook. She also makes an appearance in *Isle of Dogs.*

"Violence is filtered through her intellectual sophistication and inbred civility, meaning that the senseless cruelty of what she sees is all the more horrific. [She] approaches the cases with the sensitivity of a physician, the rational thinking of a scientist, and the outrage of a humane woman who values, above all else, the sanctity of life." (In a column in *Mystery Scene* magazine, quoted in *Contemporary Authors.*)

"So I do think she's kind of like the lady next door that you watch in the garden, but then you read about her in the newspaper and find out that she's this brilliant forensic pathologist who works crimes." (*Walden Book Report,* July 1998.)

Science Museum of Virginia. For its Life Sciences section, Patricia Cornwell donated $250,000 to develop a forensic exhibit. Said Cornwell, "This won't be a theme park sort of thing showing gory, bloody bodies. Still, it's important for young people and adults as well to realize that crime involves real people. Crime is not like a video game. In a way this will be another venue for me to present something that's really important to me. I want to make people feel like science is something that is accessible and part of their lives. If I wanted to do this any place in the world, Richmond and the Science Museum would be the place I'd choose." (*Times-Dispatch,* January 11, 1997.)

Seay, Pamela. Appointed as Cornwell's chief of staff of Cornwell Enterprises Inc., to administer her charitable foundation and the day-to-day operations of the company, which has eight staffers. She replaced Chris Bailor, who assumed new duties as the head of security and chief research assistant. (*Times-Dispatch,* January 27, 1995.)

Spielman, David. A New Orleans photographer who photographed Cornwell for *Southern Writers* (University of South Carolina Press, 1997). Spielman's photograph shows Cornwell sitting on top of a desk in her office in Richmond. Wrote Spielman in his book, "Patricia Cornwell lives in a high-security world. The best-selling author of seven mystery novels, she has received threats on her life and encountered more than her share of overzealous admirers. Her homes in Richmond, Virginia, and Los Angeles are well-protected. And the offices of Cornwell Enterprises in suburban Richmond . . . are unobtrusive but quite secure." In a story for the *Atlanta Journal-Constitution,* Spielman noted: "Patricia Cornwell has a reputation as that of a very difficult writer to get to. And even if you were lucky enough to get to her, you weren't going to have very much time anyway." To his surprise, Spielman found Cornwell more than accommodating.

Stryker saw. An autopsy saw that retails for eight hundred dollars. Cornwell gave a new one as a gift to Dr. Marcella Fierro, who took it out of the box and "swiveling her wrist, [she] demonstrates how the blade can easily slice through human muscle and bone. She explains that the saw doesn't work too well on flesh, which is supple and forgiving. "It's no good in the kitchen,' she says. They laugh." (A profile by Linton Weeks for the *Washington Post,* which appeared in the July 11, 1996 "home edition" of the *Los Angeles Times.*)

Terry, Mary Sue. A Democrat, she was the gubernatorial candidate in a race for governor against George Allen, a Republican.

Cornwell initially supported Terry, to the tune of twenty-five thousand dollars, but changed her tune and switched her support to Allen. "I was very inexperienced. I was your innocent," she said, speaking about Terry, as reported by the local paper. After switching her allegiance, she gave a press conference and on television commercials buttressed her argument that Mary Sue Terry, who ultimately lost the race, was not the right person for the job. Said Cornwell in the ads, "No one wants a woman for governor more than I do; so much so that I made a large contribution to Mary Sue Terry, only to discover she's only another politician. I've decided, not this woman, not this year. Then I say a bunch of good stuff about George [Allen]." (*Times-Dispatch,* October 22, 1993.)

Union Theological Seminary. Located in Richmond, Virginia, this is where Charles Cornwell (Patricia Cornwell's ex-husband) studied to become a minister. Patricia Cornwell made the move to Richmond as well.

Virginia Blood Services. In 1996, VBS drew blood from fellow Richmonders urged to donate by the city's most famous resident, Patricia Cornwell. In a clever approach, VBS staffers who were Cornwell fans sent her a fake manuscript titled "Postmortem Drip: Body of Blood," with "Dr. A. (Positive) Scalpeletta asking her friend Cornwell to do public service announcements for Virginia Blood Services." Their effort was not in vein—err, in vain; Cornwell rolled up her sleeves and not only pitched in but also gave blood as well. Remarked Cornwell, "It was for a great cause and I was glad to do it. . . . The real crime is not caring. Do what I do, give your blood. Give it whenever you can." (March 1, 1996).

Virginia Chamber Gala, seventy-fifth Anniversary celebration. Held on December 8, 1999, this black-tie gala's theme was "Celebrate Virginia for Virginians" and included Bruce Hornsby (a popular musician from Williamsburg) and Patricia Cornwell, among others.

Virginia Film Commission. In 1993, then-Virginia governor L. Douglas Wilder appointed Cornwell as the chairman of the new Virginia Film Office Advisory Board. Cornwell said that she'd "do everything in my power to see that movies made from my books will be filmed in Virginia. I'll do what I can to see that that is written into the contracts. It only makes sense and it would be a great way to recognize the people who made the books possible." (*Times-Dispatch,* December 4, 1993.)

Virginia Institute of Forensic Science and Medicine. Established in 1999 and located in Richmond, Virginia, this institute is the first of its kind in the world, and broke ground after Cornwell donated $1.5 million. James Kouten noted that "we give our students experience in real-world working labs so they are fully qualified. We give them one year on the actual type of equipment they will work on when they go out into the real world in a private or public lab to do forensic work. That allows them to become hands-on, fully qualified individuals in that discipline." The brainchild of Paul Ferrara (head of Virginia's Division of Forensic Science), the idea was shepherded by Cornwell to Gov. Jim Gilmore after Dr. Marcella Fierro provided her input. The result is a one-of-a-kind institute that, as Cornwell put it, will be a world-class resource, "the Johns Hopkins of forensic science and medical training." According to the *Times-Dispatch* (July 3, 1999), "It will offer a one-year program leading to certification as a forensic scientist, and the institute's students will include biologists, toxicologists and pharmacologists."

Virginia Literacy Foundation. To benefit this charity, Patricia Cornwell donated, from the proceeds of her first children's book, *Life's Little Fables,* fifty thousand dollars. She is also a board member of this charity.

Virginia Press Association. In 1995, the VPA honored Cornwell as their Virginian of the Year. At the ceremony accepting the award, Cornwell said, "People ask me what was the most profound experience that led you to where you are now. It was not working in a morgue. . . . It was being a journalist." (*Times-Dispatch,* June 25, 1995.)

Wesley, Benton. Fictional FBI profiler in the Kay Scarpetta novels who was romantically involved with her. Wesley met his match in *Point of Origin.*

Wiecking, David, former Chief Medical Examiner of Virginia. Nicknamed "The Chief," Wiecking, then sixty, retired in August 1993 after twenty-one years as the chief medical examiner. Of him, Cornwell said, "There's a little of him in Scarpetta," citing similarities between his background and her fictional heroine's background. (*Times-Dispatch,* August 23, 1993.)

Williams, Ray, police detective. When Patricia Cornwell was a volunteer police officer, she rode with Williams, a homicide detective. *See* Jim Gaudet.

Wyrick & Company. A book publisher in South Carolina that, in June 1997, hired Patricia Cornwell's former husband, Charles Cornwell, who left his position as an associate pastor at First (Scots) Presbyterian Church in Charleston to return to the fold. "I just couldn't pass up the opportunity to get back into something that is truly enjoyable for me," he told the *Times-Dispatch* in a phone interview (June 19, 1997).

THE QUOTABLE PATRICIA CORNWELL

Art of writing fiction. "I asked Cornwell if she had to 'get into character,' as actors must do when playing a role. She replied that writing fiction is a much more complicated process. In addition to getting into the minds of all the characters, she also must act as the playwright, director, set designer, lighting and props coordinators, and sound engineer. Rather than having live actors, realistic props and colorful scenery as in a play or movie, she has to do it all with word pictures." (Ron Bower, "Operators: Point of Origin.")

Authenticity and fiction. "I have one rule. It has to be within the realm of possibility." (Patricia Cornwell, quoted by Katherine Calos, "Show Biz: Cornwell on TV," *Richmond News Leader.*)

Authenticity of the Scarpetta novels. "The heroine, Dr. Kay Scarpetta, does truly function as a medical examiner. She is involved not just with the autopsy, but also with the integration of findings from other disciplines to arrive at the cause of death. In addition, she does not solely confine herself to the cause of death, but gathers additional information which might potentially help the prosecution of the case." (Dr. Thomas E. Henry, "A Reality Check for Fictional Doc," *Denver Rocky Mountain News.*)

Betrayed friendships. "I'm heartbroken that people I love and that I'm extremely good to betray me. And then I lose another friend. So it's really my loss more than their loss. . . . Betrayal, yes. Terrible betrayals. It is bizarre! I don't know what it is about my Karma. Someone said to me not so long ago, 'What is it about you that draws all this stuff to you!' And I don't know. I don't know." (Patricia Cornwell, in "Death Becomes Her," by Judy Bachrach in *Vanity Fair.*)

Body Farm. "Nothing I had ever seen prepared me for the images that assaulted me the minute I walked into that overgrown several acres of land behind the fence. There were about 40 bodies out there the first time I went, and I had the eerie sensation of having walked into something like a Civil War battleground." (Patricia Cornwell, quoted by the Reuters News Media.)

Celebrity, high price of. "The point of what I am saying: It's not a big deal! These things happen! It's too bad these things happen! It's too bad these things had to become public. But that's the price of being a celebrity." (Patricia Cornwell, commenting on the Bennett scandal, in "Death Becomes Her," by Judy Bachrach in *Vanity Fair.*)

Compassion. ". . . If everyone would reach out to the hurting person right before his eyes, the world would change, because if you make a difference in even one life, you have changed that person's world, and in the process, your own." (Patricia Cornwell, "Twice Rescued," *USA Today.*)

Copycat killer crime. "I find it an incredible irony that of all books, it would be mine. I think nobody out there is more sensitive to violence than I am or tries harder to deal appropriately with it in a novel." (Patricia Cornwell on a copycat crime in which a Florida killer was found to have had a copy of *Postmortem* in his apartment. Katherine Calos, "Florida Killing Fits Book, Police Say," *Richmond News Leader.*)

Cornwell's philanthropy. "I think the Richmond Police Department and the entire Richmond community are extremely fortunate to have a fine friend like Patricia Cornwell. She continues to contribute to the community in more ways than can be counted." (Deputy Richmond Police Chief Fred Russell, "City Police Dogs Sport Bulletproof Vests," by Jim Mason, *Times-Dispatch*.)

Crime novels. "Most crime novels are just puzzles to be solved. I couldn't do that. I feel too outraged by murder and how it affects the people left behind. What I find interesting is when you make the dead speak through science and medicine, and that person tells you through her wounds and through the trace evidence under her fingernails what happened and when it occurred." (Patricia Cornwell, quoted by Anita Chaudhuri, "Prime Subject.")

Critics. "When you've had really big success, critics are just looking for a chance to blast you out of the water. I think my characters are colorful, and I think my fans agree. They wouldn't keep buying my books if they didn't." (Patricia Cornwell, quoted by Don O'Briant, "Pistol-Packing Author's Dreams Are Just as Grisly as Her Thrillers.")

Dark times before *Postmortem*. "By now I was desperate. I was working full-time in a morgue, we're still dirt poor, living in a seminary, and I thought I'd ruined my life. Here I'd been an award-winning journalist and biographer and look at me now. I was a failure." (Patricia Cornwell, quoted by Mary Cantwell, "How to Make a Corpse Talk," *New York Times*.)

Davidson College. "I feel Davidson College did so much for me that I am delighted over the chance of giving something back. The college teaches you to be very self-reliant and to believe that if you can do well at Davidson, you can do well anywhere in the world." (Patricia Cornwell, press release, 1992.)

Financial predators. "There are predators. I've been accused of all sorts of things, from basing a book on some real murdered child to sexual harassment of an employee who was fired for good reason. They think I'll give money to get rid of them. I'd rather spend $300,000 fighting a smear on my character than pay $50,000 for someone to just go away. I've probably spent $1 million defending myself. Those cases have always been thrown out [of court]. I'll fight every time." (Patricia Cornwell, quoted by Jeff Guinn, "Kay Scarpetta, Examined: Author Patricia Cornwell Comes to Grips with Pain in Her Latest Novel.")

Glamorizing serial killers. "In America we've become so focused and so curious about these aberrant people, we almost celebrate them. They have women who want to marry them, for crumb's sake." (Patricia Cornwell, quoted by Mary Cantwell, "How to Make a Corpse Talk," *New York Times*.)

Homicide. "Homicide is the ultimate abuse of power." (Patricia Cornwell, quoted by Linton Weeks, "Murder-Minded: Crime Writer Patricia Cornwell Isn't Afraid to Tackle the Grisly," *Washington Post*.)

Humor and *Hornet's Nest*. "It's a police novel. It's very humorous. It's got its points but it's fun. You can't write about cops and not laugh. It's very satirical in some ways. I hope [people] will not go into it thinking this is a Scarpetta novel because they won't know what to make of it, because it is definitely not. There is no vague similarity between Scarpetta and this. It's more about what it's like to be on the streets with the police." (Patricia Cornwell, quoted by John Edwards, "Author Eschews Labels Except Maybe Eccentric," *Richmond* magazine, November 1996).

Literary production. "The best I did was write 200 pages in 10 days. Next morning I woke up, my left hand was paralyzed for four months. Radial-nerve damage. But I wasn't unbalanced. I was just manic like an artist gets manic." (Patricia Cornwell, in "Death Becomes Her," by Judy Bachrach in *Vanity Fair*.)

Loyal fans. "After five books, I guess you truly develop fans. They form relationships with the characters and, they think, with you as well. In the main, that's very, very good. But there's also a negative side. . . . We've had a vast array of flaky people." (Patricia Cornwell, quoted by Bill Lohman, on the occasion of a book signing in Richmond; "Making a Killing: Fans Come by Hundreds for Latest Cornwell Mystery," *Times-Dispatch*.)

Paranoia. "People think I'm paranoid, but that's the way it is out there. In New York the other night at a signing, a guy showed up with a knife on his belt. He was told to get rid of the knife or leave, so he left. Maybe it was nothing, but look at what happened to celebrities like John Lennon and Monica Seles." (Don O'Briant, "Pistol-Packing Author's Dreams Are Just as Grisly as Her Thrillers," *Atlanta Journal Constitution*.)

Persistence. "I have this very cagey way of worming myself in. I'm an infection. You try to pacify me, and before you know it, you can't get me out of your system." (Patricia Cornwell, quoted by John Monk, in "Mystery Woman for Years, Patricia Cornwell's Novels Were Rejected," *Charlotte Observer*.)

Privacy and Cornwell's sexual orientation. "It will be the great question mark. I don't care what I am or am not. I will never discuss it. I didn't talk about what Charlie [her former husband] and I did when I was living with him. There are some things that are not anybody's business and again to be perfectly blunt about it, if you come right out and say I am heterosexual or I am homosexual or I am bisexual, then you are giving people a license to categorize you in a political way and to make you their poster child to be used either for or against people. . . . If you have a nondiscrimination category, that is my politics, my religion and that is my personal life." (Patricia Cornwell, quoted by John Edwards, "Author Eschews Labels Except Maybe Eccentric," *Richmond* magazine, November 1996).

Returning to Charlotte, North Carolina. "It was very emotional, coming here. I've only been back once since I left in 1981 but this was where I got my first job, my start in life, where I got married. In some ways, I still feel like the kid running down the escalator with a radio on my belt, racing to get a story." (In an interview at the cafeteria of the *Charlotte Observer,* conducted by Polly Paddock, "From Observer Writer to International Author.")

Rolling over a rented Mercedes in California. "It was a necessary experience. Things were out of control. I was going to live or die. I was going to be bankrupt or I was going to make it." (Patricia Cornwell, quoted by Geraldine Fabrikant, "Cornwell Writes a New Chapter: Novelist Struggles to Get a Grip on Chaotic Personal Finances," *New York Times.*)

Ruth Graham. "When I was working my way through Davidson College as a waitress, Ruth would send me letters with a $100 check in them. She was like a mother to me." (Patricia Cornwell, quoted by Don O'Briant, "Pistol-Packing Author's Dreams Are Just as Grisly as Her Thrillers," the *Atlanta Journal Constitution.*)

Ruth Graham and writing. "The fact that she was interested [in my writing] changed my whole life." (Patricia Cornwell, quoted by Jenn Burleson, "Celebrities Turn Out for Fund-Raiser to Honor Ruth Graham's 80th Birthday.")

Scarpetta and Cornwell. She is "in my heart of hearts what I would like to be. A very moral person . . . a child of light, so to speak, who is doing battle with . . . irrationality, inhumanity and evil." (Patricia Cornwell, quoted by John Monk, in "Mystery Woman for Years, Patricia Cornwell's Novels Were Rejected," *Charlotte Observer.*)

Scarpetta, Kay. "I think what Scarpetta represents to me [is] what I consider the modern enlightened human being. Because she . . . does not have prejudices, but most of all she's not trussed up by stereotypes and assumptions. And she is the absolutely essential representation of someone who does not and will not abuse power." (Patricia Cornwell, quoted by Beatriz Terrazas, "Soul Researching: Patricia Cornwell's Latest Novel Emerged from Her Own Dark Places," *The Dallas Morning News*.)

Scarpetta on screen. "We've been in negotiations for years, [but] you have the major obstacle, which is me. . . . I want to preserve [readers'] fantasies of Scarpetta and my own fantasies of her." (Patricia Cornwell, quoted by Kathy Passero, "Stranger than Fiction: The True-Life Drama of Novelist Patricia Cornwell," *Biography*, May 1998).

Security. "Patricia Cornwell lives in a high-security world. The best-selling author of seven mystery novels, she has received threats on her life and encountered more than her share of overzealous admirers." (William W. Starr, *Southern Writers*, University of South Carolina Press.)

Unwanted attention. "I think the fact that I am a high-profile single woman, coupled with my subject matter, is a very volatile combination. When I get letters from inmates saying they'll be out soon, I'll go: 'Arrgh, I'll have to take my 9mm with me everywhere I go.'" (Patricia Cornwell, quoted by Anita Chaudhuri, "Prime Subject.")

Virginia Institute of Forensic Science and Medicine. "To me, the best thing I can do is give back to help victims, if I do things that might result in one less person being murdered or hurt or victimized in any way by having evidence processed more quickly." (Mark Holmberg and Bill McKelway, "With Donation, Life Will Imitate Art," *Times-Dispatch*.)

Writing. "I don't do it as a job. I don't write an outline or plot everything out. My office looks like a bomb hit it, totally unstructured. I do all the research first, and none of the writing, then I sit in front of what I've gathered and go to work. I take notes all the time, can't turn it off, use spare moments to jot things down. Then I go into seclusion; I go under, and I write a book." (*Costco Connection,* January 1999.)

Writing, on editing her books. "Very little gets lost in editing. It's not like movies where the director gets the final cut. I get the final cut. Nobody changes what I'm doing without my consent. The book that you see is pretty much what I turn in." (*Court TV* transcript in 1999, with Catherine Crier.)

Writing, on passion. "I think the most important thing is that you have to believe in what you're doing. It can't just be cranking out another book—it's your mission."

Writing, on when she started. "Probably since I was old enough to hold a crayon. All my life, really. It's always been my most natural form of expression." (*Court TV* transcript, with Catherine Crier.)

Writing, on where the ideas come from. "Everybody asks me that. I guess the answer is primarily from research." (*Court TV* transcript, with Catherine Crier.)

AN INTERVIEW WITH
PATRICIA CORNWELL

I'm a sucker, obviously, for companion-style books, especially the ones like *Deadly Women: The Woman Mystery Reader's Indispensable Companion,* which is jam-packed with articles by the biggest female names in the field. Published in 1998 by Carroll & Graf, this book also contained a short interview with Patricia Cornwell, conducted by Paul Duncan at the Waldorf Hotel in New York City.

Paul Duncan: Where does the character of Kay Scarpetta come from?

Patricia Cornwell: I have a suspicion that—and this may sound bizarre—one of her genetic coils is from my own relationship with Ruth Graham when I was growing up. She is a very powerful woman, very beautiful and very, very kind. She has a heart of gold and is a compassionate person but, in her own way, is reserved. She was certainly a heroic character to me at a period of time in my life when I had no power, when I was very young. That's the sort of person you want to come save you when something bad happens.

PD: Kay is not similar to anyone?

Patricia Cornwell: It probably has something to do with the fact that I didn't have anyone in mind when I came up with her. Also, because I'm so rooted in reality—to the real professionals and the real cases—I tend to get somewhat removed from literary, TV, or film characters. They, to me, are not reality, so they have no bearing on my work. This means I have a difficult time trying to explain my characters because people like to categorize them by comparing them to other characters.

PD: However, having created this popular character—a female medical examiner who works for the FBI at Quantico—all sorts of variations of her have started to appear in the past five years. The most notable is probably Dana Scully in *the X-Files,* who has expressed some of the same ideas and thoughts as Kay Scarpetta.

Patricia Cornwell: This is one of the reasons why Peter Guber and I are not wasting any time in producing the first Scarpetta film. Unfortunately, my books are the inspiration for other people to come up with other strong female protagonists, particularly in the FBI or medical fields. I won't even watch or read these other things that people tell me about because they'll probably just aggravate me.

One of the reasons I've been fortunate enough to have access to a lot of places and information is because I have a platform of legitimacy from my profession and background. You also earn your credibility through word of mouth and by meeting people. I can't continue to enjoy the world these people live in unless they know they can trust me. They read the books, think I'm okay and the doors open.

PD: You work to get the facts right?

Patricia Cornwell: It's an unforgiving world. If you get something wrong, people turn off you just like that. Besides that, I want to get it right for myself, keep it honest. It's very important to me personally, to get it right, to know what it feels like and to experience it as much as I can.

PD: With access to all this information, and with her two years' experience as an award-winning crime reporter for the *Charlotte Observer,* I would have thought that Patricia would be writing fact, not fiction.

Patricia Cornwell: Sometimes fiction is truer than fact. Actually, I do both, because the scaffolding of all my stories is fact, whether it is a procedure, or the type of case, or the kinds of individuals. It is all rooted in experience and research. That's the fact. The fiction of it is the way that I want the characters to work the cases.

People have asked me over the years why I don't write True Crime and I tell them that I could not bring myself to victimize people all over again. If you have a son or daughter murdered in what turns out to be a sensational crime about which books are written, and you have been on the side of the fence where I have been—seeing relatives sitting in the waiting rooms and the looks on their faces as they come to find out what's happened to their child—I don't want to write about things in gory detail that could upset those relatives all over again. There are cases where people find it cathartic to write about their experiences, and I don't bump the people who do it, it's just that I couldn't, and I don't want to.

PD: The books have very little violence in them. All we see are the effects, both physical and emotional, of violence committed off-screen.

Patricia Cornwell: That's because that's all that Scarpetta sees. It's very rare that Scarpetta will witness a violent act unless she herself commits it, as she's had to do in several books when she's had to defend herself. I only show violence when the bad guys are getting it, not when the victim is getting it.

PD: Is that planned, or is it just the way it's worked out?

Patricia Cornwell: That's the way I feel. Violence is a reality to me. I mean, I've had my hands on these dead bodies. I've been to the murder trials. I've been to the crime scenes. I've seen people roll through doors who've had their lives viciously ripped from them. I have no use for the people who commit those kinds of acts. My sympathy is for the victims. That's why I'm very comfortable with Scarpetta because she is their defender. That's the way I feel. I couldn't do it any other way.

PD: Scarpetta is very single-minded. She's on a crusade.

Patricia Cornwell: I'd say she and I both have lives consumed by what we do and what we believe. It's that I express mine in a different way than she does. She actually works the cases and I tell the story of the cases. I have said many times that what I really consider myself to be is a scribe to the people out there doing the real work, whether it is the forensic pathologists, the FBI agents, the police, the scientists, the prosecutors. . . . Someone needs to tell their stories, go in their labs and find out exactly what they're doing today. "Well, I'm using a gas chromograph to do this . . ." or ". . . the scanning electron microscope to determine which element this is . . ." They need someone like me to do that, and that's really what I consider my job.

PD: She is so driven or obsessive about her job that it seems, perhaps, sad that she has so little life outside her job.

Patricia Cornwell: It's not so much obsessive or driven as it is being devoted. For one to say that Scarpetta is obsessive or driven is like saying that a priest is. It's like a calling. She has taken on a mantle to help people who have no power. She's like a missionary, or a minister, or priest to the people who can no longer speak in a language that other people can understand. That's the way I regard what I do too.

People can also say the same thing about me. I'm divorced. I haven't remarried. I have no kids. You never read in the papers about me dating someone, and so on. It's not that I don't have a private life, or friends, and attachments—I think I have a very rich life in that way—but I deal with people in snatches. I can't have weeks on end with people I like unless I happen to be working with them. It's for the same reason. I'm not driven to be the number-one crime writer in the world—it's just that I'm [as] devoted to what I'm doing as Scarpetta is to what she's doing.

In the same way, I have to be as devoted to her so that I can tell her story and always learn the latest advances in technology or medicine that would be applicable to what she does so that I'm knowledgeable enough to deal with it in a book. And that takes a lot of time.

PD: Certainly, the temptation is to compare Patricia and Kay.

Patricia Cornwell: We're the same, but we're different. Certainly, some things are the same—how could they not be because they're coming out of me? So we probably share the same genetic code, by and large, but we're not exactly the same people. Maybe she's another manifestation of what I would be like if I did what she did for a living? Certainly, there are parallels.

PD: I think it would be difficult to write about somebody like her if you didn't share some of the same qualities. Like, for example, a devotion to justice, integrity, and decency; fighting for people who can't fight for themselves, trying to make the world a little better.

Patricia Cornwell: You can't fake that. You either feel it or you don't. I couldn't make you feel what she feels if I didn't feel it.

For each book, I come up with a case I want her to work and then I go through the pilgrimage with her, and I simply put things down pretty much the way I see them, and the way I know them from reality. In reality, of course, nobody is pure good and nobody is pure bad, but there are certainly good and evil people. Without a doubt Temple Brooks Gault is evil. That doesn't mean that he doesn't have good qualities. I don't know what they are and I don't care what they are, and I'm sure Kay doesn't care what they are either.

If you work in these professions, when people do things which are this heinous, you're not interested in their good qualities. You just want to figure out enough about them so that you can catch them, or at least give them a name so you can find them.

As far as Kay is concerned, she is not perfect, but she is purely good in terms of her integrity and morality where justice is concerned. She is having an affair with a married man, Benton Wesley—that's not moral. That's not even smart. She knows it too and she has trouble with it. She's not always done the right thing with Lucy, and she knows it. And Lucy knows it, too. But Kay tries.

I think it's on the personal front that it's more difficult which, I think, is true for most of us. You will never catch me being dishonest in the business world or even in my profession, but sometimes I might be dishonest in my personal life because I don't say something I should say because it's too hard for me to say it. That's where Kay's weaker.

PD: Reading *Cruel and Unusual, The Body Farm,* and *From Potter's Field,* these books read as a trilogy.

Patricia Cornwell: In those three books, as a matter of fact, I was trying very hard to get Kay to loosen up a little bit. I think you see that because she has more emotional situations on her hands.

PD: So there was no design for the three books?

Patricia Cornwell: No. I start each one with a case and I never know where each is going to go. For instance, *The Body Farm* was a really hard book for me to write because I set it in my own childhood, in the foothills of Western North Carolina. In a way, it was almost like killing off myself as a little girl, by putting myself imaginatively in that environment. If you're a little girl with no power, like Emily Steiner was, buried beneath the cold earth and people don't know the truth about your death, who would you want to find out who did it? You'd want Scarpetta.

She can't make the child alive again, but she can make her talk. Kay can do something for the living, to make it easy for them to cope with the evil which has occurred—that's really what she does in each of her books. Maybe we see it more and more in subsequent ones because it becomes more defined to me what her mission is. After all, just like you, I get to know her better each time. I know her a whole lot better now than I did in *Postmortem* and, I suspect, three years from now I will know her even better than I do now.

PD: I wouldn't be able to attend an autopsy. I would see the bodies as people and think of their past lives and emotions. I would find that too upsetting.

Patricia Cornwell: That is why you would probably be a good forensic pathologist. That's exactly what the good ones do. They don't look on the body they're cutting as a thing—the bad ones do because it's easier to divorce themselves from their humanity. The dead won't talk to you if you don't know them as a person.

If you really want to hear what they have to say you have to believe in their humanity. Yes, it is a sacrifice because it takes a lot out of you, but I think it takes more out of you not to do that because I think a part of you dies by degrees if you refuse to give a person their humanity. Even if they are dead.

I think one of the reasons people stay with Scarpetta for four hundred pages is because she does give people their humanity— she gives them names. She went through the whole of *From Potter's Field* determined to give the dead woman her name. When the man was beating his horse, she went up to him and asked him the horse's name and then asked him, "Do you beat Snow White every day, or just on Christmas Day?" She always gives a name to the victim, whether it's a horse or a bald lady found in

Central Park. That's what a good forensic pathologist will do. So you might be surprised at yourself. You might do better with it than you think.

I mean, it's not fun, but quite honestly the only way to endure some of the most difficult cases is if you give them their humanity. For example, one day I was with my friend Dr. Marcella Fierro, who's now the chief medical examiner—she's one of the best forensic pathologists in the world, and I've been very lucky to have her as a mentor. We were going down to the morgue in the elevator and there was this horrible smell from a body we had found in the river. It had been there for several weeks in the middle of summer. I had smelt bodies before, but this was the worst. It was really, really wretched. I was going down to help, to scribe the labels. I looked at Marcella and said that sometimes I really didn't know how she could stand this. She looked at me and said that she just tried to remember who he was.

And when you think of that, suddenly you no longer see this bloated, hideous corpse but a man wearing a hat, T-shirt, shorts, and tennis shoes, and he's out on the river fishing with his son. I saw him for the rest of the morning and I was a good trouper and I did my job. If you cannot give that much humanity back to that person, why in the world would you want to spend that much time with what's left [of] him?

This is the world of Patricia Cornwell. It's a dangerous, sinister swirl of innocent victims, murderous monsters, decomposed corpses, unflagging forensic explorers and fanatical law enforcement officers who crave justice.

—LINTON WEEKS, *WASHINGTON POST*

SECTION II

THE FICTION: A LOOK AT THE WORKS OF PATRICIA CORNWELL

BODY OF WORK

Appropriately termed Patricia Cornwell's "body of work" on her official Web site, the body count, as it were, is up to seventeen books: eleven novels featuring Kay Scarpetta, three featuring Judy Hammer and Andy Brazil, one biography in multiple editions, one children's book, one novella, and a nonfiction book. Cornwell is a steady producer: 2001 saw the publication of a Kay Scarpetta cookbook, written in collaboration with Marlene Brown, engagingly titled *Food to Die For: Secrets from Kay Scarpetta's Kitchen*.

Though the audience for the Hammer books is increasing and there's always room on the bookshelf for a Scarpetta-related cookbook, Cornwell's fans hunger most for a new Scarpetta novel—a hunger that will be satisfied when Cornwell serves up her twelfth in the series, as yet untitled, due out in 2003.

In this section we'll look at each published book and discuss it thematically, without providing a detailed plot synopsis. The telling of the tale is best left to the author, though the story behind the story—the research involved in writing the novel—is something of interest to readers, and this kind of book is the appropriate place to discuss it.

I've used as standard a format as possible for each book at the time of this writing: editions in print, editions out of print, notes, clarifying book dedications, listings of the major geography that serve as fictional locales, the story behind the story, awards won, and selected reviews.

New fans of Cornwell will find it an especially daunting task to keep track of all the characters, the plot permutations, the abbreviations, codes, and geography of Scarpetta's eleven books, each building on what has gone before.

To assist the new reader and for fans who'd like to revisit the places and people in each novel, included in each book's section is an alphabetical look at the people, places, and things in each novel. Obviously, a detailed concordance of the people, places, and things would comprise a separate book and is beyond what I think most readers would want or need; I have selectively picked what I think are the most salient and noteworthy pieces of information.

Spoiler alert: Read the novels first and use this section as a reference guide, since there are unavoidable spoilers in these listings and, let's face it, part of the fun of reading her books is discovering the surprises on your own.

I suspect that Cornwell, like most bestselling authors, casts a wary eye on reviewers in general. The barometer of her success can best be seen in the sales of her books and not the critical reviews, which tend to be highly idiosyncratic: The sales are not subject to debate, but obviously the merit of the books themselves are. Therefore, Cornwell puts more credence in what her readers, not her critics, say, and is known to listen carefully to her faithful fans who send correspondence.

RUTH, A PORTRAIT: THE STORY OF RUTH BELL GRAHAM, 1997

Note: In 1983, Cornwell published *A Time for Remembering, the Ruth Bell Graham Story;* in 1997, she republished the book in a revised and expanded edition as *Ruth, a Portrait: the Story of Ruth Bell Graham.*

Editions

1. Hardback, Hodder & Stoughton (UK edition), signed, $30; available only from Cornwell's official Web site. (*Note:* The U.S. hardback edition is in print but currently out of stock at the publisher's.)
2. Trade paperback, $10.95, Galilee Book (imprint of Doubleday).
3. Large print edition, G. K. Hall.
4. *A Time for Remembering, the Ruth Bell Graham Story* (Harper & Row, 1983). Hardback. First edition, $200–250 (*Note:* Because this is the kind of book likely to be given as a gift, the owner is likely to sign his name and inscribe it to the recipient. In this case, the book is devalued signifi-

cantly; I've seen two copies of the first edition for sale in good condition thus marred, decreasing the value to $100.)

Dedication

"To the wise old woman."

This is a reference to the book's subject, Ruth Bell Graham.

Behind the Story

In terms of Cornwell's life, Ruth Bell Graham's positive influence cannot be overstated. Then in her early twenties, Cornwell persevered against considerable opposition—including Ruth and Billy Graham—to write the authorized biography of Ruth Bell Graham, whom she credits as *the* major influence in her life: "If any single person in this world made a difference in my life, she did," writes Cornwell in an essay for *USA Today* ("Make a Difference Day").

To Cornwell's credit, her perseverance paid off and the book, despite going through several drafts, made its way into print.

Perspective

Not only is this Cornwell's first book, it's the only book she revised and updated. Reviews on the book were positive and, had she chosen to do so, Cornwell could have written more biographies of religious figures, but her writing career took her in a different, more lucrative path: book-length fiction.

According to the *Charlotte Observer*, of the first printing of sixty-five thousand copies, twenty-five thousand copies were purchased by the Grason Company, the mail-order division of the Billy Graham Evangelistic Association.

In an introduction to the new edition, Cornwell writes that "it had been suggested that I update the biography I had decided to write long ago when I was twenty-four and too young to have any business asking."

The biography is a long, loving look at a woman who is perhaps best known as the wife of Rev. Billy Graham. As this portrait shows, however, the story of Ruth Bell Graham's life is every bit as inspirational as her husband's, and its telling is done by Cornwell with genuine admiration, giving Ruth Bell Graham the recognition she so richly deserves.

An illuminating book, *Ruth, a Portrait* sheds light on one of the most visible people in the Christian community worldwide.

Reviews

"The unlikely pairing of an award-winning crime novelist and the wife of the world's best-known evangelist results in a newly revised and updated biography of Ruth Bell Graham that is both fascinating and intimate." (*Christian Retailing* magazine.)

"The book is filled with observations that enrich readers' understandings of what makes Ruth the ideal partner for her husband— and an outstanding Christian role model in her own right." (*CBA Marketplace.*)

"Cornwell's biography illuminates the life of a woman whose devotion to husband and family is an expression of her devotion to God." (*Publishers Weekly.*)

POSTMORTEM: A KAY SCARPETTA MYSTERY, 1990

Editions

1. Trade hardback: out of print. Value, with dust jacket: first edition, $925; signed, $950. Scribner.
2. "Turtleback" for Young Adult market.
3. Paperback: $7.99, Pocket Books.
4. Unabridged audiotape: read by C. J. Critt, $39.95, Harper-Audio; also Books on Tape.
5. Abridged audiotape: read by Lindsay Crouse, $18, Harper-Audio.
6. Amazon.com listed *Postmortem* in a series called "The Best Mysteries of All Time." Impress Publications Ltd is the publisher and the publication date was listed as November 2000.
7. Smithmark, a reprint house, republished *Postmortem, Body of Evidence,* and *All That Remains* in an omnibus edition.

Dedication

"To Joe and Dianne"

Geography

Richmond, Virginia.

Story Behind the Story

Some story elements inspired by the real-life crimes of the South Side Strangler (Richmond, Virginia), John B. Waterman.

Awards Won

John Crease Award (British Crime Writers Association), Edgar Award (Mystery Writers of America), Anthony Award, Bouchercon (World Mystery Convention), Macavity Award (Mystery Readers International).

Perspective

Stephen King's *Carrie,* Anne Rice's *Interview with the Vampire,* Tom Clancy's *The Hunt for Red October*—all are first novels that put their creators on the literary fast track to bestsellerdom.

In 1990, Patricia Cornwell joined that exclusive list with the publication of *Postmortem.*

An award-winning book, *Postmortem* immediately established Patricia Cornwell—then best known in literary circles for her authorized biography of Ruth Bell Graham—as a first-rate story-teller, with the promise of more books to come. (*Postmortem,* in fact, is subtitled *A Kay Scarpetta Mystery.*)

A competent and compassionate medical examiner, Dr. Kay Scarpetta relies not on brawn but on brain to piece together the identity of the killer who stalks women in Richmond, Virginia. The recipient of five major awards in the field, *Postmortem* owes much of its verisimilitude to Cornwell's personal history. In the liner notes for *Postmortem,* she wrote: "It is important to me to live in the world I write about. If I want a character to do or know something, I try to do or know the same thing."

Unlike some other writers whose literary inspirations are principally other writers in the field, Cornwell drew her inspiration from the real world: Her background as a crime reporter for the *Charlotte Observer* and the time she spent as a volunteer police officer gave her a "feel" for the area of law-enforcement coupled with a journalistic style that lent itself to writing crime suspense fiction. Insofar as background is concerned, using Richmond instead of New York City, Los Angeles, Miami, or Chicago—all used by other writers—allowed her to lay claim to a city that no contemporary writer had explored.

The result: an archetypal protagonist in a setting new to most readers, using brainpower, not firepower, to solve crimes.

It's fair to say that although Cornwell wasn't the first woman to write crime novels featuring female protagonists, she was the first to popularize the use of a female medical examiner—a fresh twist that quickly earned her a legion of fans.

Postmortem, however, drew some criticism, as well: The basic premise hit too close to home for some Virginians. As reporter Mark Bowes (*Richmond Times-Dispatch*) put it: "In the fall of 1987, Richmond was a city in fear. During several terrifying months, a man who would become widely known as 'the South Side Strangler' slipped undetected into the homes of three local women, raping and killing them in ritualistic fashion. The Strangler became Richmond's most notorious serial killer, a sadistic sexual predator who left behind tortured corpses, frantic investigators and a terrified public."

The notoriety surrounding the Strangler and the linkage between him and the similarities in Cornwell's novel prompted one bookseller to take a moral stand even before its publication, refusing to stock it. In a piece for the *Richmond Times-Dispatch,* Ray McAllister interviewed Charles Wilson, who observed: "I guess I just think that the book shouldn't have used the real murders that sort of took place. It's not that I'm against a murder mystery but this one just hit a little too close to home. I think the book is well-written and I think it's involving and entertaining. But I would hate for the family members [of the Strangler's victims] to drive by and see a big display for this book, which is obviously painful to them."

The newspaper, of course, asked Cornwell of her reaction to Wilson's comments. Cornwell responded: "This book has been compared to Thomas Harris [author of *Silence of the Lambs*] already. I never show any violence happening in this book. I show crime scenes and autopsies."

In a piece for the *Richmond Times-Dispatch,* Robert Merritt pointed out the similarities between the real-world Strangler and Cornwell's fictional accounting. Merritt concluded, however, that her book was ". . . not a fictionalized account of the 'South Side Strangler.' It draws from reality, but it uses the case as a launching pad for a different story with a different solution."

In later interviews, Cornwell would defend her position as a writer and say that she writes about specific types of crimes, and not specific cases—a good way to avoid needless litigation, as she would later find out when the similarities between reality and her fictional worlds collided again in *All That Remains.*

In so far as her career was concerned, the success of *Postmortem* presented a formidable problem: Would the second Scarpetta novel be as successful—critically or financially?

Prepublication Blurbs

"Taut and true. A thriller on the cutting edge of criminology."
—Jerry Bledsoe, author of *Bitter Blood*

"I loved the book. This is a real page-turner. I didn't know until the end who the murderer was."
—Julie Nixon Eisenhower

"*Postmortem* is my favorite kind of mystery—strong female protagonist with a formidable expertise, solid prose, and intriguing story line powered by suspense. Looking forward to a sequel and please don't take too long."
—Sue Grafton (author of the "alphabet" mysteries—*A Is For Alibi*)

"*Postmortem* is an unbelievable outing for a first novelist—for any novelist, for that matter. The story is taut, riveting—whatever your favorite strong adjective, you'll use it about this book. Cornwell gives an insider's look at big-city politics that matches *Presumed Innocent* in its gritty realism—with the addition of a believable, well-paced story and volatile, wholly human characters."
—Sara Paretsky, author of the V. I. Warshawski novels

"Patricia Cornwell is brilliantly informed in the lore of the crime lab and medical examiner's office, and a natural at the intricacies of a pulse-stopping, blood-chilling, heart-stopping plot!"
—Ann Rule, author of *Small Sacrifices* and other police procedurals

Reviews

"Gripping . . . Cornwell makes looking through a microscope as exciting as a hot-pursuit chase." (*Washington Post Book World.*)

"Excellent . . . well-paced, well-written . . . beautifully done." (*New York Newsday.*)

"A well-plotted, well-written, gripping mystery with a chilling climax. After I catch my breath, I'll look forward to Dr. Scarpetta's next case." (*Winston-Salem Journal* [North Carolina].)

"Cornwell, a former reporter who has worked in a medical examiner's office, sets her first mystery in Richmond, Virginia. Chief medical examiner for the Commonwealth of Virginia, Dr. Kay Scarpetta, the narrator, dwells on her efforts to identify 'Mr. Nobody,' the strangler of young women. The doctor devotes days and nights to gathering computer data and forensic clues to the killer, although she's hampered by male officials anxious to prove themselves superior to a woman. Predictably, Scarpetta's toil pays off, but not before the strangler attacks her; a reformed male chauvinist, conveniently nearby, saves her. Although readers may be naturally disposed to admire Scarpetta and find the novel's scientific aspect interesting, they are likely to be put off by her self-aggrandizement and interminable complaints, annoying flaws in an otherwise promising debut." (*Publishers Weekly.*)

Cornwell's First Interview

The first major interview with Cornwell ever published appeared in *Publishers Weekly.* This interview was conducted after the publication of the paperback edition of *Postmortem* but before the hardback publication of her second book, *Body of Evidence.*

PATRICIA D. CORNWELL:
A *PUBLISHERS WEEKLY* INTERVIEW
By Joanne Tagorra

With its stately homes and neatly manicured lawns, the posh Richmond, Va., neighborhood of Windsor Farms presents a veneer of invulnerability. One would hardly imagine it the perfect setting for a murder mystery. However, author Patricia Cornwell—who moved to this exclusive enclave just two months ago—uses Windsor Farms as the unlikely scene of a brutal murder in her second novel, *Body of Evidence,* out this month from Scribner. Hailed by the *Los Angeles Times* as "the new mistress of mystery" for her first book, *Postmortem,* which introduced the feisty female chief medical examiner of Virginia, Dr. Kay Scarpetta, Cornwell obviously means it when she says, "I have to live in the world I write about."

Cornwell has extended this credo to her professional life as well. A former crime reporter and a computer analyst for the Virginia chief medical examiner's office in Richmond for the past six years, she has skillfully translated the grisly details of her daily work experience at the morgue and her hands-on knowledge of forensics into fiction, giving her novels a rare authenticity. This element of Cornwell's work, along with her page-turning plots and her convincing portrait of the street-wise yet sensitive forensic pathologist, Kay Scarpetta—a highly educated, highly placed woman confronted with the prejudices of a male-dominated system—has won the author high praise from critics.

Postmortem, a main selection of the Mystery Guild—just published in paperback by Avon—won the John Creasey Award from the British Crime Writers Association for the best first crime novel of the year. And *Body of Evidence,* a main selection of the Mystery Guild and an alternate selection of the Literary Guild and Doubleday Book Club, promises to secure Cornwell's growing reputation. Several major houses are set to bid for the book's paperback rights at auction this month.

Talking with *PW* in the living room of her sprawling Tudor-style home, the author's petite, athletic frame seems dwarfed by the spaciousness of her new surroundings. Blonde and blue-eyed, casually dressed in jeans and a ski sweater, the 34-year-old Cornwell's all-American appearance is an odd contrast with the room's exotic and eclectic trappings: oriental rugs and hanging tapestries that, she explains, "came with the house." Admittedly, she is still uneasy with her new role as homeowner, particularly in one of the oldest and most exclusive sections of the city.

But she is also amused by the irony of how her life has come to imitate her art and vice versa: in *Body of Evidence,* for example, which—inspired by a newspaper item—revolves around a series of gruesome murders, the central victim is a successful young writer who, after being harassed, threatened and stalked by her killer, inexplicably allows him to enter her home in secluded Windsor Farms. "It's really very strange," Cornwell says, her Southern accent fairly evident. "At the time I was working on *Body of Evidence,* I had no earthly idea I'd be living here when the book came out. The coincidence didn't even strike me until after I had moved."

In Cornwell's just-completed third novel, of what promises to be an ongoing series, Dr. Scarpetta will also become a resident of Windsor Farms. "I guess you can understand why she has to get out of the house she's been living in," jokes Cornwell, referring to the fact that in both *Postmortem* and *Body of Evidence,* the chief examiner narrowly escapes with her life at the hands of the killers she has been pursuing.

Elements of Cornwell's life are an underlying force in her novels, particularly evident in the character and perspective of Kay Scarpetta. Explains the author: "I try to use experiences from my own life to give her, and the books, greater authenticity. She's from Miami, where I grew up, so I don't have any trouble describing her mother's garden, for example. And I understand being divorced and childless. I couldn't see her happily married with a family—that hasn't been my experience. These things don't overpower the story; they're just things I know."

Dr. Scarpetta's debut as the powerful female protagonist in *Postmortem* was the result of what Cornwell describes as a "long, literary evolution." The author—who admittedly has never been an avid mystery reader—first decided to try her hand at the genre back in 1984. Cornwell had been an award-winning police reporter—her first exposure to the crime scene—for the *Charlotte Observer* following her graduation from Davidson College, where she was an English major, in North Carolina in 1979. In 1981, she moved to Richmond with her then-husband, a Davidson professor who had enrolled in the Union Theological Seminary, and began work on a biography of Ruth Graham Bell (the wife of evangelist Billy Graham). . . . The book, *A Time for Remembering,* was published by Harper & Row in 1983, and Cornwell was left with a gap in her literary life.

"I had always wanted to be a novelist," explains Cornwell, "but I also had all this background and first-hand experience as a crime reporter that I wanted to use. So I decided to try to combine these two impulses and write a mystery novel."

Cornwell had already started on her first book in 1984 (she would end up writing three before she hit it right with *Postmortem*) when a physician friend in Richmond suggested she talk with a medical examiner to get an insider's view of the morgue and the workings of the examiner's office, including its sophisticated crime-solving techniques and forensic investigations. "I had never met a medical examiner when I was on the police beat. I had never even been to a morgue. I called the deputy chief medical examiner here in Richmond, Dr. Marcella Fierro, and she was kind enough to grant me an interview," Cornwell recalls.

Cornwell talked to Fierro for three hours, walking her through a death scene in her book. "I was shocked by two things," she says. "One, by how fascinating it was, and two, by how absolutely little I knew about it. I realized I had no idea what a medical examiner would do—Did they put on gloves, wear lab coats and surgical greens? They do none of the above."

Propelled by her "ignorance," Cornwell says she "became compulsive." Following another interview with Fierro—who has since become a good friend and colleague—she began "hanging around" the examiner's office. "I infused myself with that place, asking questions, doing anything they would let me do." As part of her stint there, Cornwell also started observing autopsies.

Finally, the chief medical examiner hired Cornwell to do technical writing for the office on a part-time basis, which, she explains, gave her "some legitimacy." In the meantime, she also became a volunteer police officer in Richmond. "Though a lot of it was mundane," she says, "I got a taste of what it's like to be out there in the rank and file." For three years, Cornwell rode with homicide detectives once a week on their 4 P.M. to midnight shifts: "I would follow their footsteps into a house where a dead body was laid out and watch them look for shell casings and fingerprints, observing everything they did."

In the course of a five-year period, Cornwell ended up a full-time employee at the chief medical examiner's office—which she describes as "the closest thing we have in this country to Scotland Yard"—working as a computer analyst. During that same period, Cornwell wrote the three books that "nobody wanted. The main character was a male detective, a kind of poor man's Adam Dalgliesh," she explains, referring to the celebrated P. D. James protagonist. "He just didn't work."

Cornwell's first two novels were rejected by all of the major publishing houses. "I couldn't even get anyone to look at the third," she recalls. "And I couldn't find an agent to take me on." Frustrated and despairing, Cornwell sent 50 pages of her manuscript to P. D. James with a letter asking her to read them. "She promptly sent it back, saying that she did not have time to read and critique other people's manuscripts, but she also wrote me a very nice, encouraging letter. And irony of ironies," muses Cornwell, "in less than a month I'll be doing a joint book signing with her in Chicago."

Indeed, Cornwell was about to give up her career as a mystery novelist when—ever-persistent—she sought out the advice of an editor at Mysterious Press, Sara Ann Fried, who had always written her "very nice" rejection letters. "I needed to know if it was worth it to keep trying, and she was very encouraging. And she also gave me some very sage advice. She said that I should write about what I knew, instead of esoteric poisonings set in river mansions somewhere. And she advised me to make Scarpetta the main character. The male detective just wasn't believable."

Just about the time Cornwell started to toy with ideas for her next novel, in the summer of 1987, a grim series of stranglings began in Richmond. "One of the victims was a woman physician. That really hit home for the other female physicians in the office, but also for the men, several of whom had known her through her work."

Cornwell began to consider how Dr. Scarpetta would deal

with such a situation. "I wondered, if I made her the main character, what she would do. I wanted to approach it from a psychological perspective—Scarpetta projecting onto the life of this murdered female physician and identifying with her. That's how *Postmortem* evolved," she explains, stressing that the book is totally fictitious. "I never studied the details of the cases because I didn't want to be influenced by them."

About a year later, in the winter of 1988, Cornwell had just finished *Postmortem* when her boss asked her to attend the opening of the new Dade County medical examiner['s] office in Miami—where the author was planning a family visit. "What else do you do on vacation if you're me?" Cornwell asks, laughing. "You go to the dedication of a new morgue."

Fortuitously, Cornwell ran into Edna Buchanan, the Pulitzer Prize–winning police reporter for the *Miami Herald* and author of *The Corpse Had a Familiar Face* (Random House). The two spent the afternoon together, and Buchanan suggested Cornwell contact her agent, Michael Congdon. "I had already finished the first draft of *Postmortem,* so I sent him the manuscript. He sat on it for several months and then he called and said he would take me on as a client."

In the fall of 1988 the book began to make the rounds. "Interestingly," Cornwell notes, "it went the same way my first three books had gone—four or five houses rejected it immediately. Finally, in January, Scribner took it," and Cornwell began a productive working relationship with editor Susanne Kirk. As she prepares for a one-month publicity tour, and awaits the results of the paperback auction, she is hard at work on her fourth novel, in which, she says, "I've come up with something out of thin air—unlike anything I've ever read." As for the rest of the series, "I'm much less infatuated now with the forensic tricks and scientific information—though they will always be an important aspect of my books—and much more interested in the psychological and spiritual nuances of Scarpetta's life: what she thinks when she's looking out the window drinking her coffee, what it feels like to be her, instead of what it's like to know what she knows."

According to Cornwell, readers can expect to see a mellower, less strident Scarpetta in future books. "I get more interested in her with each novel, and as long as I continue to grow and change, so will she. She really is a part of me and that's why she's so real. Again, it's just a part of trying to live what I write."

Postmortem A to Z

Amburgey, Dr. Alvin. A health commissioner whose office as part of HHSD (Health and Human Services) was located across the street from Scarpetta's.

Armando. Dorothy Farinelli's first husband, whom she subsequently divorced. She married him when she was eighteen; he was twice her age. He was from Miami and lived a questionable lavish lifestyle.

"Auntie Kay." Lucy Farinelli's nickname for her aunt, Kay Scarpetta.

Bertha. Takes care of Lucy at Scarpetta's home.

Blank, Jacob. Dorothy Farinelli marries this children's book illustrator.

Blue Ridge Mountains. Prominent mountain range in western Virginia, visible from Charlottesville, the home of UVA (the University of Virginia).

Boltz, Bill. A Commonwealth attorney investigating the murder of Lori Petersen.

Brookfield Heights. Trendy place for the upwardly mobile to buy row houses, priced up to one hundred thousand dollars.

Cagney. Former medical examiner in Richmond whose office Scarpetta occupied after he died of a heart attack.

Channel 12. Local TV news crew that shows up to cover the murder of Lori Petersen.

CID. Criminal Investigation Division. A division of the U.S. Army tasked with investigating crimes perpetrated by military personnel.

CME. Abbreviation for chief medical examiner.

Coffee. The beverage of choice at Neils Vander's lab. He always offers a cup of java to Scarpetta, who always accepts it—a known vice.

DBA. Database administrator.

DMV. Department of Motor Vehicles.

Dorothy. Coworker at Scarpetta's office who was "absolutely hysterical" when Lucy reformatted her computer disks, including irreplaceable files, such as a book in progress.

EOT. End of tour.

ER. Emergency room.

Farinelli, Dorothy. Lucy's mother, who lives in Florida.

Farinelli, Lucy. Ten-year-old niece of Kay Scarpetta, whom she takes under her wing.

FIP. The fingerprint image processor used to detect "fingerprint characteristics."

FMP. Fingerprint matching processor; high-speed computer capable of comparing "eight hundred matches per second."

Forensic Science Bureau. One of several laboratories located in the same building as Scarpetta's office.

Fortosis, Dr Spiro. University of Virginia professor of medicine and psychiatry, whom Scarpetta uses as a sounding board for the conflicted feelings she experiences when dealing with the Strangler cases.

Ginter Park. Cecile Tyler lived here, "the oldest residential neighborhood in Richmond."

Grand Rounds lecture. "Women in Medicine." Scarpetta gives a lecture at Virginia Medical College; one of the attendees was Lori Petersen, a victim of the Strangler.

***Herald,* the.** The hometown newspaper (the *Miami Herald*) that Lucy alludes to in a discussion of sensationalistic crime with her aunt, Kay Scarpetta.

HHSD. Health & Human Services Department.

James River. A major river that cuts through southeast Virginia. It divides Richmond roughly in half.

Kitchen. Scarpetta's favorite room in her home in the west end of Richmond. "When all else fails, I cook," says Scarpetta.

Lewis, Patty. One of the victims of the Strangler. She lived in a brownstone in Brookfield Heights.

Magpie. A Dumpster-diving street person who retrieves a blue jumpsuit that is an important piece of evidence in the Strangler case. The Dumpster is located near the home of one of the Strangler's victims, Henna Yarborough. The jumpsuit has the distinctive odor of maple—a by-product of the Strangler, who is typed as a secreter.

Main Street. Where fine clothing stores are located.

McCorkle, Roy. The Strangler. A "Mr. Nobody," a twenty-seven-year-old hired by the city of Richmond as a communications officer. He attacks Scarpetta at her home and she is saved by Marino, who is armed with a .357 and shoots the Strangler dead—four rounds.

ME. Abbreviation for medical examiner.

MO. Modus operandi.

Mont Blanc pen. Benton Wesley's preferred writing instrument, this pen is distinctive: black with a white cap, symbolizing the mountain located in Europe. Cornwell herself used to give these pens out as gifts; she would buy them from the military exchange store at Quantico.

Monticello. The home of Thomas Jefferson (Charlottesville, Virginia). Scarpetta promised her niece, Lucy, that she'd take her here, but work interfered—the death of Lori Petersen.

MP-4 Polaroid camera. Used to take instant photos of fingerprints.

Ninhydrin. Chemical "helpful for visualizing latent prints."

OCME. Office of the Chief Medical Examiner. The principal individual in the Commonwealth of Virginia charged with investigating suspicious deaths.

PC. Personal computer.

PERK. Physical evidence recovery kit, used in the field to retrieve samples for criminal investigations.

Petersen, Lori. A homicide victim found by her husband in the Berkley Downs area of Southside Richmond. Police Sgt. Pete Marino called Kay Scarpetta to summon her for an investigation. Petersen worked in the emergency room at the University of Virginia Medical College. A Harvard graduate, Petersen was young, smart, and a gifted doctor. She is the fourth victim of the killer known simply as the Strangler.

Petersen, Matt. The husband of Lori Petersen; he reported her death to the police. He's a Ph.D. candidate at the University of Virginia (Charlottesville, Virginia).

Plymouth Reliant. Peter Marino's car. Usually filled with fast-food wrappers and scented with an air freshener.

Police Headquarters. Located in downtown Richmond. Described by Cornwell as "built of stucco that is almost indistinguishable from the concrete in the sidewalks."

Ruger .38. Firearm owned by Dr. Scarpetta.

SEM. Scanning electron microscopy.

Sheepskins. Scarpetta has "diplomas and certificates" from Cornell University, Johns Hopkins, and Georgetown.

Sixth Street Marketplace: Richmond, Virginia. A modern mall where Scarpetta shops, located downtown near the banking district.

Slip, the. Area of Richmond known for bars and restaurants; a trendy area where Yuppies congregate.

Squirrel. Derogatory term used by police detective Pete Marino in describing Lori Petersen's murderer. It's one of his favorite terms—the killers are nuts.

Steppe, Brenda. One of the victims of the Strangler.

Stryker saw. A heavy-duty bone cutter used in the morgue. (*Note:* Cornwell gave a new one to her friend and mentor, Dr. Marcella Fierro.)

Tanner, Norman. Director of Public Safety (Richmond, Virginia).

Tony. Kay Scarpetta's ex-husband, Tony Benedetti. They were married six years, and among other character flaws, he could never remember (or didn't care to remember) the little details of what she liked or didn't like, especially in terms of food or fashion.

Turnbull, Abby. A reporter covering the police beat and investigating the murder of Lori Petersen.

Tyler, Cecile. One of the four victims of the Strangler. A young black woman, she had worked as a receptionist at an investment firm in Richmond.

Vander, Neils. Fingerprint examiner for the Commonwealth of Virginia. Scarpetta calls him after she gets the call from Marino. He assists her in the postmortem of Lori Petersen.

VICAP. Violent Criminal Apprehension Program. Computer tool used by the FBI to profile criminals.

Virginia Commonwealth University (VCU). College in Richmond with campuses throughout the city.

VMC (Virginia Medical College). Scarpetta is on the faculty of this college; Lori Petersen worked here.

Wesley, Benton. FBI profiler who works in a Richmond field office. A former high school principal, he held a master's degree in psychology.

Williams, Tennessee. American playwright who is the subject of Matt Petersen's Ph.D. dissertation.

Yarborough, Henna. Taught journalism at VCU; a victim of the Strangler.

BODY OF EVIDENCE, 1991

Editions

1. Paperback, $6.99, Avon Books.
2. Large print edition, G. K. Hall & Co.
3. Unabridged audiotape: read by C. J. Critt, $39.95, Harper-Audio. Also available from Books on Tape. And, read by Lorelei King, an edition from Chivers Audio Books.
4. Abridged audiotape: read by Lindsay Crouse, $18, Harper-Audio.
5. E-book downloadable from the Internet, $7.95, from audible.com.
6. Hardback, first edition (out of print), $110.

Dedication

"For Ed, Special Agent and Special Friend."

This is a reference to Ed Sulzbach, an FBI profiler. In an unpublished interview conducted in 1991 with Catherine Milligan, Cornwell said: ". . . One of my closest friends and a tremendous influence on my work has been Ed Sulzbach, who is an FBI agent and was a profiler at Quantico for a number of years—and the intellectual model for Benton Wesley. In fact, I would list Ed right up there at the very top of the list in terms of tremendous influences on my work. Without him, I would not have the FBI behavioral science element probably at all because you just can't dream up that yourself. . . ." In the same interview, Cornwell points out that this was before the Thomas Harris novels that gave FBI profiling its high visibility in contemporary suspense novels.

Geography

Principally Williamsburg and also Richmond.

Perspective

On the heels of an award-winning first novel like *Postmortem,* the question that must be resolved is whether or not the first book was a fluke—it wasn't, as readers and reviewers happily discovered.

Reviews

"Nerve-jangling . . . verve and brilliance . . . high drama . . . Ms. Cornwell fabricates intricate plots and paces the action at an ankle-turning clip." (*New York Times Book Review.*)

"Takes the reader into the fascinating world of the forensic crime lab . . . a complex, multilayered novel with enough twists and turns for two books." (*Washington Post Book World.*)

"Excellent . . . compelling . . . in *Body of Evidence* Chief Medical Examiner Kay Scarpetta must deal with a deranged killer who stalks and murders a noted historical novelist and then seems to be working back through the novelist's past . . . Scarpetta is much more than a female 'Quincy,' and Cornwell is the perfect match for her." (*Chicago Tribune.*)

Body of Evidence A to Z

.380 automatic. The firearm owned by Beryl Madison.

Aims, Frank Ethan. The missing link in the Beryl Madison case. A former in-patient at Valhalla, Aims—a lost-baggage deliveryman working out of the Richmond airport—is the final piece in this puzzle.

Amtrak. A national train line subsidized by the government. Sterling Harper boards Amtrak's *The Virginian* heading to Baltimore.

Benedetti, Tony. Scarpetta's former husband.

Chamberlayne Gardens. Retirement home in Richmond where Scarpetta goes to interview Mrs. McTigue in connection with the Beryl Madison investigation. McTigue's husband did the restoration on Cutler's Grove when Madison lived there.

CIA. Criminal investigative agents; the FBI's designation for their profilers.

Culpeper's Tavern. The tavern in Williamsburg that Cary Harper frequented on a regular basis, typically staying an hour, according to Sterling Harper, his sister, who is interviewed by Scarpetta in connection with this case.

Glaser Safety Slugs. Bullets found in a Smith & Wesson 9-mm automatic left behind by Jeb Price. The slugs expand on impact, causing extensive damage.

Hamm, Joni. A forensic lab scientist who works in a lab colocated with Scarpetta's office. Hamm is examining the trace evidence in connection with the Madison case.

Harper, Cary. A Pulitzer Prize winner and noted recluse, this novelist lived in Williamsburg, Virginia, at Cutler Grove on the James River. The real-world inspiration was likely Carter's Grove, the only plantation in Williamsburg on the James River. He had a relationship with his protégée Beryl Madison when she was in her early twenties. A one-book wonder who wrote *The Jagged Corner,* he died in the same manner as Madison—his throat was cut.

Harper, Sterling. The surviving sister of Cary Harper. She lives at Cutler's Grove in Williamsburg, Virginia.

James, Mark. Scarpetta's former boyfriend, whom she dated when they were both in law school. He turns up in Richmond on short notice, to Scarpetta's surprise and delight. The last time she had seen him had been fifteen years earlier. He initially passes himself off as a lawyer for a Chicago firm, but in fact he is an FBI agent—a fact he conceals from Scarpetta until he meets her in Florida, where she's retrieved the missing manuscript by Beryl Madison.

Madison, Beryl. Novelist living in Key West, Florida, who is murdered in her home in Windsor Farms, an upscale subdivision of Richmond. Her letters open *Body of Evidence.*

Masterwash. A car-washing facility, Southside Richmond. This is where Beryl Madison took her Honda Accord EX; consequently, Marino goes there to interview anyone who remembers seeing her there and turns up "a first-class squirrel," Al Hunt.

Miami, Florida. Scarpetta's hometown. She returns to seek out two men noted in Beryl Madison's letters—PJ and Walt. PJ turns out to be Peter Jones, from whom Madison had rented a room in his house. He also has the sought-after manuscript, which he turns over to Scarpetta—nearly a thousand pages long.

MMPI. Minnesota Multiphasic Personality Inventory; a standardized test used to determine mental disorders.

Omni Park Central. A swanky hotel in Manhattan where Scarpetta meets her former boyfriend, Mark James.

Orndorff & Berger. The law firm Mark James cites as his employer—a fabrication, as it turns out. He and Scarpetta meet Sparacino at its NYC office to discuss Beryl Madison's lost manuscript.

Pen names, Beryl Madison's. Adair Wilds, Emily Stratton, Edith Montague.

PERK. Physical evidence recovery kit.

Price, Jeb. An intruder whom Scarpetta catches rifling through her office files.

Richmond's Byrd Airport. The major airport in the Richmond area, now called RIA—Richmond International Airport.

Ruger. .38 revolver with Silvertips. Scarpetta's firearm.

Schwarzchild's. In Richmond's Regency Mall. A jewelry store where Scarpetta has a consultant. (*Note:* This is where Cornwell buys her Breitling chronograph watches.)

Smathers case. A case brought up by Sparacino, who uses it as ammunition against Scarpetta in his search for the missing Madison manuscript, which he mistakenly believes she's harboring and refusing to release. The Smathers case involved Scarpetta; personal valuables on the person turned up missing and her office was held accountable. The resultant publicity tarnished reputations, among them Scarpetta's.

Sparacino, Robert. A lawyer in NYC who specializes in entertainment law; has a well-deserved unsavory reputation. Both Cary Harper and Beryl Madison were clients of his. He is the literary executor of Madison's estate and is looking for her final book, a manuscript that he believes is in Scarpetta's hands.

Valhalla Hospital. Located in Albermarle County, this is a psychiatric facility.

Village Frame Shoppe & Gallery. On Princess Street in Williamsburg, Virginia. Scarpetta notices the gold seal of this shop on the back of a young girl's portrait painted by Sterling Harper; the portrait hangs in her home at Cutler's Grove. Scarpetta goes to this shop to glean information on it.

Westwood Racquet Club. The tennis club Beryl Madison belonged to.

ALL THAT REMAINS, 1992

Editions

1. Trade hardback, $25, Scribner.
2. "Turtleback," for the Young Adult Market, Econo-Clad Books.
3. Paperback, $7.99, Avon (reissued edition).
4. Unabridged audiotape:
   (a) Read by Donada Peters, Books on Tape.
   (b) Read by Lorelei King, Chivers Audio Books.
5. Abridged audiotape: read by Kate Burton, HarperAudio.
6. Downloadable audio, $6.95, from audible.com.
7. Advance reading copy, signed. Paperback. $55.
8. Hardback, first edition, signed. $50 to $95, signed on a signature card and laid in, $27, signed on the author's bookplate, $55, inscribed, $75.
9. First UK edition, signed. $125 to $175.

Dedication

"This book is for Michael Congdon. As always, thanks."

Congdon was Cornwell's first agent and editor, as well. Congdon, a highly regarded editor, is generally credited closely with Cornwell on her first four novels.

Geography

Principally the Greater Hampton Roads (i.e., the Peninsula); Richmond and surrounding environs.

Perspective

Cornwell is quick to point out that she writes about *types* of crimes, not specific cases, and that's been true for many years. But in this case, the similarities between fact and fiction, between real life and storytelling, precipitated a lawsuit subsequently dismissed by a judge.

Reviews

"Fresh from her triumphs in *Postmortem* (1990) and *Body of Evidence* (1991), Richmond chief medical examiner Dr. Kay Scarpetta tries for the hat trick against a killer who attacks couples in cars—five couples so far, including Fred Cheney and Deborah Harvey, daughter of national drug czar Pat Harvey. A handful of physical clues—a jack of hearts left at each crime scene, the removal of all the victims' shoes and socks, the similarity of the crimes to an isolated murder eight years earlier—are all Kay has to work with as she goes up against not only the killer but also scruffy detective Pete Marino, falling apart now that his wife's left him; her obsessive friend, reporter Abby Turnbull, who's signed a contract to write a book about the murders; the FBI, who are out to protect a killer they suspect is one of their own officers-in-training; and Mrs. Harvey, determined to punish her daughter's murderer herself. The medical detail—encompassing riddles of when and how as well as who—is as sharp and wide-ranging as ever; and although Cornwell takes a chance on a denouement that lacks the slam-bang impact of her earlier endings, she continues to show one of the most astonishing growth curves in the genre. Thanks to Cornwell's forensic expertise, her corpses continue to speak more eloquently than many crime writers' living characters." (*Kirkus Reviews.*)

"Cornwell's Dr. Kay Scarpetta is fast becoming everyone's favorite forensic specialist. . . . This time, Scarpetta must contend with a serial killer who has breached the FBI's top secret artificial intelligence system." (*Library Journal.*)

"Dazzling, one of the year's best . . . Cornwell ranks among the best writers in the genre today. . . . Everything rings true: the dialogue, the scientific and procedural details, the characters, the politicking, and the inter-agency squabbling . . . A riveting tale showcasing master prose, a labyrinthian puzzle, a multidimensional protagonist with a credible supporting cast and an authentic milieu . . . After reading Cornwell's thriller, most others will pale in comparison." (*Milwaukee Journal Sentinel.*)

"Many journalists consider themselves admirably equipped to turn out crime fiction. Occasionally, they're even right. . . . [This] is the third in Cornwell's dead-on series about Dr. Kay Scarpetta . . . a brainy physician-attorney and sensational cook made mortal by her lousy tennis game and miserable love life. . . . Scarpetta is variously assisted and thwarted by a colorful supporting cast, including her irascible cop sidekick, Pete Marino." (Katrine Ames, *Newsweek.*)

"Ms. Cornwell, who once held a job in a medical examiner's office, smartly relies on strong action, realistic lab procedures and a working atmosphere thick with paranoia to cover the bald spots in her writing. One minds, of course, when characters spout clichés or go wandering off into the plot thickets to disappear without a trace. But if the living appear a little peaked, the dead are quick enough to lend their morbid vitality to this thriller." (Marilyn Stasio, *New York Times Book Review.*)

"The first Dr Kay Scarpetta novel, *Postmortem,* stayed impressively clinical throughout and the effect was riveting. *Body of Evidence . . .* remained strong on intrigue but allowed a certain lushness of style to deform the plot. . . . [In this novel], the author is back on form, with plenty of bodies awaiting autopsy, and barely a love affair in sight. . . . Kay Scarpetta needs to muster all her energy and alertness. She never emerges from these deadly imbroglios with her emotions unscathed, but generally succeeds in giving an impression of competence and right-thinking—and the novels are satisfactorily abundant in complications and side-issues." (Patricia Craig, *Times Literary Supplement.*)

"With her third published mystery, Richmond novelist Patricia Daniels Cornwell exhibits new-found security and skill in her chosen genre. She's a pro. Her writing now seems effortless, as if she could go on like this for years. If she does, there won't be a mystery fan anywhere who won't have read her." (Ann McMillan, *Richmond Times-Dispatch.*)

All That Remains A to Z

7-Eleven. Convenience store chain popular in southeast Virginia. Deborah Harvey was last seen at one of their stores five miles west of the New Kent rest stop off I-64, where she and her boyfriend, Fred Cheney, are later found dead.

ACTMAD. Abbreviation for the American Coalition of Tough Mothers Against Drugs, supposedly a "clean" charity. Mrs. Harvey had been investigating the organization because of its shadowy connections and dubious practices.

Anchor Bar and Grill. A bar in Williamsburg, the location of the last known sighting of two murdered women—Jill Harrington and Elizabeth Mott, whose bodies were later discovered in a church cemetery. (Mott's Volkswagen was found "in a motel parking lot off Route 60 in Lightfoot.") (*Note:* There is no real bar named the Anchor Bar and Grill in Williamsburg.)

Aura. Psychic energy not visible to most but can be seen as a color band around a person. Psychic Hilda Ozimek tells Scarpetta and Marino the colors of their auras.

Bell JetRanger. Drug czar Pat Harvey arrives on the scene in this helicopter. (*Note:* Cornwell owns, and flies, a Bell JetRanger. She is reportedly looking to trade hers in for a more powerful one with increased range.)

BOLO. Be on the lookout.

Buckroe Beach. Located in Hampton, this is approximately five miles from Interstate 64 where Ben Anderson's Dodge pickup truck is found.

Carter's Grove. A part of Colonial Williamsburg, this plantation house is a major tourist attraction flanking the James River.

Colonial Parkway. The most scenic road on the Peninsula, the parkway extends from the edge of the James River and meanders its way through marshlands, dense forests, and Colonial Williamsburg, extending deep into York County.

Colonial Williamsburg. The restored colonial town, a favorite destination of Scarpetta's. (She and her former boyfriend Mark had discussed spending a weekend here.)

Commissioner of Health and Human Services. Scarpetta's boss, Dr. Paul Sessions, who receives correspondence from Pat Harvey regarding the murder of her daughter Deborah. Scarpetta will soon be under a microscope herself.

Couple Killings. The name given to the series of killings centered around Williamsburg, Virginia. (*Note:* The similarities between the fictional Couple Killings and the Colonial Parkway Murders led to a lawsuit filed against Cornwell by distraught parents whose children had been victims of the Parkway murderer, who remains at large. The case was ultimately dismissed.)

Dealer's Room, The. A bookstore in Merchant's Square that Scarpetta thinks may have been a favorite haunt of the serial killer who leaves a playing card behind. This bookstore, owned by Steven Spurrier, carries the usual stock (general fiction and nonfiction), but also carries out-of-print books and military publications.

Department of Animal Health. In Richmond, colocated with Scarpetta's office. This is the animal morgue.

Farm, The. The nickname for the CIA training facility, Camp Peary, located at exit 238 of Interstate 64 near Williamsburg.

Fort Eustis. An army post, the home of its Transportation Corps. Located northwest of Newport News.

Georgetown University. Scarpetta graduated from this university in D.C. with a law degree after obtaining her M.D.

Globe and Laurel. A restaurant in northern Virginia; located near Triangle, near a Marine Corps base. The restaurant, owned by Maj. Jim Yancey, was brought to Scarpetta's attention by Mark James.

Gloucester. A small town located north of the York River. This is the last place another couple, Bruce Phillips and Judy Roberts, was seen.

Harvey, Pat. The mother of Deborah Harvey. Pat Harvey is the National Drug Policy director, the "drug czar."

Hollywood Cemetery. In Richmond, located south of the city and north of the James River. The remains of presidents and major Confederate military figures are interred on these grounds.

Hornsby, Bruce. Popular musician from Williamsburg. When Turnbull and Scarpetta are driving around Williamsburg, they are listening to his song, "Harbor Lights," on the radio.

Hot apple cider. On the Duke of Gloucester Street, in the fall and winter, costumed vendors have food stalls where snack food is sold; cold apple cider is served during the hot months, and hot apple cider during the cold months. Hot apple cider is a favorite beverage of Scarpetta's.

HYDRA-SHOK®. The 9-mm bullet used to shoot Deborah Harvey in her back.

I-64 East. A major interstate in southeast Virginia, running from Richmond through Hampton Roads.

Jack of hearts. A playing card left by the killer, his calling card left behind at the scene of each of the four couples' murders.

James, Mark. Scarpetta's boyfriend back when she attended law school at Georgetown. He would later abandon his law practice to work for the FBI. On the rebound after her disastrous marriage to Tony, Scarpetta finds solace with Mark James—a "passionate fling," as she explains it to her friend Abby Turnbull.

John Marshall Courts Building. Located in downtown Richmond.

Jordan, Ellen. A young girl who works at the 7-Eleven and was the last person to see Fred Cheney and Deborah Harvey alive. Turnbull and Scarpetta interviewed her as part of the ongoing investigation.

Langley Field. Langley Air Force Base, the home of ACC (Air Combat Command). It's usually called LAFB, not Langley Field. Located near Hampton, on the Peninsula.

Law School at William & Mary. The Marshall-Wythe School of Law is located near the main campus of William & Mary. Jill Harrington graduated from here.

Main Street Station. A Richmond landmark, this was formerly a railroad station; it is now an upscale shopping mall.

Martin's Hundred. An archaeological dig in Colonial Williamsburg that Scarpetta frequented.

Mercedes. The car Scarpetta drives. It is dark gray.

Merchant's Square. Retail shops flanking both sides of the Duke of Gloucester Street in Williamsburg.

Monument Avenue. In Richmond. A street appropriately named, with its statues of Confederate generals on horseback.

Morrell, Jay. A state policeman in charge of the Cheney-Harvey investigation.

New Kent rest stop. Off Interstate 64, westbound, this is where the bodies of Fred Cheney and Deborah Harvey are found, along with their abandoned car, a Jeep Cherokee.

Newport News. Benton, who has flown in to investigate the killings, flies into the airport in this town, surrounded by Hampton (on its southeast side) and James City County and Williamsburg on its northwest to east side.

Newport News airport. Located in Denbigh, this airport is where Steven Spurrier is arrested as he is heading to the parking lot.

Old Dominion University. Located in Norfolk, Virginia. Ben Anderson and Carolyn Bennett attended this liberal arts college; they were both juniors.

Old Towne. In Williamsburg. An apartment complex popular with young people, especially college students from the nearby William & Mary.

Ozimek, Hilda. A psychic hired by the Harveys in a search for their missing daughter, who is unfortunately one of the victims of the Couple Killer.

Palm Leaf motel. Located in Lightfoot, Virginia, off Route 60. This nondescript motel is where Elizabeth Mott's Volkswagen is found.

Peninsula Search and Rescue. (Yorktown, Virginia). They are called in to assist in this case. The dog handlers are Jeff and Gail; the dogs are Salty and Neptune.

Providence Forge. A small town in Virginia, southeast of Richmond. Jim Freeman, one of the victims, came from here.

Quantico. In Virginia. This is the Marine Corps base where the FBI training academy is colocated, due south of Washington, D.C. Benton Wesley trained Mark James at Quantico.

RIA. Richmond International Airport. The major airport that serves the city and the surrounding area. (South of RIA is the Newport News–Williamsburg International Airport.)

Richmond skyline. As you drive into the city from any direction, the skyline is prominent—Richmond is one of the few cities in southeast Virginia large enough to have a dominating skyline. (Portsmouth and Norfolk both have similar skylines.)

Richmond Times. The local newspaper in Richmond. (The real paper's name is the *Richmond Times-Dispatch.*)

Route 199 in York County. A major road that winds its way through York County and James City County. Three miles south of this route, the "skeletonized bodies" of Ben Anderson and Carolyn Bennett are found.

Silversmith Shop. Located on the Duke of Gloucester Street, this shop sells handmade silver goods, ranging in price, depending on the goods, from inexpensive charms and trinkets to expensive jewelry. In this shop Scarpetta buys a "sterling silver pineapple charm and a handsome chain." (The pineapple is a symbol of Colonial Williamsburg.)

Six Mile. Town in South Carolina where the psychic Hilda Ozimek lives.

Smithsonian's National Museum of Natural History. Located in D.C., this is where Scarpetta had attended a "forensic anthropology course" in years previous; Scarpetta goes to see Dr. Alex Vessey to have him examine bones from the Cheney-Harvey case.

Southside. The south side of Hampton Roads—Norfolk, Virginia Beach, Portsmouth. Fred Cheney's father is a businessman who hails from this area.

Spindrift, North Carolina. The intended destination of the late Fred Cheney and Deborah Harvey—one of four couples who fall prey to the Couple Killer.

Spring Street. The nickname for the state penitentiary located in downtown Richmond. (*Note:* The penitentiary has since been torn down and relocated.)

Stingray Point. Located on the Chesapeake Bay, this is the location of the family home of Carolyn Bennett, one of the victims of the Colonial Parkway Killer.

Tag number R. A special license plate designation for rental cars only. (*Note:* This may have been the case some years ago, but currently there is no such designation to mark rental cars, for obvious security reasons.)

Trellis, The. Located on the Duke of Gloucester Street in Williamsburg, The Trellis is one of the best restaurants in town and is perhaps best known for its desserts, mostly chocolate.

Turnbull, Abby. *Richmond Times* reporter who now works for the *Washington Post.*

Turncoat, Abby. The derisive name Pete Marino calls Abby Turnbull, a *Washington Post* reporter Scarpetta knows.

U.S. 17. The major road that leads from Gloucester over the York River Bridge and to the Peninsula (Yorktown, Newport News). Locals call it simply Route 17.

USAir. Major airline dominating the Southeast. Scarpetta and Marino catch a flight on this airline from RIA to Charlotte, North Carolina, on a prop job, and then connect to fly out to Six Mile, South Carolina, to see a psychic, Hilda Ozimek.

Vessey, Dr. Alex. Works at the Smithsonian's National Museum of Natural History. Examines the bones from the Cheney-Harvey case and determines that they have not been cut but, in fact, hacked—an important clue to the killer.

Virginia Beach. A city on the south side of Hampton Roads. During the summer this is the major destination of tourists who must drive on a congested Interstate 64 to reach the beach, where the boardwalk, miles of sand, and high-rise hotels beckon to tourists principally on the East Coast.

West Point. A town southeast of Richmond, located off Interstate 64. Not to be confused with the U.S. Army's military academy.

Westwood Racquet Club. An indoor facility in Richmond where Scarpetta goes after her friend Anna suggests she go to unwind, work out her frustrations. (*Note:* Cornwell initially attended college on a tennis scholarship.)

Williamsburg. The colonial capital and home to the College of William & Mary. Abby Turnbull takes a wrong turn off the interstate (at exit 238) and drives up to the Camp Peary gate—a CIA training facility. Afterward, FBI agents show up at her office in D.C. and ask why she had driven to the installation.

Williamsburg-Tidewater area. Locals call this Hampton Roads; if locals refer to the Greater Hampton Roads area, they are referring to a large chunk of southeast Virginia, from Middlesex County to the north and the North Carolina border to the south—ten cities and five counties.

Windsor on the James. The home of Pat Harvey is located near the small rural town of Windsor near the James River; Harvey's estate, which overlooks the river, is estimated by Scarpetta to be five acres in size.

York River State Park. Two skeletonized bodies are found in this park, which flanks the York River.

Zenner, Anna. Dr. Jill Harrington's physician and a personal friend of Scarpetta's.

CRUEL AND UNUSUAL, 1993

Editions

1. Paperback: $7.99, Avon Books.
2. Unabridged audiotape: Books on Tape.
3. Abridged audiotape: read by Kate Burton, $18.
4. Downloadable audiotape: read by Kate Burton, $6.95.
5. Advance reading copy, $45.
6. Hardback, first edition, $35, signed, $65–90.

Dedication

"This book is for the inimitable Dr. Marcella Fierro. (You taught Scarpetta well.)"

This is a reference to one of Cornwell's mentors and good friends, the chief medical examiner for the Commonwealth of Virginia.

Geography

Principally Richmond.

Awards

Gold Dagger Award, from the British Crime Writers Association.

Reviews

"Morbidly entertaining. . . . The elaborate plot shows expert engineering, and the lucid descriptions of forensic procedures that make her story so grimly fascinating are delivered in an authoritative voice." (*New York Times Book Review.*)

"Taut, high tech and eerily credible . . . with each book, her scalpel is getting sharper." (*Newsweek.*)

"Engrossing . . . An extremely effective novel of suspense, in all its varieties. . . . Cornwell embroils Kay Scarpetta in a grisly case involving a recently executed murderer whose fingerprints turn up at a new crime scene."

"Cornwell's accustomed forensic flair, plus the bonus of an unusually baffling and intricate plot, make this her best book yet—and a new high point in her meteoric rise." (*Kirkus Reviews.*)

"Once again, the real star of the show—the element about which Ms. Cornwell writes more skillfully than any other novelist going—is forensic technology. . . . What is new about *Cruel and Unusual* is its attention to the persona of a killer. Here, the author brings a murderer to life the same way she brings her most successful characters to life—by examining what remains after he is dead. Her use of forensic detail to create a character is utterly convincing, so that you feel no pity for the killer—which I suspect the author would find inappropriate if not immoral— but shared humanness." (Ann McMillan, *Richmond Times-Dispatch.*)

Cruel and Unusual A to Z

AFIS. Automated Fingerprint Identification System.

Assessment Protocol. A questionnaire used by the FBI when interviewing a violent offender. Benton Wesley administered an AP on Ronnie Joe Waddell when he was on death row.

Behavioral Science Unit. At the FBI Academy in Quantico, Virginia. Profiler Benton Wesley worked out of this office.

Deep water terminal. In Richmond, off the James River. A terminal for container ships and other large vessels.

Deighton, Jennifer. An astrologer found dead of carbon monoxide poisoning in her car garage near the Richmond airport.

DOA. Dead on arrival.

Donahue, Frank. State penitentiary warden found dead.

Downey, Minor. A special agent with the FBI. Scarpetta consults with him at his office in D.C. His specialty is investigating bird-related accidents.

Drone. Derogatory term used by Pete Marino to describe criminals.

Firing range. An indoor pistol-firing range in Richmond on Midlothian Turnpike. Lucy has been spending time here, practicing her firing skills after Marino gave her lessons in firearms.

Fort Myers, Florida. Scarpetta flies here to meet with Jennifer Deighton's former husband, who is a holistic healer.

Grueman, Nicholas. The attorney of the late Ronnie Joe Waddell. Back history: Grueman was a law school professor who had Scarpetta as one of his students. A lot of bad blood exists between him and Scarpetta, who must now deal with him in the aftermath of Waddell's execution. He later admits he regards her highly and tried to motivate her by his own means and defense in the case at hand.

Hale, Charles. A ticket agent at Victoria Station. He is injured in the blast that kills Scarpetta's former boyfriend Mark. Hale comforts the dying man and does what he can to stop the bleeding. For this act of human charity, Scarpetta returns the favor.

Heath, Eddie. A thirteen-year-old boy murdered in Richmond; last seen on the north side of Richmond at a convenience store on Chamberlayne Avenue.

Homestead. Located in West Virginia near Hot Springs. Scarpetta, her niece, Lucy, and Benton Wesley meet here for R and R. Its real-world inspiration is Greenbrier, a sixty-five-hundred-acre resort at White Sulphur Springs, West Virginia.

Luma-Lite. In Scarpetta's lab. This high-powered arc lamp replaced the laser used to enhance evidence identification.

Marino, Doris. Pete Marino's ex-wife who, after thirty years of marriage, leaves him.

Naismith, Robyn. A young black woman, a former Miss Virginia, an anchorwoman for Channel 8. She was murdered by Ronnie Joe Waddell.

Norring, Governor. The governor of the Commonwealth of Virginia, who can grant a stay of execution or clemency for Ronnie Joe Waddell, who is scheduled to die in the electric chair for his convicted murder of Robyn Naismith. He also questions Scarpetta behind closed doors when questions of impropriety arise regarding her late employee, Susan Story.

Richmond Times-Dispatch. The hometown newspaper in Richmond, Virginia.

Ruger. One of several firearms owned by Scarpetta.

Scarpetta's schooling. During the Special Grand Jury investigation, she answers a question from a juror about her education, which includes "Saint Michael's, Our Lady of Lourdes Academy, Cornell, John[s] Hopkins, and Georgetown." It totals, as she states, seventeen years, including a one-year residency.

Seaboard Building. Located near the morgue in Richmond. Fingerprint, DNA, and serology identification is performed here.

Special Grand Jury. Scarpetta, accused of improprieties that she can't or won't explain, is summoned to appear on January 20 to explain her actions. In the interim, she's suspended with pay, and Fielding is appointed the acting chief medical examiner of Virginia, pending the grand jury's decision.

Suffolk. A farming town on the south side of Hampton Roads. Ronnie Joe Waddell grew up here. It's best known for being the peanut capital of the world.

Sullivan, Hilton. An alias for Temple Brooks Gault.

Twenty-two. The caliber of the bullet that links two seemingly unrelated homicides—Eddie Heath's and Susan Story's.

Victoria Station, London. Scarpetta's former boyfriend, Mark, died here after a terrorist bomb exploded.

Virginia Museum. Popular arts museum in downtown Richmond. Scarpetta met Virginia governor Joe Norring at a black-tie reception here.

Virginia Power. The utility company that checked out the setup for the electric chair before Waddell's execution. (*Note:* VEPCO, Virginia Electric Power Company, is now called Dominion Power, named after the state's name, Old Dominion.)

Virginia State Penitentiary. Located near the James River in Richmond, this correctional facility housed, among others, inmates on death row, including Ronnie Joe Waddell. (*Note:* This penitentiary has been razed and its inmates have been moved to a modern correctional facility.)

Waddell, Ronnie Joe. His "meditation" opens *Cruel and Unusual*. He is put to death by the state for the murder of Robyn Naismith.

Windsor Farms. An upscale housing subdivision in Richmond. Scarpetta's new residence. (*Note:* Cornwell used to live here, as well.)

THE BODY FARM, 1994

Editions

1. Paperback, $7.99, Berkley Publishing Group.
2. Large print edition, Simon & Schuster.
3. Abridged audiotape: read by Jill Eikenberry, $9.98, Simon & Schuster.
4. Downloadable audio, read by Jill Eikenberry, audible.com.
5. Advance reading copy, $25–65.
6. Hardback, first edition, $30–45, signed, $45–65.
7. First UK edition, signed, $65.

Dedication

"To Senator Orrin Hatch of Utah for his tireless fight against crime."

A chance meeting at a gym between Cornwell and Hatch resulted in a friendship; Hatch subsequently sponsored a bill that later passed through, the Federal Crime Bill in 1994, which restored funding to the FBI Academy at Quantico, Virginia.

Geography

Black Mountain, North Carolina; the Body Farm at the University of Tennessee.

Story Behind the Story

This is the first Scarpetta novel in which Cornwell sets the major plotline geographically near the place where she grew up in western North Carolina. This novel also popularized *The Body Farm* (University of Tennessee), which until then had assumed a low-key existence.

In various profiles and interviews for this book, Cornwell noted that going back home to work on this novel was a very emotional experience for her. Going back, I think, achieved closure for her; she could put her turbulent past behind her and move into the future as a grown woman and a bestselling author.

The novel begins with Dr. Kay Scarpetta awakening to the sound of gunfire. She's at the FBI Academy at Quantico, Virginia, where she's been given a case file that haunts her: the death of Emily Steiner, only eleven years old, whose murder shocks the sleepy town of Black Mountain, a small town of seven thousand in North Carolina, east of Asheville.

A malevolent beast has come to Black Mountain, and appropriately, its soul is black. The town's citizens are outraged, shocked, and saddened; they know that if a human monster is in their community and killing children, then nothing is sacred—no one is safe.

Scarpetta, with her supporting cast (Benton Wesley and Pete Marino), flies in via helicopter to the on-edge town to work the case, which also takes Scarpetta to a little-known research facility, informally dubbed "the Body Farm," in which human remains decompose and provide clues as to the causes of death.

Meanwhile, Scarpetta's niece, Lucy, is working at the FBI's ERF (Engineering Research Facility), setting up CAIN (Crime Artificial Intelligence Network).

As expected, Cornwell serves up a satisfying stew: the supporting cast, spearheaded by Scarpetta, chase down every lead, examining every clue; a malevolent villain, hell-bent on human destruction; the eerie, unsettling locale of the Body Farm, with its real-world counterpart; and the small towns of North Carolina that Cornwell herself knows so well.

Supplementing her trademarked forensics investigations, the descriptions of a helicopter in flight are written with the authority of someone who has spent considerable time in the cockpit. (As part of the research for this novel, Cornwell learned how to fly a helicopter and, later, bought her own Bell JetRanger, which can be seen on the back cover of the paperback edition of this book—shot around sunset.)

Reviews

"Cornwell's plot is visceral, graphic, and frightening in a way that's vaguely reminiscent of *Silence of the Lambs.* Her writing is masterful, and she provides evocative backgrounds, provocative characters, and enough ghoulish specifics about autopsies and dead bodies to induce weeks of nightmares. . . . This deserves a place in every mystery collection." (Emily Melton, *Booklist.*)

"Following the disappointing *Cruel and Unusual* (Scribner, 1993), one wondered whether Cornwell was getting bored with her popular Kay Scarpetta series. After all, that novel featured a tired, confused plot and cardboard characters. But, happily, Cornwell is back at the top of her form here. Sure, there are still the red herrings and the plot contrivances, but what makes *The Body Farm* stand out is the deeper characterizations, especially in the depiction of Scarpetta's relationship with her troubled niece, Lucy. 'It seems this is all about people loving people who don't love them back,' says Scarpetta, referring to the murder of an 11-year-old girl, which she is investigating as an FBI consultant. But this is also the novel's haunting theme: homicide detective Pete Marino, jealous of Scarpetta's affair with FBI unit chief Benton Wesley, becomes involved with the dead girl's mother; Lucy, in love with a calculating fellow FBI student, is accused of violating agency security. Emotionally satisfying reading." (Previewed in "PrePub Alert," Wilda Williams, *Library Journal,* June 1, 1994.)

"The book nearly redeems itself when it dwells on the irreversibly tragic effects of violence on the human spirit. [It] may not be the best novel in the Scarpetta series. But for those who can no longer tolerate detective stories crammed with gratuitous killing, mayhem and cruelty, it may be a welcome relief." (Bill Kent, *New York Times Book Review.*)

"Cornwell casts a wider, surer narrative net in the latest case set for her increasingly complex heroine, Kay Scarpetta, Chief Medical Examiner for the Commonwealth of Virginia. As an FBI consultant, Scarpetta investigates the North Carolina murder of 11-year-old Emily Steiner, whose mutilation suggests the M.O. of an escaped killer met previously in *Cruel and Unusual.* Forensic clues from the body's second autopsy prompt Scarpetta to request that certain experiments be made at the University of Tennessee's Decay Research Facility, known as the Body Farm. Meanwhile, she, Pete Marino of the Richmond, Va., police, and her new love interest, FBI Unit Chief Benton Wesley investigate the apparent suicide (from autoerotic asphyxiation) of the local FBI agent in charge of the case. Then, Scarpetta's computer-whiz niece Lucy, working at FBI headquarters at Quantico, is charged with violating security. During her travels between North Carolina and Virginia, Scarpetta worries about both the less-than-forthcoming Lucy and Marino, who becomes emotionally entangled with Emily's beautiful stricken mother. Results at the Body Farm lead her to a convincing, if abrupt, resolution. Deeper characterization and a more intricate plot mark this fifth in a consistently compelling series." Five hundred thousand first printing; paperback rights to Berkley Books, audio rights to Simon & Schuster; Literary Guild selection (*Publishers Weekly*).

Of Body Farms and All That Remains

For most of two decades, the University of Tennessee Anthropology Research Facility has gone unnoticed by the general public, and it's just as well. What goes on at the facility is grisly stuff, not for the fainthearted, but essential to the growing body of work that comprises forensics today.

With the 1994 publication of Patricia Cornwell's *The Body Farm,* the research facility came to the attention of her millions of fans. The research facility harvests cadavers.

According to Greg Barrett of *USA Today,* ". . . 300 or so corpses—unclaimed from the county morgue, donated by family or willed by the deceased—have written the text on forensic anthropology's method for gauging 'time of death.'"

How a body decays speaks volumes on how that person lived . . . and died. Beyond the general public that feels a sense of desecration when it's aware that such a place exists, there are a specific group of people who wish it never did exist—the criminals put behind bars because of the clues the cadavers yield to the researchers.

Cornwell likened the grounds of the research facility to the grounds of a battlefield, which seems altogether appropriate. To see dozens of bodies in various states of decay, most perhaps naked and exposed to the elements, is a sobering sight. The stench must be unbearable, but Cornwell, who prides herself on researching on site, made the trek to this remote facility to get the details right in *The Body Farm*.

As *USA Today's* Greg Barrett points out, there's stiff resistance to establishing other so-called body farms, though there's a definite need for them. What the bodies undergo in the sweltering Tennessee heat is quite different from how the same body would decompose in, say, a cooler climate like Maine, or Oregon, or even Florida.

Despite the identified need, it's not likely that there would be a second body farm in the United States. One, most people say, is enough. For most people, who have never seen the inside of a morgue, the notion of naked bodies decomposing in the open is repugnant, even though they'd admit under pressure that there's a forensic need for such a place. There is, unfortunately, no other way to accurately identify what happens to a decomposing body over a period of time.

The so-called "strange harvest" (as *USA Today* termed it) is indeed grisly fare, but forensics experts would agree that if this is what it takes to harvest the truth, which helps secure convictions, then the harvesting must continue, not so much in the name of science but in the name of justice.

The Body Farm A to Z

500+E Mercedes Benz. Scarpetta's car wrecked by her niece, Lucy. It is of 1992 vintage, an eighty-thousand-dollar car.

Asheville Memorial Hospital. Dr. Jenrette meets Scarpetta here to perform an autopsy on Max Ferguson.

Begley, Hal. A judge in North Carolina who agrees to Scarpetta's request to exhume Emily Steiner.

Bell JetRanger. Helicopter that Scarpetta, Marino, and Benton fly in to Swannanoa, North Carolina, to investigate the Steiner case.

Black Mountain, North Carolina. A small town east of Asheville in the western part of the state. Population approximately seven thousand.

Body Farm. A research facility at the University of Tennessee, the only one of its kind, where decomposed bodies are studied to yield forensic clues.

CAIN. Crime Artificial Intelligence Network. A computerized system for tracking criminals. Lucy, a computer expert, is working as an intern at the ERF (Engineering Research Facility) for the FBI. She's raising CAIN.

Creed, Lindsey. A janitor with a checkered work history who is under suspicion for the Emily Steiner murder.

Dorothy. Lucy Farinelli's mother.

ERF. Engineering Research Facility. At Quantico, a new division that Lucy has set her vocational sights on.

Eye Spy. Located at the Springfield Mall in Richmond. Lucy's coworker Carrie Grethen has connections to this store, which causes her to be terminated from the ERF. The store caters to James Bond wannabes and sells spy surveillance equipment. This is also where Scarpetta confronts Grethen and, when leaving, spies Temple Gault entering.

Ferguson, Max. SBI agent found dead, hanging from the ceiling, of autoerotic asphyxiation—a suspicious death since it did not appear to be by his hand.

First Precinct, Richmond. Pete Marino, recently promoted to captain, has been assigned to the roughest part of town, covered by the First Precinct.

Gault, Temple Brooks. He's on the Ten Most Wanted lists nationwide.

Graham, Billy. World-famous evangelist who lives near Asheville. (*Note:* The Grahams played a pivotal part in Cornwell's life.)

Grethen, Carrie. Coworker of Lucy at the FBI's ERF.

HRT. Hostage Rescue Team. Elite FBI unit training at Quantico.

Jenrette, Dr. James. Performed the autopsy on Emily Steiner.

Katz, Dr. Thomas. He's in charge of the Body Farm.

Maxwell, Wren. A friend of Emily Steiner's whom Scarpetta and Marino talk to, with the hope that he can tell her about Steiner.

Montreat. The FBI sends a Bell JetRanger to pick up Scarpetta at this small town in western North Carolina, the home of Ruth and Billy Graham.

Newport, Rhode Island. Lucy seeks refuge in this port town as Scarpetta looks for, and finds, her at the Seaman's Institute.

OPR. Office of Professional Responsibility. The division of the FBI that conducts internal investigations. Lucy is under investigation for possible security breaches while working for the FBI's ERF.

Orange duct tape. An unusual color of duct tape, used to bind Emily Steiner.

Shade, Lyall. Anthropologist at the University of Tennessee.

Shuford Mills. In North Carolina. This company is a leading manufacturer of duct tape. The orange duct tape is a custom job.

Socks. A stray kitten that Emily Steiner adopted; Socks died of a broken neck.

Steiner, Emily. Eleven-year-old from Black Mountain, North Carolina; she was sexually assaulted and murdered.

Third Presbyterian Church. Behind this church is the cemetery in which Emily Steiner is buried.

Travel-Eze. Scarpetta, Marino, and Benton stay at this motel on U.S. 70 for $39.99 a night.

University of Virginia. College in Charlottesville. Lucy is about to graduate from here and hopes to be hired by the FBI.

Windsor Farms. The subdivision in Richmond where Scarpetta lives.

Wolfe, Thomas. American writer who lived in Asheville, best known for his novel *Look Homeward, Angel*.

Yellow Brick Road. The formidable obstacle course at the FBI Academy.

FROM POTTER'S FIELD, 1995

Editions

1. Paperback, $7.99, Berkley Publishing Group.
2. Large print edition, G. K. Hall & Co.
3. Abridged audiotape, read by Blair Brown, $24.
4. Downloadable audio, read by Blair Brown, $11.95.
5. Hardback, first edition, $23, signed, $50–65.
6. First UK edition, $50.

Dedication

"Dr. Erika Blanton (Scarpetta would call you friend)."

Geography

New York City and Richmond.

Reviews

"Cornwell is at the top of her form in this riveting novel as Dr. Kay Scarpetta continues the search for serial killer Temple Gault. . . . Mystery presentations don't get any better than this." (*AudioFile.*)

"For first-time readers of Patricia Cornwell, *From Potter's Field* is not the best introduction to this best-selling mystery writer. Her fans (count me one), though, will love it. . . . There are, however, two major flaws in Cornwell's story. The killer takes on proportions bigger than life. His motives are irrational. . . . It is difficult to imagine someone so evil, so intelligent, and yet so reckless. Scarpetta's indecisiveness over continuing her long-lasting affair with a married colleague also is not credible. At this stage of her life, an individual whose clinical proficiency in performing autopsies has won her high praise from the FBI just wouldn't let her personal life conflict with her professional life in such a messy way." (Jim Bencivenga, *Christian Science Monitor.*)

"Once again, Cornwell proves herself one of today's most talented crime fiction writers, an author who keeps her readers on the edges of their seats with magnificent plotting, masterful writing, and marvelous suspense. This is certain to be one of the most popular thrillers of the year." (Emily Melton, *Booklist.*)

"Cornwell's Dr. Kay Scarpetta is fast becoming everyone's favorite forensic specialist; her latest outing, *The Body Farm,* was #2 on the *New York Times* Best Sellers list. This time, Scarpetta must contend with a serial killer who has breached the FBI's top secret artificial intelligence system." (*Library Journal.*)

"Scarpetta, however, with her edgy intelligence, remains one of the most satisfactory heroines of popular fiction. She's touched by the tragedies represented by the corpses she dissects, and she struggles with the complicated relationships in her life." (Elise O'Shaughnessy, *New York Times Book Review*.)

"Readers new to Cornwell will be impressed by her wonderful plot and interesting characters. Those who have read the previous five Scarpettas may find this a slow starter but, by the middle, it is impossible to put down. . . . As always, Cornwell's knowledge of medical examining practices is used efficiently and smoothly." (Kate North, *New Scientist*.)

"Chief Medical Examiner Kay Scarpetta plays a tense cat-and-mouse game with a serial killer, an old enemy, in her sixth outing (following *The Body Farm*), and he has her badly rattled. The story begins as a rotten Christmas for Scarpetta: Temple Gault has struck again, leaving a naked, apparently homeless girl shot in Central Park on Christmas Eve; Scarpetta, as the FBI's consulting pathologist, is called in. Later, a transit cop is found shot in a subway tunnel, and, back home in Richmond, Va., the body of a crooked local sheriff is delivered to Scarpetta's own morgue by the elusive, brilliant Gault. The normally unflappable Scarpetta finds herself hyperventilating and nearly shooting her own niece. In the end, some ingenious forensic detective work and a visit to the killer's agonized family set up a high-tech climax back in the New York subway, which Gault treats as the Phantom of the Opera did the sewers of Paris. There's something faintly unconvincing about Gault (in a competitive field, it's tough to create a really horrific serial killer), and Scarpetta, stuck with her own family troubles and involved in a rather glum affair with a colleague, seems to be running low on energy. Still, this is a compelling, fast-moving tale, written in a highly compressed style, and only readers who know that Cornwell can do better are likely to complain. Literary Guild, Doubleday Book Club and Mystery Guild selections." (*Publishers Weekly*.)

From Potter's Field A to Z

.38. A handgun owned and carried by Scarpetta.

10–7. Police code for "end of tour." Gault uses a pager belonging to Davila to send Scarpetta this code.

10–20. Police code for "current location."

911. A pager code used by Benton and Scarpetta to notify one another that Temple Gault struck again.

Aero Services International terminal. Place where Marino and Scarpetta meet Wesley, who flies in on a Bell JetRanger.

American Express. A travel and entertainment credit card belonging to Scarpetta. Loaned to Lucy, the Gold card was stolen by Carrie and passed on to Gault, who brazenly uses it.

Benelli, Mr. A rich heir who owns an apartment at the Dakota, currently occupied by Temple Gault.

Browning High Power. A handgun owned and carried by Scarpetta.

Brown, Lamont. A victim of Gault.

CAIN. Used by Commander Penn, it alerted her to Gault's MO; she then contacted Scarpetta. It's a searchable database accessible by law-enforcement officials worldwide to identify and track criminals.

Central Park. In New York City. A white female in her thirties is found dead here, and in the nude. Gault is under suspicion; hence the 911 that Scarpetta receives from Benton.

Dakota. John Lennon was shot to death by an obsessed fan in front of this apartment building in Manhattan. Lennon owned several apartments in the Dakota.

Davidson College. Gault attended this college for one year. (Cornwell graduated from this college; her former husband, Charles Cornwell, taught English at Davidson, as well.)

Dolcetto D'Alba. A favorite wine of Scarpetta's.

First Avenue. Opposite Bellevue Hospital, this is the location of New York's Office of the Chief Medical Examiner, whose workload is the biggest in the country—eight thousand autopsied.

Fort Lee. An army post located southwest of Richmond. It is the home of its Quartmaster Corps, in charge of logistical supplies. Scarpetta goes to Fort Lee to visit the post's Quartermaster Museum.

Gault, Jayne. Temple Gault's twin sister.

Gault's victims. A man in a bar in Abingdon, Virginia; Eddie Heath; Scarpetta's morgue supervisor; the prison warden who befriended him; and Helen, a prison guard. The latest: the woman found nude in Central Park.

Green Top. A gun store in Richmond.

Gruber, Dr. Curator of the Quartermaster Museum.

Hilton Head, South Carolina. Scarpetta travels here to see Anna Zenner, a psychiatrist. (*Note:* Cornwell owns property at Hilton Head.)

James Galleries. In Richmond. A gallery whose inventory includes the work of an artist who prints gruesome symbology on lab coats, to Scarpetta's disgust. However, it is Gault's use of Scarpetta's credit card here that prompts her visit—he passes himself off as her son, Kirk. (The card presumably reads "K. Scarpetta.")

Janet. Lucy's new friend.

Jonas, Dr. Examiner on the scene at Davila's crime scene.

Live Oaks Plantation. The home of Peyton Gault, Temple's father.

LUCYTALK. The ID Lucy uses to log onto CAIN.

Marino, Richard. Pete Marino's son, nicknamed "Rocky."

Medical College of Virginia. Scarpetta is taken here after hyperventilating and having muscle spasms.

Museum of Natural History. In Manhattan. Because Gault comes to this museum to look at its shark exhibit, Scarpetta and Marino go to look for clues—anything that might help in their search for him.

Penn, Frances. One of three commanders of the New York Transit Police. She is "in charge of education, training and crime analysis."

Phillip Morris Plant. A prominent landmark in Richmond. Off I-95, it has a multistory cigarette pack jutting skyward.

Potter's Field. In New York City. The place where unclaimed bodies are buried, usually the unidentifiable or indigent. It is currently situated on Ward Island.

Ramble. An isolated part of New York City's Central Park where Gault had taken his victim.

A senior portrait of Patricia Daniels Cornwell
from the Davidson College yearbook

Office of the *Charlotte Observer,* where Cornwell wrote from 1979–1981

The Virginia Biotechnology Research Park, in Richmond, which houses the Chief Medical Examiner's Office

Cornwell's signature in a book is a highly sought after item for collectors and fans; here she signs *The Last Precinct* in 2000

Pasteur & Galt Apothecary Shop in Williamsburg,
the real-life inspiration for The Apothecary Shop
in *All That Remains*

The King's Arms Tavern in Williamsburg, one of several inspirations for Culpepper's in *Body of Evidence*

Cornwell's Bell JetRanger helicopter, in which she often pilots herself to book signings and other events

Patricia Cornwell
signs *Point of Origin*
in Richmond
(2000), where she
always draws a
huge crowd

S500 Mercedes. Scarpetta's new car, replacing her 500-E, which Lucy drove when she was run off the road.

Second Avenue subway station (Manhattan, in the Bowery). Jimmy Davila (a policeman with the Transit Police Homeless Unit) is found dead here, shot between the eyes.

SOP. Standard operating procedure.

Taceant Colloquia Effugiat Risus Hic Locus Est Ubi Mors Gaudet Succurrere Vitae. Inscription on a wall at the New York Office of the CME. Very roughly translated: "No laughter in this place of death."

Tavern on the Green. A favorite watering hole in Manhattan for the literary crowd.

Tucker, Col. Paul. Richmond's chief of police. Supervises six hundred policemen.

VIP Heliport. In New York City. Marino, Scarpetta, and Wesley land here to investigate Gault's handiwork.

CAUSE OF DEATH, 1996

Editions

1. Trade hardback, $25.95, Putnam.
2. Paperback, $7.99, Berkley Publishing Group.
3. Large print edition, Simon & Schuster.
4. Unabridged audiotape, read by Kate Reading, $35.95, Random House.
5. Abridged audiotape, read by Blair Brown, $23.50, Random House.
6. Abridged audio on CD, read by Blair Brown, Random House.
7. Hardback, first edition, signed, $50–60.
8. Limited edition of 185 copies in matching slipcase, $135–150, published by Putnam. (*Note:* This is the first limited edition of any of Cornwell's books.)

Dedication

"To Susanne Kirk—visionary editor and friend."
Kirk was her new editor at Putnam.

Geography

Richmond and Hampton Roads (Southside).

Perspective

Just as Cornwell learned how to fly a helicopter, for research on *The Body Farm,* she had to learn how to scuba dive for this book, which opens with a murder at the inactive naval shipyard.

Reviews

"No one handles the technical stuff better than Ms. Cornwell—and not just the slicing and dicing at the morgue. Her crisp, authoritative style extends to advanced computer technology and the chemistry of nuclear power. It's a good thing, too, because I wouldn't give you two cents for the silly villains in this piece." (Marilyn Stasio, *New York Times Book Review*)

"First, the good news: the omni-competent Kay Scarpetta is back, along with her sidekicks, in a murder mystery that's tighter than her last escapade, *From Potter's Field.* Chief medical examiner for the state of Virginia and an FBI consultant, Kay finds ample opportunity to demonstrate her skills in the autopsy room and outside it, too: here, she also dives with a Navy SEAL rescue squad and, through her computer-genius niece Lucy, an FBI agent, takes an up-close-and-personal look at a robot operated via virtual reality. But there is bad news: the work lacks the extraordinary, can't-go-to-bed-'til-you're-finished suspense of Cornwell's earlier novels, e.g., *Cruel and Unusual.* The killers here, members of a nihilistic, fascist cult who think their founder akin to God, are identified early on but never developed as characters. Their crimes, while heinous, don't baffle and tease the reader (or Kay) in the manner of the villain Temple Gault, who was dismissed in the last book. While Cornwell's authoritative presentation of forensic sleuthing, FBI procedures and high-tech crime-fighting compensates mightily for the overneat dovetailing of characters' paths and even the implausible role Kay plays in the climax, the hurried, almost slapdash pace of the climactic scenes is disappointing from so accomplished a writer. But even at less than her best, Cornwell remains a master of the genre, instilling in readers an appetite that only she can satisfy." One million first printing; $750,000 ad/promo; Literary Guild, Mystery Guild, and Doubleday Book Club main selections. (*Publishers Weekly.*)

Cause of Death A to Z

Bell Tire Service. A tire repair facility on Virginia Beach Boulevard in Virginia Beach. After Scarpetta and her niece's car tires are vandalized, they plan on having their cars towed here for repair.

Birdsong. A special finish applied to pistols to enhance their usefulness by waterproofing and painting to make them blend in. Modification typically requested by special ops military/civilian personnel.

Black Talon. Especially destructive bullets no longer in manufacture.

Book of Hand. The literary product of Joe Hand, this is the Bible of the New Zionists.

Chesapeake. A major Southside city.

Cop killers. Teflon-coated bullets that can pierce armored vests. Also called KTWs.

CP&L. Commonwealth Power & Light, the statewide utility company. (The real-world company is called Dominion Power.)

Dead fleet. The mothballed navy ships anchored in the James River off Newport News.

DMV. Division of Motor Vehicles.

DOS 6. Disk operating system, version 6.0. Software manufactured by Microsoft, this is a precursor to its Windows software. Lucy, a computer whiz, is an expert with DOS.

DRUGFIRE. FBI "firearms evidence imaging system." A computerized program, a subset of CAIN, used to "link firearms-related crimes."

Eddings, Theodore A. He is the fatality reported by a bogus policeman and Detective Roche. A reporter based in Richmond, Virginia, he worked for the AP (Associated Press).

Elizabeth River. A major river that divides Norfolk and Portsmouth.

Exploiter. Eddings's air hose snagged on the screw on this submarine.

Fan, the. A fashionable part of Richmond, on Monument Avenue, so named because of the layout of the streets.

FEMA. Federal Emergency Management Agency.

Hand, Joe. Leader of the New Zionists.

Hill Café. Located on Twenty-eighth Street in Richmond, it's a favorite with police.

HRT. Hostage Rescue Team. The FBI's elite team to which Lucy is attached, to her dismay, not as an active member but a technical consultant because of her computer expertise.

Inactive naval shipyard. An anonymous caller, hiding behind a bogus name, calls Dr. Mant at home to report a death at this location.

Janet. A friend of Lucy's and a fellow FBI agent, she's assigned to the D.C. field office.

Libby Hill Park. A prestigious neighborhood of Richmond, known for its old homes.

Mant, Dr. Philip. The chief medical examiner of the Tidewater District, in whose home at Sandbridge Scarpetta is staying.

Naval Criminal Investigative Service. Captain Green of the NIS meets Scarpetta at the inactive naval shipyard after she got the call about the discovery of Eddings's body.

New Zionists. A radical group with a reinforced compound in Virginia. The group is feared to be plotting terrorist activities.

Old Point. A nuclear power plant in Virginia taken over by terrorists, the New Zionists. (The real power plant is located at Surry County, across the James River from Williamsburg.)

Qaddafi. Libyan president who has known ties to terrorist organizations. Linked to the New Zionists.

Roche, Det. C. T. From the Chesapeake Police Department, he calls Dr. Mant at home to report the body found at the inactive naval shipyard. Instead of Mant, he gets Scarpetta, who is temporarily a house guest because she's covering for him at work. Roche, however, earns her scorn by mixing business with pleasure: When investigating the car vandalism, he also makes a pass at Scarpetta, which she soundly puts down.

Rotunda. At the University of Virginia in Charlottesville. This structure is Scarpetta's favorite design by Thomas Jefferson.

Sandbridge. A subdivision of Virginia Beach, facing the Atlantic Ocean. Principally known for its expensive beach homes, many of which are protected by a seawall. Scarpetta is staying at a home in Sandbridge, at the residence of the CME, chief medical examiner, of the Tidewater District.

SEM. Scanning electronic microscope.

Sentara Norfolk General Hospital. Located near the Elizabeth River, this is the home base of its airmed chopper, *Nightingale.*

Sessions, MG Lynwood. Called in to discuss the case at hand, the selling of submarines from the inactive shipyard.

Sulgrave. A street in Windsor Farms, the home of Mrs. Eddings, the mother of the reporter who was found dead in the Elizabeth River.

Tidewater District. Covering southeast Virginia, the office of the CME (chief medical examiner) is located in Norfolk near the Elizabeth River waterfront. Its entrance is in the back of the Department of Health Building.

U-238. Depleted uranium found on the bottom of someone's shoes tracked into Scarpetta's Mercedes Benz.

Virginia Beach. Major seaside resort in Southside Hampton Roads. Best known for its miles of beach facing the Atlantic, it's the reason why traffic on the I-64 is clogged, sometimes bumper to bumper, during the summer months, up through Labor Day.

Virginian-Pilot. The major newspaper serving the Southside, which used to be served by an evening paper, the *Ledger-Star,* which suspended publication, as have many evening papers nationwide because of shrinking circulation.

Wesley, Connie. The wife of Benton Wesley. Their marriage on the rocks, they are filing for divorce.

Yellow Brick Road. The formidable obstacle course at the FBI Academy in Quantico, Virginia.

Young, Off. S. T. An unknown person poses as a Chesapeake policeman, calls Dr. Mant, and gets Scarpetta instead.

UNNATURAL EXPOSURE, 1997

Editions

1. Trade paperback, $7.99, Berkley Books.
2. Large print edition, Simon & Schuster.
3. Unabridged audiotape, read by Kate Reading, $34.95, Random House.
4. Abridged audiotape, read by Blair Brown, $24, Random House.
5. Abridged audio on CD, read by Blair Brown, $27.50, Random House.
6. Hardback, first edition, signed, $40–55.
7. Limited edition of 175 copies in matching slipcase, published by Putnam. $185–225.

Dedication

"To Esther Newberg/ *Vision, No Fear*"
Newberg is Cornwell's agent at ICM.

Geography

Rural Virginia (Wakefield) and Tangier Island (off the Virginia coast).

Reviews

"Whoever shot the latest unidentified female victim Dr. Kay Scarpetta's called out to examine—whoever cut off her head, dismembered her, and bagged her torso for disposal in a Virginia landfill—may have been doing her a favor. Though Virginia's chief medical examiner doesn't realize it until she's called out to an even more horrific death scene—an inoffensive old woman on Tangier Island who seems to have died of smallpox—the earlier victim had signs of the same ravaging illness, supposedly eradicated in 1977. The violence to the first victim, and the care taken to conceal her identity, would point to murder even if Scarpetta hadn't started to get sinister computer messages from somebody called 'deadoc,' who soon goes on to order the President: 'apologize if not i will start on france'[sic]. Arrayed against deadoc are the Richmond homicide squad (headed by Scarpetta's old friend Capt. Pete Marino), the Virginia State Police, the FBI (including Scarpetta's on-again lover Benton Wesley and her niece Lucy), the Center[s] for Disease Control [and Prevention], and the U.S. Army Medical Research Institute of Infectious Diseases. But in true Cornwell fashion, the good guys are their own worst enemies: The state cops and the FBI are mired in turf wars; a slick state investigator's determined to arrest the wrong perp and smear Lucy for an old lesbian affair; the USAM-RIID, woefully underfunded, has furloughed so many unessential employees that there's hardly a nurse to care for Scarpetta when she comes down with a fever she can only pray isn't smallpox.

Cornwell's tenth shows her best-selling formula—in-your-face forensics, computer terrorism, agency infighting, soap-opera romance, penny-dreadful villain—wearing a little thin. But fans, swept up in a fever of their own, won't care a bit." (*Kirkus Reviews.*)

Unnatural Exposure A to Z

AFIP. Armed Forces Institute of Pathology. Before Colonel Fujitsubo assumed command of USAMRIID, he commanded AFIP.

AFIS. Automated Fingerprint Identification System.

AKA. Used online, Lucy's code for Scarpetta—Aunt Kay Always.

AOL. America Online. Scarpetta's online provider; it's the biggest of its kind in the world.

Atlantic waste disposal landfill. In southeast Virginia, off Route 460 (a major road connecting Petersburg to Suffolk), near Wakefield. Scarpetta is notified when a body is found here—a white woman, decapitated.

Balls of Fire. Marino's bowling team.

Bass, Dr. The head of the Body Farm in Knoxville, Tennessee.

Bev's Kicked by a Horse Cocktail Sauce. Homemade sauce sold at P. T. Hastings.

Biotech Park. In downtown Richmond near the Coliseum, the new location of Scarpetta's office (the old one: the Consolidated Building).

BL-4 containment. Bio Level 4. In the lab environment, Ebola and other viruses for which there are no known cures are isolated and studied under the most stringent conditions with appropriate security/decontamination procedures in place.

BMW. Wesley Benton drives a silver BMW.

BWI. Baltimore-Washington International Airport. Located midway between the two cities.

Case 1930–97. The unidentified body of the woman found at the Atlantic landfill.

CASKU. Child Abduction Serial Killer Unit. The head of this unit is Benton Wesley, who is now divorced from Connie.

CDC. Centers for Disease Control. This one is located in Atlanta, Georgia, on the grounds of Emory University, a major research center in the United States for biohazards. It has a BL-4 containment facility.

Crowder, Dr. Phyllis. Scarpetta drives to Newport News to visit Crowder, who is complaining that she has the "wretched flu." Crowder, however, has contracted something far more deadly.

DEADOC. The name used by someone logging onto AOL. Dead doctor.

Dugway Proving Ground. Located in Utah in the Great Salt Lake Desert, the U.S. Army's testing facility for chemical/biological defense.

Graceland. Pop icon Elvis Presley's estate, a popular tourist attraction. Scarpetta and Marino tour Graceland.

Grigg, Detective. From the Sussex Sheriff's Department, Grigg called Scarpetta to alert her about the body found on the premises of the Atlantic landfill.

HALT. Homicide Assessment and Lead Tracking system. A database shared by the FBI and state police.

HEPA. High-efficiency particulate air filter. Used to filter air and prevent the transmission of airborne biohazards too small to be filtered out by less discriminate filters.

HRT. The FBI's Hostage Rescue Team, for which Lucy is a computer specialist.

I-64. Major interstate in southeast Virginia, connecting Richmond to Southside Virginia.

James, Mark. Scarpetta's former boyfriend who was in the wrong place at the wrong time and is killed by an IRA bomb.

Kitchen, Mr. The owner of the Atlantic landfill.

KSCARPETTA. Kay Scarpetta's AOL sign-on name.

Lucky Strikes. Detective Grigg's bowling team.

McFee, Julie. A solicitor (i.e., lawyer) from London who was with Mark James when the bomb exploded. She and James had been romantically involved—a fact Benton had known about for some time but did not share with Scarpetta until after James's untimely demise.

No. 3 Store Street (Ireland). The location of the Coroner's Office.

Pathology Electron Microscopy Lab. Colocated with Scarpetta's office, this lab has, among its assets, a TEM (transmission electron microscope), the only one in Richmond.

Pleasants, Keith. An employee at the Atlantic landfill, he gives Scarpetta a tour of the trash site. Based strictly on circumstantial evidence, Investigator Ring suspects Pleasants as the landfill killer.

P. T. Hastings. A seafood restaurant in Richmond's Carytown, where Scarpetta stops to buy food for dinner. It has, she says, the best seafood in town.

Quarantine. Isolation imposed on a geographic area or person/s when suspected of biohazard contamination. Scarpetta is under quarantine because of possible exposure.

QUINCY. Lucy's AOL name.

Riley, Dr. Alan. He works at MCV and is treating Wingo for HIV.

Roy, Rob. Sheriff in Sussex County; he meets Scarpetta at the Virginia Diner in Wakefield. She discusses her meeting with Keith Pleasants and is convinced he's innocent—in fact, she posts bond for him, to Sheriff Roy's surprise. After discussing the circumstances, the sheriff concurs.

Sentara Norfolk General Hospital. Where Dr. Crowder is taken after Scarpetta pays her a visit and confronts her with undeniable evidence linking her to the outbreak.

Shelbourne Hotel (Dublin, Ireland). Unable to sleep, Scarpetta, staying at this hotel, calls back home to Marino, who is playing poker with his buddies. It's business, though, not pleasure for Scarpetta, who is comparing similarities between serial dismemberments in Virginia and in Dublin, as well.

Shockoe Slip. In Richmond, a popular shopping/dining district tailor-made for the upwardly mobile.

SINBAD. Scarpetta's AOL password, named after her mother's "rotten cat." Her niece, Lucy, chides her for never changing her password.

Tangier Island. Located in the Chesapeake Bay between Virginia and Maryland. Scarpetta fears an outbreak of a virus on this island after an islander exhibits unidentifiable eruptions on her body. A remote island, it is accessible by boat or by aircraft. (No ferries run between the mainland and this island.) Its main source of revenue is shellfish—specifically, blue crabs.

Ukrop's. Popular grocery chain store that Scarpetta wishes were near her home.

USAMRIID. U.S. Army Medical Research Institute of Infectious Diseases (Fort Detrick, Maryland). Scarpetta speaks with Colonel Fujitsubo, who runs the facility, and briefs him on what she suspects may be an outbreak of unidentified origin on Tangier Island. Its mission: The identification of and defense against biohazards nationwide.

Vander, Neils. A section chief of fingerprint examination who assists Scarpetta in matching a morgue photo of the dead woman found in the landfill with one she received by E-mail attachment via AOL. It's a match.

Virginia Diner. In Wakefield, a popular roadside diner frequented by locals and tourists alike.

VR. Virtual reality. At the FBI's ERF, Lucy takes Scarpetta on a virtual reality tour, a computer landscape in which she's immersed and which, understandably, she finds disorienting.

WHO. World Health Organization. Disseminates consumer alerts internationally. An alert is issued on Vita spray.

Wingo. An employee of Scarpetta's, he confesses to her that he's HIV positive and she offers to help.

POINT OF ORIGIN, 1998

Editions

1. Hardback, $25.95, G. P. Putnam's Sons.
2. "Turtleback" binding, Young Adult market, Econo-Clad Books.
3. Paperback, $7.99, Berkley Publishing Group.
4. Large print edition: Thorndike Large Print, Basic Series, Simon & Schuster.
5. Unabridged audiotape, read by Kate Reading, $39.95, Random House.
6. Abridged audiotape, read by Joan Allen, $24.95, Putnam Publishing Group.
7. Hardback, first edition, $40–45.
8. Limited edition of five hundred slipcased copies, published by Putnam. $150–185.

Dedication

"With love to Barbara Bush (for the difference you make)."

Cornwell is a good friend of the Bush family; her Web site (now under construction) had photos of her with the Bushes; on her Web site, she also endorsed Pres. George W. Bush.

Geography

Richmond.

Reviews

"Does Kay Scarpetta ever have a nice day? No sooner has she been taken from the arms of her FBI lover Benton Wesley by a disquieting note from her niece Lucy's murderous ex-lover Carrie Grethen, locked up ever since *The Body Farm* (1994), than she gets called to the scene of a particularly horrific arson. Nineteen horses are dead at the farm of black publishing mogul Kenneth Sparkes, a longtime adversary of Scarpetta's, along with what looks like the body of Sparkes's onetime lover Claire Rawley. All indications are that the fire started in the commodious master bathroom, but since there's no sign of accelerant or fuel, Scarpetta's forced to fall back on her specialty, testimony from the corpse, which eventually leads her back in time to a series of equally inexplicable arson-murders. By now, Carrie Grethen has escaped and written to every newspaper on the East Coast that she was seduced by Lucy and framed by Scarpetta and Wesley; Scarpetta is at loggerheads with Teun McGovern, Lucy's new boss at Alcohol, Tobacco, and Firearms; and Scarpetta's irascible buddy Capt. Pete Marino is indulging himself in intimations of mortality that turn out to be only too well-timed. As in Scarpetta's recent cases (*Unnatural Exposure,* 1997, etc.), the final face-off between good and evil comes as something of an anticlimax after the trademark grueling forensics, showing once again that Cornwell's most compelling characters tend to be dead." (*Kirkus Reviews.*)

"Cornwell's ninth novel in the Kay Scarpetta series finds Scarpetta, Benton Wesley, Pete Marino, and Scarpetta's niece, Lucy, investigating a series of arson cases also involving human victims. To further complicate the plot, Scarpetta's old nemesis, Carrie Grethen, featured in *Cruel and Unusual* (Scribner, 1993; Avon, 1995 reprint) and *From Potter's Field* (LJ 8/95), has escaped from a maximum-security psychiatric facility and is threatening Scarpetta and those close to her. Though this new work contains many of the characteristics of Cornwell's best Scarpetta novels—well-drawn characters, nail-biting suspense, and shocking plot twists—Scarpetta herself seems to be growing increasingly weary of it all, and the series seems to be losing momentum. It will be interesting to see where Cornwell takes it next. Still, readers who have enjoyed Cornwell's other installments should like this one, too. Recommended for public libraries and popular reading collections." (Previewed in "PrePub Alert," *Library Journal,* March 1, 1999. Leslie Madden, Georgia Institute of Technology Library and Information Center, Atlanta.)

Point of Origin A to Z

ATF. A federal agency overseeing the regulation of alcohol, tobacco and firearms. Lucy is now an ATF agent.

AWOS. Automated Weather Observation Service.

AXIS. Arson Incident System. A database that catalogs known fire incidents. By cross-checking, the modus operandi (MO) may help identify the arsonist by his handiwork.

Breitling Aerospace watch. An expensive chronograph Scarpetta gives Benton for Christmas. (*Note:* Cornwell wears this brand, which she buys from an upscale store at the Regency Mall.)

CFI. Certified fire investigators.

Cole's Restaurant Supply. In Richmond. Scarpetta pays a visit to this store to buy their biggest pot, which she needs for the morgue. When asked by the clerk, she says she needs it to "boil different things."

ESA. Enterprise Systems Architecture. An ATF computer network that is a "national arson and explosive repository."

Farrier. A blacksmith who shoes horses.

Feebs. The ATF's derogatory term for the FBI.

Fire simulator. A computer model that, once the variables about a known fire are entered, approximates how and when a fire started. In the case at hand, the fire simulator "proved" that the fire could not have started in the master bedroom at Sparkes's estate.

Fire starter. A magnesium block used to spark fires, available at sporting goods stores like Jumbo Sports in Richmond, which Scarpetta visits.

FTIR. Fourier Transform Infrared Spectroscopy.

Halliburton. An aluminum case favored by photographers; Scarpetta has a well-used Halliburton in which she stores her tools of the trade, including a camera.

Heloair. Located near RIA (Richmond International Airport), this company rents helicopters. Lucy, who flies helicopters, joins Scarpetta; they soon lift off in a Bell JetRanger and head to Kirby Forensic Psychiatric Center.

King's Dominion. A theme park off Interstate 95, twenty miles north of Richmond; it is located at Doswell, Virginia.

Kirby Forensic Psychiatric Center in New York. Carrie Grethen is a patient in this facility, from which she writes cryptic letters to Scarpetta.

Lehigh Valley Hospital (Pennsylvania). Scarpetta meets Dr. Abraham Gerde to discuss the discovery of another suspicious fire-related incident, Kellie Shephard's. Shepherd was found dead in her bathtub.

Lucy Boo. Scarpetta's nickname for her niece, Lucy Farinelli, until she started kindergarten.

PAD. Preventive aggressive device. A restraining device often used at psychiatric facilities that consists of a leather belt with chains to secure the wrists and ankles.

Point of origin. The specific location where a fire started.

Q-dot calculations. The mathematics used to "estimate the physics and chemistry of a fire as it related to what the investigator observed at the scene or was told by witnesses," says Scarpetta, in a conversation with Teun McGovern.

Rawley, Claire. A beautiful young blonde whose body was found in a tub at Sparkes's estate.

Richmond Times-Dispatch. The local newspaper.

Ruthers Road. In Richmond. Marino lives in a "small aluminum-side white house" on this street. At Christmas, his light-festooned house is so garish that it has achieved the notoriety of being on Richmond's "Tacky Tour."

Sea Pines (Hilton Head, South Carolina). Scarpetta and others gather here to pay respects to the late Benton Wesley, who died in the line of duty. She scatters his ashes from the air in a helicopter flown by Lucy.

Sparkes, Kenneth. Media mogul whose horse farm in Warrenton, Virginia, was targeted for an arson attack.

Tally-ho. Aviation lingo for "above the horizon." Used by a pilot to describe the location of other aircraft relative to his own.

Unabomber and Cunanan. Carrie Grethen, who escaped from Kirby Foresnsic Psychiatric Center, is compared to these two men—the former killed via mail bombs, the latter killed fashion designer Gianni Versace—by Benton, in a conversation with Scarpetta.

Westpark. Lucy and her roommate Janet (with the ATF) share an apartment in this building. Scarpetta and Marino pay them a visit, bringing dinner.

Whackers. Derogatory term used by ATF agents to describe civilians who rubberneck at fires—fire buffs, as Scarpetta calls them.

SCARPETTA'S WINTER TABLE, 1998

Scarpetta's Winter Table, trade hardback, ninety-one numbered pages, $19.95; Wyrick & Company, 1998. Photos by Alice Cassidy.

If the Scarpetta novels are main dishes, *Scarpetta's Winter Table* is a holiday appetizer. Unlike her Scarpetta novels, published by Putnam, this book was published by a small house in Charleston, South Carolina. But, you wonder, why Wyrick & Company?

The telling clue can be found in the book's dedication: "To Charlie/Editor and Friend." My educated guess is that the reference is to Charles Cornwell, Patricia's former husband, currently an editor at Wyrick & Company.

As you'd expect, Patricia Cornwell's own design company, Bell Vision Visual Communications, designed the jacket and the book itself; Alice Cassidy, likely a staff photographer, provided the pictures. In other words, the "look" of the book bears Cornwell's unmistakable imprint. Unfortunately, the book printing does an injustice to Cornwell: The photographs have a muddy appearance—little tonal range and contrast—and detract from what is otherwise a delightful book that will whet your appetite.

Here's some food for thought: Why not celebrate a Scarpetta Christmas by dishing out some of Kay Scarpetta's, Lucy Farinelli's, and Pete Marino's favorite foods and beverages?

Here's what's on the menu: Scarpetta's Holiday Pizza, Childhood Key Lime Pie, Wholesome Chicken Soup, and Famous Stew. Lucy's Bloody Marys, Friendly Grill, and Felonious Cookies. Marino's Cause-of-Death Egg Nog, Last-Minute Chili, and Southern-Style New Jersey Omelet.

For Cornwell fans hungry for more, a sequel is available. In collaboration with Marlene Brown, Cornwell authored *Food to Die For: Secrets from Kay Scarpetta's Kitchen.*

BLACK NOTICE, 1999

Editions

1. Hardback, $25.95, Random House.
2. Paperback, $7.99, Berkley Publishing Group.
3. Large Print edition, $13.95, Random House Large Print.
4. Unabridged audiotape, read by Kate Reading, Putnam Publishing Group.
5. Abridged audiotape, read by Roberta Maxwell, Putnam Publishing Group.
6. Hardback, first edition, signed, $45–65.
7. First UK edition, signed, $93.50.
8. Limited edition of two hundred slipcased copies, published by Putnam. $145.

Dedication

"To Nina Salter/ *Water and Words.*"

Geography

Lyon, France; Richmond.

Perspective

Black Notice is in two significant ways a departure from the established canon of Scarpetta stories.

First, its fictional time frame is set immediately after that of its predecessor, *Point of Origin,* so the two go hand in hand; in fact, *Black Notice* has the distinct feel of being the second part of a long tale, not simply the next story in this ongoing series.

Second, this novel shows a side of Scarpetta that her fans have wanted to see for years: a private side, her vulnerability, which contrasts sharply to the professional persona of Dr. Kay Scarpetta, the Chief Medical Examiner for the Commonwealth of Virginia.

A major turning point in Scarpetta's life ("I stared out the window at a neighbor raking leaves and felt helpless, broken and gone."), she must come to grips with an ugly reality of life: That even those whom you hold near and dear are not protected against the randomness of the universe or the depredations of criminals.

Also, *Black Notice* takes Scarpetta to Interpol (France), which gives a much needed change of locale to the Scarpetta canon, since most of Cornwell's novels are set in Richmond.

Reviews

"Virginia Chief Medical Examiner Kay Scarpetta has never liked Christmas; and this year, when she's still mourning the death of her FBI lover Benton Wesley (*Point of Origin,* 1998), looks like her worst holiday season ever. While she can't identify or name the exact cause of death, the corpse found in a sealed shipping con-

tainer aboard a cargo ship from Belgium is the least of her problems—even though Cornwell leads from strength by presenting
one of her most extended (and unnerving) postmortems. Just as
Scarpetta and her longtime police ally Capt. Pete Marino are running into industrial-strength flak from Richmond's new deputy
chief, ambitious, manipulative Diane Bray, someone in Scarpetta's
office is sabotaging her more underhandedly: a series of petty thefts
is only the nuisance that finally awakens her to a fraud counter-
manding her orders and masquerading as her over the Internet.
And her niece Lucy Farinelli, an agent working out of Alcohol,
Tobacco, and Firearms' Miami office, is undercover with a bunch
of seriously bad people. The web of evil that binds all these plots
together (think drug smuggling; think Interpol; think werewolves)
isn't believable for a minute, but expertly mired in Scarpetta's fath-
omless professional battles, you won't have a minute to think about
it till you've turned the last page. It's fascinating to watch Scarpetta
and her supporting cast, instead of growing, like V. I. Warshawski,
become more and more themselves, like Sherlock Holmes—especially in such a brilliantly paced adventure as this one." (*Kirkus
Reviews.*)

"It's like a splash of cold water on a hot day to be plunged, after
the irritating third-person satire of Cornwell's last novel, *Southern
Cross* (1998), back into the bracing narration of medical examiner
Kay Scarpetta. As in the nine Scarpettas past (*Point of Origin,* etc.),
here it's not the novel's events, startling as they are, that propel the
story so much as the deep-hearted responses of Kay, as real a hero
as any in thriller fiction, to the "evil"—her word—that threatens.
Evil wears several faces here, from petty to monstrous. Most insid-
ious is the office sabotage—insubordination, thefts, fraudulent E-
mails—that's making the grieving Kay look as if she's lost her grip
since her lover's murder in *Point of Origin*. More destructive are

the overt attempts by calculating Richmond, Va., deputy police chief Diane Bray to ruin Kay's career as well as that of Kay's old friend, Capt. Pete Marino. Then there's the wild rage at life that's consuming Kay's niece, a DEA agent. Finally—the plot wire that binds the sometimes scattered plot—there are the mutilation killings by the French serial killer self-styled "Loup-Garou"— werewolf. The forensic sequences boom with authority; the brief action sequences explode on the page—in the finale, overbearingly so; the interplay between Kay and Marino is boisterous as always, and there's an atmospheric side-trip to Paris and an affecting romantic misadventure for lonely Kay. A thunderhead of disquietude hangs over this compulsively readable novel, sometimes loosing storms of suspense; but to Cornwell's considerable credit, the unease arises ultimately not from the steady potential for violence, but from a more profound horror: the vulnerability of a good woman like Kay to a world beset by the corrupt, the cruel, the demonic." One million first printing; $750,000 ad/promo; Literary Guild, Doubleday Book Club, and Mystery Guild main selections; unabridged and abridged audio versions; foreign rights sold in eight countries. (*Publishers Weekly.*)

Black Notice A to Z

Anderson, Det. Rene. In charge of the crime scene where the body is found at the Port of Richmond.

Black notice. A color-coded notice issued by Interpol to indicate an unidentified body, like the one found at the Port of Richmond in a container off the *Sirius*.

Bray, Diane, Chief of Police, City of Richmond. She feels the city needs new blood, like Detective Anderson; and the old hands like Marino who can't, or won't, modernize are considered relics. For this reason she takes him off homicide and reassigns him as a watch commander.

Buckheads. A restaurant located in the Beverly Hills Shopping Center. Scarpetta considers it "the city's finest chophouse." Well-known for its steaks and seafood.

Carson, Al, Deputy Chief, Head of Investigations. He has resigned, which consolidates power in Deputy Chief Bray, to Marino's distaste.

Chandonne, Thomas. Interpol believes the body found in the container is that of this man, who decided to bypass the cartel, cutting them out of the illegal deals he ran, including drug trafficking and gunrunning. When he's found out, however, he's terminated with extreme prejudice by the cartel.

Charles de Gaulle Airport. Scarpetta and Marino arrive at this Paris airport to meet with Jay Tally.

CHUKOCME. Chuck's E-mail address with AOL. An employee of Scarpetta's with the dream of being a police officer, he meets clandestinely with Detective Anderson and Deputy Chief Bray, who pump him for information about Scarpetta. Chuck finally comes clean with Scarpetta after she confronts him.

Commonwealth Club. A prestigious "men-only" club where the power elite meet. Women are allowed as guests of members, but not in the locker room, where a lot of wheeling and dealing is done.

COMPSTAT. Computer-driven statistics. A computer model developed by the New York Police Department.

Deputy Chief Bray suggests Lucy, whom she's trying to recruit, would be ideal to implement it in Virginia.

Container Man, the. The deceased man found in the container at the Port of Richmond is given this nickname, for lack of other ID.

Crestar. Major bank in the Southeast. (After a recent bank merger, it's now called SunTrust.)

David, Terry Jennifer. Lucy's driver's license shows this alias. She's ATF (Bureau of Alcohol, Tobacco and Firearms) working with DEA in Florida on search-and-seizure missions in HIDTA.

DEA. Drug Enforcement Agency.

Dear Chief Kay. A chat room on AOL in which someone is impersonating Scarpetta.

DOA. Dead on arrival.

Dodge Ram Quad Cab pickup truck. Marino's wheels.

Francisco, Ted. An agent with the ATF field office in Miami, he calls Scarpetta to inform her that Lucy's partner, Jo, was shot in the line of duty and taken to Jackson Memorial under an assumed name.

Glynco, Georgia. The location of a national academy used to train federal agents of all stripes—basic training.

HIDTA. High intensity drug trafficking area.

Hypertrichosis. A very rare medical condition in which the person is covered with fine body hair over his entire body, along with other accompanying anomalies. The appearance of such a hirsute person suggests a werewolf.

Institut Medico-Legal. Autopsies in Paris are conducted here under the supervision of the medical examiner, Dr. Ruth Stvan.

Interpol. International police. Headquartered in Europe. Coordinates law-enforcement activities worldwide. Uses color-coded notices to highlight "wanted and missing people, warning, inquiries," says Scarpetta.

Jo. A DEA agent, a friend of Lucy's—her "psycho partner," as Lucy puts it.

Lord, Sen. Frank. He hand delivers a letter from Benton to Scarpetta as per Benton's instructions.

Loup-garou. A French word meaning "werewolf."

Luong, Kim. A murder victim, she worked at a convenience store in Richmond.

Miami field office, ATF. Lucy has been reassigned here.

One-Sixty-Fivers. Lucy's term for the gun traffickers so named because of the ammunition they prefer, "one-sixty-five-grain Speer Gold Dot."

OSHA. Occupational Safety & Health Administration. Federal agency in charge of safety considerations in the workplace.

Port of Richmond. Location of a cargo container, off-loaded from the *Sirius,* in which a body is found.

Regency Mall. A major shopping mall off Parham Road in Richmond.

ROOSTR. Chuck's password to log online AOL.

Rubyfruit. A bar in Greenwich Village, New York, run by a former policewoman, Ann. Seeking solace and refuge, Lucy retreats here to get away from the emotional turmoil she wants to leave behind, at least temporarily.

Shaw, Joe. Director for the Port of Richmond.

Sig-Sauer 232 pistol. The firearm Lucy keeps in an ankle holster.

Smith & Wesson revolver. Scarpetta's firearm.

Tally, Jay. The "ATF liaison at Interpol." He is with Senator Lord and requests that Scarpetta and Marino catch a Concorde to France on short notice.

Vander, Neil. Fingerprint expert who runs the fingerprint ID lab.

VCIN. Virginia Criminal Information Network.

Wagner, Sinclair. Secretary of OSHA.

THE LAST PRECINCT, 2000

Editions

1. Hardback, $26.95, Putnam Publishing Group.
2. Large print edition, $26.95, Random House Large Print.
3. Unabridged audiotape, read by Kate Reading, Putnam Publishing Group.
4. Abridged audiotape, read by Roberta Maxwell, Putnam Publishing Group.
5. Abridged audio on CD, read by Roberta Maxwell, Putnam Publishing Group.
6. Limited edition of 175 slipcased copies published by Putnam. $145–200.

Note: Signed first editions, with Cornwell's bookplate, are currently selling for approximately $40; flat-signed copies, $45 and up.

Dedication

"To Linda Fairstein—/Prosecutor. Novelist. Mentor. Best Friend. (This one's for you.)"

By avocation, Fairstein is the author of the Alex Cooper mystery series: *Likely to Die, Final Jeopardy,* and *Cold Hit.* By vocation, she's a New York prosecutor and handles sex assault crimes and domestic violence.

Geography

Richmond.

Perspective

For some years Cornwell has dutifully turned in each Scarpetta novel on time, allowing the publishers to crank up the promotion and publicity to maximum effect. Nothing, though, can happen until the book is turned in . . . but this book refused to be shoehorned in the plot Cornwell had originally conceived, including considerable research done on-site at Jamestown, Virginia, near Williamsburg. (Just like a good cook, she lets nothing goes to waste; the research was put into the third Judy Hammer novel, *Isle of Dogs.*)

Cornwell felt that in recent years the emphasis has been on the forensics, on how the murders are solved; consequently, we see too much of Scarpetta on the job, competent and professional, with a blurring of her private life.

This novel concerns itself largely with Scarpetta's private life, which is what the fans want: a balance between Scarpetta on and off the job. The result is a book that properly can be called a turning point in her fiction: a balanced book that shows the vulnerability of Scarpetta, who at times, in the past, has come across as a Wonder Woman single-handedly fighting crime.

Reviews

"What could be more open and shut than a case in which a widely sought killer tricks his way into the home of Virginia's Chief Medical Examiner, attacks her with a hammer of exactly the same sort he'd used in killing Richmond Deputy Police Chief Diane Bray, and is still on the scene when police arrive? But when Dr. Kay Scarpetta, the intended victim of notorious Jean-Baptiste Chandonne, hears the statement the suspect (dubbed Le Loup-Garou, the Werewolf, for the fine, undisguisable hair covering his entire body) has given the police, she realizes that despite her obvious suffering and terror, attested by the elbow she broke just after throwing some providential formalin into her assailant's eyes, the case boils down to her word against his. As she and her embattled loyalists—ATF niece Lucy Farinelli; neanderthal Richmond Police Captain Pete Marino; New York sex crimes ADA Jaime Berger—toil to link Chandonne's current murder spree first to the killing of a Big Apple weathercaster two years ago, then to the execution of Scarpetta's FBI lover Benton Wesley, the news gets steadily worse until Scarpetta finds herself entering a grand jury chamber not as an expert witness but as a homicide suspect." (*Kirkus Reviews.*)

"*The Last Precinct,* Cornwell's 11th novel featuring Dr. Kay Scarpetta, is really Part 2 of *Black Notice* (LJ 7/99), her previous work in this series. The story opens on the night following a vicious attack on Scarpetta by Le Loup Garou (the Werewolf). As she recovers from her injuries, Scarpetta begins another healing process as well by beginning to deal with her past, examine her present life, and contemplate a career change. As always, bodies are delivered to the morgue, and as Scarpetta unravels the mysteries of their deaths, she begins to suspect a connection between a few of her patients and the Chandonne crime family, of which Le Loup Garou is a member.

This may be Cornwell's least action-oriented, most reflective work featuring Scarpetta. Readers unfamiliar with the series may find it confusing, but fans will want to read it. Recommended for all public libraries and popular reading collections." (Previewed in "Pre-Pub Alert," *Library Journal,* February 1, 2000. Leslie Madden, Georgia Institute of Technology, Atlanta.)

" '*My central nervous system spikes and surges, my pulse pounds. I am sweating . . .* ' If only readers would share this response with Cornwell's immensely popular Kay Scarpetta, Virginia's chief medical examiner. But most won't. Kay has plenty of reason to be upset. She's standing in a room in a shabby motel where a body has been found, severely tortured. She's under official suspicion of having murdered maleficent uber-cop Diane Bray (in Kay's last outing, *Black Notice*). She's suspected of trumping up charges against accused serial killer Jean-Baptiste Chandonne, also introduced in [*Black Notice*]. She's reeling from the aftershock of Chandonne's murderous attack on her; she mightily misses her slain FBI agent/lover Dan Belson; she's learned that her gay niece, Lucy, is quitting law enforcement for a private PI firm called the Last Precinct—and it's Christmas time. Kay has a lot of support in the midst of this law-and-disorder soap opera, from, among others, Lucy, tough cop/sidekick Pete Marino and Kay's aged friend, psychiatrist Anna Zenner—and that's part of the problem with this novel. Excessive emoting and way too much talk (including long therapeutic sessions between Kay and Anna) derail momentum time and again; the pages feel soggy with tears. Cornwell does provide intense intrigue, but it's a strain to follow as she connects events and loose ends from several novels. Within this narrative swamp, there's one new and very memorable gator, though—New York prosecutor Jaime Berger, obviously modeled on real-life ADA (and novelist) Linda Fairstein, to whom Cornwell dedicates the novel; she's sharply drawn and charismatic. Cornwell will win few if any new fans with this overlong, sluggish offering, but her giant readership is so hardcore and so enamored of Kay that the publisher's first printing of one million seems, if anything, conservative." (Eight-hundred-thousand-dollar ad/promo; Literary Guild, Mystery Guild, and Doubleday Book Club main selections; national satellite tour; foreign rights sold in the UK, Germany, Italy, France, Holland, Japan, Finland, Turkey, and Spain, *Publishers Weekly*.)

The Last Precinct A to Z

Admin leave. Administrative leave. Lucy is on admin leave from the ATF.

Bell 407. The helicopter Lucy buys. It carries six passengers and a pilot and costs, according to Bell's Web site, approximately $263 per flight hour to operate. (*Note:* This is the same helicopter Cornwell owns. She is reportedly looking to trade it in for a newer, faster model with extended cruising range.) Lucy's chopper is "black with bright stripes," just like Cornwell's.

Berger, Jaime. A prosecutor from New York; she wants to discuss with Scarpetta the murders of Kim Luong and Diane Bray. (*Note:* My educated guess is that Berger is modeled, in part, after Linda Fairstein, Cornwell's friend and fellow best-selling novelist who runs the sex crimes unit of the New York County District Attorney's Office.)

Biotech II. The newly built research facility in which Scarpetta's lab is housed—a $30 million complex with 130,000 square feet. It is located in the Biotechnology Research Park near the Coliseum in downtown Richmond.

Caggiano, Rocky. Peter Marino's son, a lawyer, who changed his name. He graduated from William & Mary and its law school, Marshall-Wythe.

Chandonne, Jean-Baptiste. The intruder who attacked Scarpetta as chronicled at the end of *Black Notice.*

Fort James Motel and Camp Ground. Located on Route 5 West in James City County (near Williamsburg). A body is found at this overpriced tourist trap.

Gilmore, Gov. Jim. The former governor of the Commonwealth of Virginia, who is adamantly opposed to former mayor Giuliani's policies of exporting trash to landfills in the Commonwealth.

Godspeed, Discovery, Susan Constant. Anchored in Jamestown, these replicated ships are modeled after the ones that carried the English settlers to Jamestown in 1607. (Of the three, two are permanently anchored.)

Jamestown. Located on the banks of the James River near Williamsburg, Jamestown has the distinction of being, as Cornwell noted, "the first permanent English settlement in America." (Jamestown, with its ongoing archaeological digs, is a favorite place of Cornwell's. She, in fact, celebrated a Thanksgiving at Jamestown, arriving in style in two helicopters, including her own. Her guests included film stars Dan Aykroyd and his wife, Donna Dixon. Jamestown, in fact, was supposed to be a major part of *The Last Precinct,* but the book took a different direction plotwise and the research done at Jamestown will be used in another book, possibly the twelfth Scarpetta novel.)

Jefferson Hotel, The. The most opulent hotel in Richmond, highly rated by independent hotel/inn reviewers.

Recently restored to its former magnificence, The Jefferson—one of the most expensive hotels in the city—is where Lucy is staying. (When Scarpetta tells Marino where Lucy is staying, he is incredulous and asks if she's won the lottery. She hasn't, of course, but investments in Internet "inventions and stocks" made her a multimillionaire able to afford her own chopper.)

John Marshall Courts Building. Where Scarpetta testifies before the special grand jury in connection with the Diane Bray case.

JR102. The most famous grave excavation at Jamestown, the remains of a young man, a contemporary of John Smith. The man was shot to death.

Last Precinct, The. The company McGovern starts after resigning from the ATF. When all else fails, you can turn to her firm for help.

Le Loupe-Garou (the Werewolf). Jean-Baptiste Chandonne's name for himself.

Lockgreen. An upscale subdivision in Richmond. Scarpetta lives here. (She moved from Windsor Farms.)

McGovern, Teun. Formerly with the ATF, based in Philadelphia, she was Lucy's supervisor. McGovern, however, turned down a move to Los Angeles to be a Special Agent in Charge (SAC) and resigned to start up her own company.

Morgenthau, Robert. A brilliant DA in Manhattan for whom Berger works.

Mosby Court. One of seven housing projects in Richmond.

Red notice. Issued by Interpol on Jay Talley—a fugitive on the run.

Regency Mall. A popular mall in Richmond where Scarpetta does her Christmas shopping. Scarpetta is supposed to meet Lucy in front of Waldenbooks, and spies Marino on the elevator.

Righter, Buford. A commonwealth attorney who hails from an old Virginia family and who is a middle-of-the-roader, competent but uninspiring—a lawyer in need of a spine donor. In a discussion about the Chandonne case, Scarpetta calls him a "coward."

Special Agent in Charge. Supervises a field division. McGovern was hand-picked to be one in Los Angeles.

Special Grand Jury. Scarpetta, who has been set up, is being investigated to see if sufficient evidence exists to indict her for Diane Bray's murder.

Schwarzchild's Jewelers. An upscale jewelry store on the second floor of the Regency Mall, where Scarpetta had gone months earlier to buy Lucy a gold "Whirly-Girls necklace." (*Note:* This is where Cornwell buys her Breitling chronograph watches.)

TLP. The Last Precinct.

Zenner, Dr. Anna. A psychiatrist, she is, as Scarpetta puts it, "my most trusted friend."

HORNET'S NEST, 1996

Editions

1. Paperback, $7.99, Berkley Publishing Group.
2. Large print, G. K. Hall Large Print.
3. Abridged audiotape, read by Chris Sarandon, Putnam.
4. Hardback. (Out of print.)

Dedication

"To Cops."

Geography

Charlotte, North Carolina.

Perspective

Success for a popular novelist, says writer Harlan Ellison, can come at too dear a price: Readers will *demand* more of the same in endless variations, wanting more tales of their favorite character, themes, and settings. In short, they want the same reading experience and will reward the writer who delivers what they want.

It's a reader's heaven . . . and a writer's hell—the theme of Stephen King's *Misery*, in which a bestselling novelist is literally forced to resurrect a character he killed off, because he wanted to end one series to begin fresh with another.

Insofar as Patricia Cornwell is concerned, her fans and critics speak in one voice when they clamor for more Scarpetta tales.

Cornwell, who is planning to publish the twelfth Scarpetta novel in 2003, has signed contracts for four more. Scarpetta will be around for a long time. The interesting question is whether or not *this* new series will, like the Scarpetta novels, find its audience.

Cornwell had gone boldly where she has not gone before in writing this police procedural, set in Charlotte, North Carolina. *Hornet's Nest* introduces us to two strong female protagonists and one strong male protagonist; respectively, Deputy Chief Virginia West, Chief Judy Hammer (who heads the Charlotte Police Department), and rookie Andy Brazil. (My guess is that Brazil will steal the show: Cornwell would do well to have a new series with a strong male protagonist, instead of repeating herself by using a strong female protagonist.)

Understandably, given her track record, Cornwell faced unreasonably high expectations from readers, critics, and booksellers alike, heightened by the publisher's cheerleading—*New Cornwell novel! New characters! New series!*

The general expectation was that this series would be, in style and tone, similar to the Scarpetta series. That expectation, however, was apparently not shared by Cornwell, because this series is substantially different from what has gone before. Though her new fictional universe seems familiar—the geography of North Carolina and the inner workings of a police department are well-trod territory in her fiction—the comic tone of *Hornet's Nest* in general is not what readers or reviewers expected.

Only time will tell if West, Hammer, and Brazil find a place in the hearts of Cornwell's diehard fans who have long embraced Scarpetta.

If this book is any indication, readers are in for some surprises, including broad swipes at humor that will either hit the mark squarely . . . or miss it entirely.

As Carl Hiassen (a working journalist who writes novels on the side) would probably observe, writing comedy is not funny business: It's deadly serious and your readers will either love the work . . . or hate it.

Cornwell's next book in this series will either convince her fans that she's on track or prove that her vision has derailed. But in the meantime, her longtime fans have bought tickets at the station to get on this first train ride, so to speak, to travel to new destinations.

As the train conductor would say: All aboard the Cornwell express!

Reviews

" 'Where's the beef?' That's a fair question to put to Patricia Cornwell, who has written a long . . . detailed and exceedingly dull police procedural that inexplicably lacks a major criminal investigation to give it focus. . . . Although a serial killer makes a promising appearance, he quickly fades out of the frame, leaving the police to drop their inquiries . . . for more mundane infractions of the peace. Until the killer returns, we have to settle for exhaustive character analysis of Hammer and West, who are interesting enough, and young Andy, who is just plain creepy. 'Brazil wasn't normal,' in the opinion of his editor. That understates the weirdness of Andy, who is driven by an unhealthy obsession with police work. Hammer and West think he's cute—which does not inspire confidence in their professional acumen." (Marilyn Stasio, *New York Times Book Review.*)

"*Hornet's Nest* is so full of friction that it sends off sparks in all directions. It doesn't, however, show any notable expertise in the area of plot-making or intrigue; but the author delivers to her committed readership all the homicides, perverts, hookers of indeterminate gender, all the street and law-enforcement jargon, all the life-and-death bustle which animate her narratives, with her customary drive and efficiency." (Patricia Craig, *Times Literary Supplement.*)

"The decision to abandon her forensic pathologist Kay Scarpetta leaves Cornwell lacking more than a fail-safe series heroine. The only credible element in this novel is the urban New South setting. The story—about two women top cops and a young male newspaper reporter in Charlotte, N.C.—is routine fare at best. The three characters—42-year-old Deputy Chief Virginia West; her boss, unhappily married Chief Judy Hammer; and handsome wunderkind journalist and volunteer cop, Andy Brazil—are preternaturally competent automatons, obsessive and utterly devoid of self-awareness. A sequence of serial killings of out-of-towners, men who are pulled from their rental cars, sexually mutilated, marked with orange spray paint and shot, creates tension in Charlotte. While Hammer struggles with city politics and a depressed, obese husband, West contends with Brazil (a "handsome and fierce" 22-year-old with 'total photographic recall'), who is on assignment to write about police activity, having impressed his editor by turning in 'a hundred of hours' overtime five months in a row.' Rather than reveal her characters through their words and actions, Cornwell forces them on us predigested ('West believed women were great'; 'Brazil did not believe prostitution was right.'). In that same descriptive mode, she takes them on roller coaster rides of extravagant emotion—rage, grief, resolve, despair—and offers set pieces in place of plot: mid-book, more than 150 pages pass without mention of the murders. We are made privy to the fantasies of West's cat, but not to the motivations behind the killings. There is nothing to believe in on these pages beyond Charlotte itself." (*Publishers Weekly.*)

Hornet's Nest A to Z

B&E. Police abbreviation for "breaking and entering."

Bird, Special Agent Gil. FBI profiler.

Black Widow. Name given to serial killer haunting Charlotte. The target: out of towners.

BMW 2002. The car Brazil drives. Not a late model, however, but a relic a quarter-century old.

Brazil, Andrew. Called Drew. Andy Brazil's father, a police detective, who was shot to death in his car.

Brazil, Andy. Attends nearby Davidson College. (*Note:* There are several parallels between Brazil and Cornwell. She also attended Davidson College, worked in the cafeteria serving line, went to school on a tennis scholarship, and worked at the *Charlotte Observer,* starting at the bottom by editing the television listings. Like Brazil, Cornwell aspired to more—to be a reporter.) Brazil has applied to the Charlotte Police Department's academy as a volunteer policeman. (Cornwell was, in fact, a volunteer policeperson for the Richmond Police Department.) Upon graduation from Davidson, Brazil aspires to be a police reporter. (Cornwell, in fact, was a police reporter for the *Charlotte Observer.*)

Bristol, Tennessee. Virginia West attended a "very small, religious school" in this town. (Cornwell, in fact, attended this college—King College.)

Carolinas Medical Center. The major hospital in the area.

Charlotte/Douglas International Airport. The major airport serving this area. (Major hub for USAir.)

Charlotte Observer. The hometown newspaper at which Andy Brazil works. (Upon graduating from nearby Davidson College, Cornwell began her writing career as a journalist with this paper.)

Coliseum. The $230 million sports facility facing the office building of the *Charlotte Observer.*

Firing Line, The. West coaches Andy Brazil at this indoor pistol range on Wilkinson Boulevard.

Gorelick, Nancy. A district attorney, "the city's top prosecutor."

Hammer, Chief Judy. Police chief of the Charlotte Police Department. She's in her early fifties.

Hornet's Nest. A nickname given to Charlotte by Lord Cornwallis, who occupied the city and was "met with hostility," as Cornwell put it.

LEC. Law Enforcement Center.

Mag-Lite. High-powered, heavy-duty flashlight.

Mercedes. The car Judy Hammer drives.

Niles. West's Abyssinian cat.

North College Street. The location of the Mecklenburg County Medical Examiner's Office, where Dr. Odom works.

Note: The book series started out in Charlotte, then moved with the second book to Richmond, perhaps because for Cornwell the backdrop of Charlotte would require additional research for future books. Obviously, it's easier to colocate both fictional worlds within the same city, which would allow cross-pollinating storylines—a shared fictional universe, as it were.

Odom, Dr. Wayne. Medical examiner in the greater Charlotte area.

Panesa, Richard. Publisher of the *Charlotte Observer.*

Presto Grill. On West Trade Street. Hammer and West eat breakfast here every Friday.

Radar. The nickname of a police dispatcher who, early in his career as a policeman with the North Carolina Highway Patrol, made frequent—in fact, too frequent—use of his radar gun. He loved to clock anything that moved . . . and things that didn't, as well.

Rickman, Joshua. Nickname, Bubba. Redneck with revenge fantasies directed toward Brazil and West, with whom he's had a close encounter of the physical kind at The Firing Line.

Scoop, The. Nickname for Brent Webb, a television reporter for Channel 3.

Search, Mayor. Despite the five recorded murders by the Black Widow, Mayor Search stubbornly insists that Charlotte is a safe town, evidence to the contrary. Fear has gripped the town, and the mayor has his head in the sand.

SICU. Surgical Intensive Care Unit. The Carolinas Medical Center.

Sophia, Princess Charlotte. The city of Charlotte, North Carolina, is named after this queen, who was married to George III. Hence its nickname, "the Queen City."

Tilly, Chad. Director of the Tilly Family Mortuary.

West, Deputy Chief Virginia. One of the deputy chiefs in the CPD, she heads the investigative division of three-hundred at age forty-two. (Like West, Cornwell was a high school tennis star.)

SOUTHERN CROSS, 1998

Editions

1. Hardback, $25.95.
2. Paperback, $7.99, Berkley Books.
3. Large print edition, $11.95, Wheeler Large Print Series, Wheeler Publishing.
4. Unabridged audiotape, $39.95, Putnam Publishing Group.
5. Abridged audiotape, $24.95, Roberta Maxwell.

Dedication

"To Marcia H. Morey/World champion in juvenile justice reform and all you've ever done/*for what you've taught me.*"

Geography

Richmond.

Perspective: *Hornet's Nest* and *Southern Cross*

Just as Lestat will be forever linked to Anne Rice, Jack Ryan to Tom Clancy, and Jake Grafton to Stephen Coonts, Dr. Kay Scarpetta will be forever linked to Patricia Cornwell.

No matter what else Cornwell writes, the longevity of Scarpetta and her popularity with the readers virtually guarantee that you cannot think of Cornwell without thinking of Scarpetta.

For Cornwell, such an association has its benefits: Readers will buy her books on name value alone, instead of having to rely on reviews, personal recommendations from friends and family, or browsing in a bookstore.

But there's also an attendant price to pay: The reader—and, indeed, the book world at large—automatically judge anything new by whether it measures up to what's been previously published. And therein lies the problem from the readers' perspective: They want more of the same; they don't want the writer to stray from the well-trod yellow brick road.

From the writer's perspective, it's a creative prison and there's always the urge to go over the top, so to speak. A scene from *The Shawshank Redemption* comes to mind: Tim Robbins plays Andy Dufresne, a wrongfully accused convict who has literally burrowed his way out of prison; he emerges out of a pipe, outside the prison yards, and stands up in exultation as the rain from heaven literally and figuratively washes him clean. He is free.

After chronicling the adventures of Dr. Kay Scarpetta since 1990, Patricia Cornwell broke the mold and decided to shape another literary creation—a new female portagonist for a separate series.

For a writer like Cornwell, there's nothing but risk in getting off the main path, as she discovered when the mixed reviews came in. Publicly, in response to queries posed during online interviews,

Cornwell said that *Southern Cross* is one of her best books, and her fans tell her that, too. Privately, the criticisms about the books must sting, particularly since the Scarpetta books have, in the main, garnered good reviews.

In a prepublication review of *Black Notice* in *Publishers Weekly* (June 14, 1999), the reviewer began by making an inevitable comparison between the two fictional worlds. Regarding *Black Notice,* "It's like a splash of cold water on a hot day to be plunged, after the irritating third-person satire of Cornwell's last novel, *Southern Cross* (1988), back into the bracing narration of medical examiner Kay Scarpetta."

Ouch!

Insofar as reviews are concerned, there's one inviolable truth: If all the critics are in agreement about a book's merits, or demerits, there's probably some truth in their comments; but if they are not in general agreement, if the reviews run the gamut from panning to praise, then it's a different matter entirely.

In the case of *Hornet's Nest* and *Southern Cross,* it's a different matter entirely. Cornwell has deliberately taken a detour in a similar fictional universe, one that overlaps with Scarpetta's world.

As you'd expect, the new series draws heavily from Cornwell's life experiences: *Hornet's Nest* is set in Charlotte, North Carolina, a city she knows well; by vocation, Andy Brazil is a rookie reporter at the hometown newspaper and, by avocation, a volunteer policeman—the same experiences Cornwell has had; the novel chronicles the life of Charlotte police chief Judy Hammer, whose professional turf is the world Cornwell covered in her beat as a police reporter.

In *Southern Cross,* the second book in the series, Cornwell brings the characters to Richmond, enabling her to establish dual geographic backgrounds with which she is intimately familiar—the Richmond PD and the city itself.

Readers expecting a cloned Scarpetta novel were inevitably disappointed, because Cornwell clearly wanted to stretch as a writer with this new series, to try new fictional techniques, to write in a burlesque style, to inject humor—a stark departure from the clinical world of Scarpetta at work.

Predictably, some of Cornwell's die-hard fans would have preferred another Scarpetta story, but Cornwell perhaps felt that going back to that well too frequently would run it dry. But by writing a new series, there's room for literary experimentation, there's room to have a little fun and not take life so seriously, and there's room to introduce new characters and situations that could not find their way into a Scarpetta novel.

With only three books in the series published to date, it's a little premature to pass definitive judgment on Cornwell's new fictional universe, which is clearly starting to shape up.

Reviews

"It's fortunate that Cornwell has a new Kay Scarpetta thriller (*Black Notice*) coming out in July, because this second novel featuring southern police chief Judy Hammer is as disappointing as last year's *Hornet's Nest*. The problem is elementary. Cornwell, who writes the Scarpetta novels in a first-person voice that blazes with passion and authenticity, lacks control over the third-person narration here. The tone is all over the place, veering from faux-Wambaugh low-jinks to hard-edged suspense, and the plotting is, too. Hammer and her team of deputy chief Virginia West and greenhorn cop Andy Brazil have moved via a federal grant to Richmond, Va., in order to set straight that city's policing. If only they could bring order to the narrative, which twists into an unwieldy welter of subplots. Early on, for instance, Hammer and

West misconstrue as malevolent an overheard phone conversation between a local redneck, Butner (Bubba) Fluck IV, and a coon-hunting pal. From there Cornwell spins seriocomic descriptions of Bubba at work, Bubba on a hunting trip, Bubba arguing with a black cop. Among these events and those of other subplots (stymied love between West and Brazil; sabotage of the cops' Web site; the jailing of a police dispatcher; etc.) runs a more dominant plotline—the only one in the novel that exerts dramatic force—about a talented boy artist strong-armed into a gang by a sociopathic teen. There's a lot of broad, often slapstick, social commentary (mostly about class warfare) larded into all the goings-on. If Cornwell's intention is to reproduce with a snicker the chaos of a big southern city, she has succeeded all too well." (*Publishers Weekly.*)

"With the phenomenal success of her Scarpetta books, Cornwell set herself something of a problem: how to strike off in new directions with different protagonists. . . . While the characterization and plotting (always Cornwell's strong suits) remain as razor sharp as ever, there is more emphasis on humour, making a piquant contrast to the high-octane action (although some might find the whimsical character names—Smudge, Muskrat, Weed, et al.—a tad too Dickensian for this kind of urban thriller). Supremely entertaining stuff, and though some may yearn for the return of her doughty pathologist heroine, Cornwell has demonstrated that she is no one-trick pony." (Amazon.co.uk, Barry Forshaw.)

"The three stars are warm, witty and somewhat frustrated. However, a warning label goes with this novel and its predecessor. Beware that this novel is not a Kay Scarpetta tale, nor is it an effort to take the renowned forensic medical examiner and relocate and

rename her. Instead, Patricia Cornwell heads in an entirely different direction that turns into a different but enjoyable reading experience." (Online review by Harriet Klausner for BookBrowser.)

Southern Cross A to Z

ABIN. Air bag identification number; used to ID stolen air
bags from cars.

Anaconda .44. The pistol Bubba carries in his Jeep.

ATF. Federal Bureau of Alcohol, Tobacco and Firearms.

BMZ. The car Brazil recently bought. It has a V6 engine and
is a Z3, replacing the aged BMW 2002 he previously drove.

Brazil, Andy. Brought by Judy Hammer to Richmond, to
"do research, handle public information and start a website."
(On Cornwell's official Web site, a banner announces that she's
the author of two series—Kay Scarpetta and Andy Brazil. The
latter suggests that he is likely to assume a greater importance
in the books that follow. Perhaps Cornwell felt that writing
about two strong female protagonists was too similar, so writing from the male perspective, and from an up-and-comer,
would be a welcome change of pace with her readers.)

Budget, Off. Jack. A black officer who stops Bubba, who
has a bumper sticker of the Southern Cross, which prompts a
discussion about its significance: Budget is, predictably, against
it; Bubba is for it. He lets Bubba go with just a warning.

CIA. Central Intelligence Agency.

COMSAT. Computer-driven statistics. "The New York
Crime Control Model of Policing."

CPR. The police department's motto: "Courtesy, Professionalism and Respect," which Hammer also had borrowed from the NYPD.

DEA. Drug Enforcement Agency.

Divinity. A young black girl who is under the thrall of a vicious thug named Weed. Divinity comes on to "Pretty Boy," Andy Brazil; she's a whore with a knife and pulls it on Brazil, who is forced to pull his Colt Mustang and point it between her eyes. She then bolts.

Ehrhart, Lelia. On the board of directors of the Hollywood Cemetery, she is serving her eighth term as its chairperson.

EOT. Police abbreviation for "end of tour" of duty.

Fan District. A neighborhood in Richmond that is laid out like a fan, radiating streets. A trendy part of town with town houses and homes of varying architectural styles.

FBI. Federal Bureau of Investigation.

Feuer, Gov. Mike. The governor of the Commonwealth of Virginia. Because of his uncommon name, he's commonly called, by the Democrats, "the Fuhrer."

Fling, Off. Wally. Administrative assistant to Chief Judy Hammer.

Fluck IV, Butner. A redneck white supremacist who vows revenge on Brazil or West after a public altercation at The Firing Line, an indoor pistol range.

Hammer, Chief Judy. She resigned from the Charlotte PD and, after a proposal went through the National Institute of Justice, worked with police departments throughout the South for one-year terms, lending her expertise.

Hollywood Cemetery. Located north of the James River, the cemetery is south of 195. Several Confederate generals are buried there, along with numerous soldiers. One of its most famous statues, Jefferson Davis, is covered with graffiti, to the outrage of the community.

Plum Street. In the Fan District. This is where Andy Brazil lives in a rental, owned by Ruby Sink.

Popeye. Judy Hammer's terrier.

Rhoad, Off. Otis. A policeman who is infatuated with his police radio, earning him the derisive nicknames of "Rhoad Hog" and "Talk in a Box" (perhaps inspired by the fast-food hamburger chain in southeast Virginia, Jack in a Box). Rhoad is appropriately named, because he also loves to give out speeding tickets with a vengeance.

Richmond. The capital of the Confederacy.

Richmond Times-Dispatch. Hometown newspaper.

Robin Inn. A popular restaurant for nearby college students, opposite West's home.

Sink, Ruby. Andy Brazil's landlady. She is the association secretary of Hollywood Cemetery, where a desecration has occurred.

Southern Cross. The battle flag of the Confederacy.

UZ. Police abbreviation for "unsafe zone," meaning high-crime area.

Wakefield, Virginia. Small rural town in southeast Virginia where a new weather radar has been installed—a WSR-88-D Doppler.

West, Dep. Chief Virginia. Brought by Judy Hammer to Richmond, to head up investigations (her area of expertise).

ISLE OF DOGS, 2001

Editions

1. Hardback, $26.95, Putnam.
2. Large print edition, $32.95, Thorndike Press.
3. Unabridged audiotape, $44.95 read by Michele Hall, Penguin Putnam Group.
4. Abridged audiotape, $24.95, read by Becky Ann Baker, Penguin Putnam Group.
5. Audio CD, abridged, $29.95, read by Becky Ann Baker, Penguin Putnam Group.

Dedication

"To Friend and Publisher, Phyllis Grann"

Geography

Tangier Island, Virginia; Richmond, Virginia.

Perspective

You can lead a horse to water, but you can't make him drink. It's an old adage that came to mind after I read a few dozen reviews posted on Amazon.com about Cornwell's third Judy Hammer/Andy Brazil novel, *Isle of Dogs.*

The Amazon.com system relies on readers to provide the reviews, which are, in fact, mostly opinions—variations of "I liked the book" or "I didn't like the book." We're not talking about the level of criticism that, say, John Simon would provide; we're talking about fans who have spent money on a book they had hoped to enjoy.

In the case of *Isle of Dogs,* the 274 reviews on Amazon.com are consistent in their criticisms of the book. In fact, the overall rating of the book is 1.5 stars out of 5—hardly what the publisher would want to see.

All the king's horses and all the king's men. . . .

To Cornwell's credit, she attempted to start a new series that would give her a break from the Scarpetta novels; and to her readers' credit, they have supported her with a vote of confidence in buying enough copies to make each a bestseller, but will the series reach a point of diminishing returns?

Rather than build an audience for the series, the latest offering, *Isle of Dogs,* may actually *decrease* her readership, if the postings on Amazon.com are a reliable barometer of the readers' sentiments, which range from "I'm still a huge fan looking forward to Cornwell's next book" to "Don't waste your money on this one," and everything in between. Clearly, her readers are giving her, and this series, the benefit of the doubt, but how many more books will Cornwell write if each new book receives such a harsh reception?

Part of the disappointment is undoubtedly due to the expectations that her longtime readers bring to any new series. They have cut their teeth on Scarpetta and like the nitty-gritty forensic world in which she lives; and perhaps they had expectations of the same kind of story, with one difference—a male protagonist.

If any Scarpetta fan picks up *Isle of Dogs* (or the earlier books) with such expectations, he will inevitably be disappointed. Though the fictional worlds are set in familiar terrain—in this case, Tangier Island, located six miles below the Virginia-Maryland state line—the landscape is completely different; the characters' names are a dead giveaway (Unique First, Fonny Boy, Dr. Faux) that Cornwell is not taking herself too seriously, which she clearly does in the Scarpetta novels, and she is saying to the reader, "I've got a sense of humor that I'd like to share with you, so have fun with this book."

Cornwell's intent—to write a comedic novel—is clear, but as is obvious, writing a humorous novel is no laughing matter: Florida-based journalist/novelist Carl Hiassen's black comedies are compulsively readable and just plain fun, but Cornwell's seems forced and—dare I say it?—simply unfunny.

In this novel we get the most diverse cast of characters imaginable: Dr. Kay Scarpetta makes a sober appearance; likewise, Judy Hammer plays it straight; Andy Brazil is the main protagonist, who also doubles as "Trooper Truth," who posts essays on the Internet that cause heartburn at the governor's mansion; a supporting case of characters named Unique First and Dr. Faux (to name but two); and talking seafood—crabs having conversations with a trout.

The end result, I fear, is a novel that misses the mark by a country mile. Neither fish nor fowl—comedic but not a comedy, tragic but not a drama—*Isle of Dogs* has its strong points (notably the informative essays by Trooper Truth), but as a comedic narrative, it leaves a bad taste in the mouth, like a soft drink that has unintentionally gone flat.

Isle of Dogs A to Z

A. Spy. The anonymous E-mail "handle" used by Major Trader in his communiques with Trooper Truth.

Bass, Dr. Bill. Director of the Body Farm.

Bell 403 helicopter. Workhorse helicopter used to shuttle the governor and his family around the commonwealth.

Biotech II. The building (Richmond, Virginia) that houses the CME (chief medical examiner) and the related forensic labs.

Bonny, Anne. The subject of an essay by Trooper Truth, she is "the Most Notorious Female Pirate Who Ever Lived."

Brazil, Andy. Formerly a policeman with the Charlotte PD (one year) and the Richmond PD (one year), he's now a Virginia State Trooper (six months). He's also the man behind the Web site, TROOPER TRUTH, posting online and stirring up a hornet's nest in law-enforcement circles.

Brees, Windy. A secretary who lives up to her namesake—she's an airhead—and who works at Biotech II.

CCV. Country Club of Virginia, located off Three Chopt Road in Richmond, where the elite meet to eat, hobnob with fellow financial wizards, etc.

Church Hill. One of Richmond's seven hills; the location of Judy Hammer's historic row house.

Crimm IV, Gov. Bedford. The governor of Virginia who suffers from gastrointestinal distress (his "submarine," as his wife terms it) and orders speed traps set on Tangier Island, to deflect public attention from controversies that afflict him.

Crimm, Regina. The youngest daughter of the governor whom Andy Brazil befriends. She accompanies Andy Brazil to the morgue where Caesar Fender is examined. Scarpetta takes her at face value and assumes she's a police officer; but on her trip to the morgue, acting as a scribe recording the results of Scarpetta's examination, Crimm's lack of familiarity with the terminology is a dead giveaway.

Custer, Moses. An ill-fated vendor whose untimely encounter with Unique First proved fatal. (His eighteen-wheeler is filled with pumpkins for sale at the Farmer's Market.)

Discovery. The name of one of the three ships (along with the *Susan Constant* and the *Godspeed*) that set sail from London in 1606 to the New World, arriving at what we now call Jamestown, Virginia.

Fan District. Historical part of Richmond where Andy Brazil lives, in a home that is neither air-conditioned nor properly heated.

Farmers' Market. Located in downtown Richmond. Moses Custer meets his demise here in the form of Unique First, who doesn't understand until it's too late that when she offers him a "unique experience," he's understandably puzzled, until he's attacked, and killed, by her cohorts.

Faux, Dr. Sherman. A dishonest dentist held hostage by an islander, Faux not only pads his bills but performs needless surgery to inflate his income. (He is finally rescued by the Coast Guard.)

Fender, Caesar. Homicide victim killed with a flare gun.

Fig. Nickname of Chef Figgie, the head cook at the Governor's Mansion.

First, Unique. A beautiful eighteen-year-old girl who enjoys a nearly orgasmic release in preying on unsuspecting victims.

Godspeed. The name of one of the three ships (along with the *Susan Constant* and the *Discovery*) that set sail from London in 1606 to the New World, arriving at what we now call Jamestown, Virginia.

Governor's Daughters. The three oldest are named Constance, Grace, and Faith; the youngest, and homeliest, is named Regina. (She is befriended by Andy Brazil.)

Ham. A Virginia delicacy Governor Crimm particularly hates. (Crimm prefers seafood.)

Hammer, Judy. Currently a police superintendent for the city of Richmond, brought in under a grant by the National Institute of Justice to set things straight with "troubled police departments." A no-nonsense, all-business policewoman whose brusque manner offends Gov. Bedford Crimm IV, who refuses to accept her calls. (He feels threatened by strong women.)

Hurricane. An islander, father of Fonny Boy. Hurricane concocts the scheme to hold Dr. Faux hostage.

Isle of Dogs. A geographical reference to a part of London famous for its alehouses. (According to Cornwell, on a 1610 map of London, it was spelled "Isle of Dogges." Its spelling today is simply "Isle of Dogs," with nautical/naval names: The White Swan, The Gun, Cubitt Arms, The Pier, The

Waterman Arms, The Lord Nelson, The Ferry House, and The Ship. *See* www.isleofdogs.com for more information.)

J.R. Nickname of the first homicide victim in the New World. Carbon-dating puts his death in 1607, according to the researchers at Jamestown Rediscovery (*see* www.apva.org).

Macovich, Trooper. A state trooper and helicopter pilot who unknowingly becomes a pawn in a deadly game orchestrated by Possom and Smoke.

Minihorse. The proper nomenclature for the miniature horses used for seeing-eye purposes, like a seeing-eye dog. (*Note:* Cornwell has donated money to provide seeing-eye minihorses to the needy.) In this story, a point of confusion as the characters talk about the minihorse as a pony, which is also the nickname of a character—Pony.

Morales, Cruz. A teenage gunrunner from New York City.

Orion flare gun. Used by Fonny Boy to effect a Coast Guard rescue. Despite Dr. Faux's sound advice—fire one flare after the other, instead of firing all three in rapid succession—Fonny Boy succeeds in getting a CG helicopter to notice them.

Picaroon. Island slang for "pirate." The term is used by islanders to describe the dentist, Dr. Faux, who is understandably viewed with suspicion. (He's not only a mainlander, which is sufficient cause for suspicion, but they know he's not what he appears to be: They see him for the thief he in fact is.)

Pony. A butler at the governor's mansion. (He is not to be confused with the seeing-eye "pony," or minihorse, that trots on the scene in the latter part of the book: A point of confusion that is milked for maximum effect.)

Popeye. A lost dog, the subject of an intensive search by Andy Brazil.

Rudd, Ricky. A NASCAR driver from North Carolina, the object of fantasy of Barbie Fogg. (She writes him weekly letters that, predictably, go unanswered because there's no return address and a fake name, to boot.)

Ruth's Chris Steak House. A popular eatery at the Bellgrade Shopping Center in Richmond, a favorite dining place of Governor Crimm.

Sawamatsu, Dr. Assistant chief medical examiner who works under Dr. Kay Scarpetta. (Sawamatsu, unbeknownst to Scarpetta, collects "souvenirs" from his dead patients—a fact Andy Brazil passes on to Scarpetta, urging her to check it out, which she promises to do.)

Scarpetta, Dr. Kay. The famous CME of the Commonwealth of Virginia. First appearance in a Judy Hammer/Andy Brazil novel. She examines Caesar Fender, who was shot to death with a flare gun.

SHC. Spontaneous human combustion. The subject of an essay by Trooper Truth, who explains that contrary to popular opinion, people don't spontaneously combust. (He cites "the Body Farm," the University of Tennessee's Decay Research Facility, the only research center of its kind, which is at the heart of a Scarpetta novel, *The Body Farm.*)

Smoke. An escapee from a maximum security prison in Virginia, he's a gang leader who attempts to hijack a helicopter en route to a NASCAR race; the helicopter, however, is manned by Andy Brazil and Judy Hammer, both of whom are in disguise and foil his nefarious plot.

Submarine. Mrs. Maude Crimm's pet nickname for her husband's gastrointestinal distress, which, to the distress of all, surfaces far too frequently.

Susan Constant. The name of one of the three ships (along with the *Godspeed* and the *Discovery*) that set sail from London in 1606 to the New World, arriving at what we now call Jamestown, Virginia. (A historical reproduction of the *Susan Constant* is permanently moored in Jamestown, Virginia. For more information, go to www.historyisfun.org. . . . Cornwell pokes fun at the Jamestown Settlement, which is "worth visiting as long as you realize that the first settlers did not construct the twentieth-century buildings, restrooms, food court, souvenir shops, parking lots, and ferry, anymore than they sailed on the fabricated ships moored in the river.")

Tangier Island. Located between the shores of Virginia and Maryland/Delaware, this remote island is the focal point of the governor's new plan to post speed limits, which clearly makes no sense, since most people on the island get around in golf carts, not cars. Such needless intrusion raises the hackles of the islanders, who hold a mainland dentist hostage with the hope that the governor will allow the islanders to secede from the commonwealth.

Trader, Major. He has the ear, and confidence, of Governor Crimm.

Trash, Trish. Hoping to establish a liaison with Unique First, TT becomes, instead, the latest victim of Unique First.

Trip. The name of the minihorse (not pony!) delivered to the governor's mansion. (Trip is the reason why the governor's limo is lined with wood chips in the trunk, just in case Trip's gotta go.)

Trivets. The first lady of Virginia, Mrs. Maude Crimm, conceals her lust for these collectibles from her husband.

TROOPER TRUTH. An anonymous Web site where, under the same pen name, Andy Brazil posts essays that stir the soup, so to speak, within the law-enforcement community and the governor's office, as well. (In *Isle of Dogs,* the postings take the form of essays throughout the book itself.)

VASCAR/NASCAR. The islanders at Tangiers confuse the two, the former a radar system, the latter a car-racing franchise.

VFR. Visual flight rules. When flying aircraft, doing so by sight instead of relying wholly on instruments (far more difficult).

LIFE'S LITTLE FABLE, 1999

Life's Little Fable is a children's book for ages four to eight. Illustrated by Barbara Leonard Gibson, this forty-page book echoes Eve's dilemma in the Garden of Eden: Faced with temptation, you must decide for yourself what is best and be prepared to accept whatever consequences may follow, good or bad.

In Cornwell's story, the protagonist is Jarrod, who lives in an idyllic world and who faces temptation in the form of the "god of the pond," who tempts him with anything his heart desires if he enters the pond. Available only in hardback, in a school/library binding, the book retails for $16.99, but the best source for the book is Cornwell herself, who offers signed copies from her Web site (currently under construction) for $11.99.

Reviews of the book have been mixed. A leading journal for children's literature, the *Horn Book Magazine,* gave it a savage review that surely must have stung. "Bring us the scalpel of Dr. Scarpetta!" the reviewer cries. "Noted crime novelist Cornwell offers up an incoherently rhyming fable about a lucky little boy who lives in a land without gravity. The writing and pictures are so amateurish that even a vanity press would think twice before publishing this one."

Kimberly Brooks, who has a B.S.ED. in elementary education, works in a library, loves Cornwell books, and considers herself an authority on children's books, wrote a review online for Amazon.com and stated: "While the art work is lovely, the story line is so vague and abstract, an adult can barely follow what the meaning of it is, let alone children. . . . I am very well-versed in Children's Literature and find this book a huge disappointment."

Frankly, I find the criticism to be a bit harsh: I think the illustrations are appropriate and, while clearly not in the same league as, say, the work of Colleen Doran, Gibson's art is charming and needs no apologies.

Similarly, I don't think Cornwell need apologize for this fledgling effort.

We've heard from the adult readers, but I wonder what children think of the book? I'm willing to bet they'd give the author a fairer hearing (or reading).

Case closed.

JACK THE RIPPER, CASE CLOSED, 2002

"That is so serious to me that I am staking my reputation on this," she said. "Because if somebody literally proves me wrong, not only will I feel horrible about it, but I will look terrible."
— Patricia Cornwell to Diane Sawyer, on ABC-TV

Editions

1. Hardback, $27.95, Putnam.
2. Unabridged audiotape, $49.95, Penguin Putnam Group.
3. Abridged audiotape, $24.95, Penguin Putnam Group.
4. Audio CD, abridged, $43.99.

Perspective

Long ago a human monster stalked London and murdered five women. Commonly known as Jack the Ripper, the killer remained at large and went to his grave secure in the knowledge that he had gotten away forever with his heinous crimes, which have baffled serious students, researchers, scholars, and law enforcement experts for over a century.

Enter Patricia Cornwell.

Cornwell had no intention to write a nonfiction book about Jack the Ripper, but in researching him for a Scarpetta novel, she became fascinated and decided to pursue her fascination to a logical conclusion: She would solve the crime by using modern techniques, including DNA identification, then publish her findings in a nonfiction book.

Though many others have published books dissecting this century-old unsolved case, none of them had the advantage of unparalleled access that Cornwell enjoyed. According to Scribner, "Enlisting the help of forensic experts, Cornwell examines all the physical evidence available: thousands of documents and reports, finger-prints, crime-scene photographs, original etchings and paintings, items of clothing, artists' paraphernalia, and traces of DNA. Her unavoidable conclusion: Jack the Ripper was none other than a respected painter of his day, an artist now collected by some of the world's finest museums."

In the spring of 2002, Cornwell appeared on *ABC News* and gave an in-depth interview to Diane Sawyer regarding her conclu-sions. Stated Cornwell, "I do believe 100 percent that Walter Richard Sickert committed those serial crimes, that he is the Whitechapel murderer."

Unlike her contemporaries, who have attempted to conclusively prove the true identity of the infamous Jack the Ripper, Cornwell has two advantages: fame and fortune. Fame can open doors and insure media coverage as well; fortune can pay for any research costs—in this case, $4 million, which included purchasing thirty paintings by Sickert and other paraphernalia, in a search for hard evidence.

What do I make of all this? I can't say, since I've not read her book, nor have I read any of the existing body of work about this infamous case. But I am absolutely sure of one thing: Cornwell has convinced herself that she has unearthed the true identity of Jack the Ripper. Unfortunately, others are not convinced, including Ripperologists (fans and scholars of the case who pride themselves on an exhaustive knowledge of the subject), who feel she's covered old ground that's been sufficiently disproved.

Adding fuel to the controversy surrounding her book: the staid London newspaper, *The Guardian,* put in its two pence worth. Arts correspondent Fianchra Gibbons observed that "even in the context of the crackpot conspiracy theories, elaborate frauds and career-destroying obsessions that London's most grisly whodunnit has spawned, Cornwell's investigation is extreme. Not only did she have one canvas cut up in the vain hope of finding a clue to link Sickert to the murder and mutilation of five prostitutes, she spent 2 million pounds buying up 31 more of his paintings, some of his letters and even his writing desk."

The end result: one of Cornwell's most controversial books. It will surely be the center of a renewed, heated debate about Jack the Ripper; but in a larger context, it also speaks to our obsessive and insatiable appetite for, and fascination with, human monsters.

Though Cornwell's book is titled *Jack the Ripper, Case Closed,* the case is anything *but* closed, according to the Ripperologists (*see* www.casebook.org).

Note: For Cornwell fans who want to learn more about Cornwell's hunt for Jack the Ripper, I recommend the following resources:

1. A transcript of an interview online, at www.abcnews.com, "Mystery Solved?", in which Cornwell states her case to Diane Sawyer.

2. The aforementioned interview itself and a benefit talk Cornwell gave at the VIFSM (Virginia Institute of Forensic Science and Medicine), available in DVD ($39) and VHS ($29). To purchase, contact: info@vifsm.org and, in the subject line of your e-mail, type "BENEFIT."

3. *The Ultimate Jack the Ripper Companion* ($35, 692 pages, published by Carroll & Graf).

4. *The Ultimate Jack the Ripper Sourcebook: An Illustrated Encyclopedia* ($16, 704 pages, published by Carroll & Graf).

SECTION III

WHAT'S NEXT FOR PATRICIA CORNWELL AND KAY SCARPETTA

WHAT MAY COME FOR KAY SCARPETTA

In an interview published in the *Writer,* Patricia Cornwell gives her readers an inkling of what is to come: Kay Scarpetta will leave the employment of the city of Richmond to pursue her work independently worldwide. From a fictional point of view, this solves the age-old problem that a long-running book series must address—how to break new ground instead of writing variations on a theme.

The Last Precinct strongly suggested that a major change was in the works. Scarpetta's growing disenchantment with the status quo and the bureaucracy seemed to have come to a head—compounded with the problems her niece, Lucy, had experienced in law enforcement with the FBI—and with the next Scarpetta novel, due out in 2003, we will likely see Scarpetta in a new light.

Prior to *The Last Precinct,* some readers were concerned that Scarpetta's character had become overly sensitive to criticism, quick to react to real (or imagined) slights; in a word, obstreperous. *The Last Precinct,* though, showed Scarpetta outside the lab and a person with foibles and fears, just like the rest of us.

That, I think, is the enduring appeal of Dr. Kay Scarpetta. Her enduring humanity, her sympathy for crime victims and their families, and her utter contempt for those who perpetrate crime—no sympathy for the devil, in other words. She is the embodiment of what we would like to be ourselves and often aren't.

In interviews, Patricia Cornwell is frequently asked if Scarpetta is a thinly disguised self-portrait. Cornwell responds, quite correctly, that creating fiction is no simple matter of transposition, so although Scarpetta is obviously filtered through her perceptions, the two are not one and the same.

"It is important to me," Cornwell has said, "to live in the world I write about. If I want a character to do or know something, I try to do or know the same thing." This, I think, gives her novels a sense of realism that raises them above the level of most suspense novels. Writers are by nature inventive, and experience isn't a necessary ingredient for bestsellerdom—Tom Clancy, the king of the technothriller, has never been in the military—but by writing what you know, and by going out and getting your hands dirty in the research process, the writing comes alive. Similarly, when the characters have their own lives, as they grow and try to make sense of their lives, we can identify: We, too, try to make sense of our own lives.

The key commonality between Cornwell as creator and Scarpetta as creation is that both have a shared vision of the world, embodied by Cornwell's personal credo: "Enlightenment. Justice. Do no harm. Fight the fight. Leave the world better than you found it." This worldview informs Cornwell's life and imbues Scarpetta's character with a sense of humanity that, I think, is lacking in her fictional counterparts who seem in comparison to be mere cogs in the storytelling machinery.

We live, unfortunately, in the Age of the Celebrity, which means that, as Shakespeare put it, the good that men do is oft interred with their bones. In Cornwell's case, the philanthropy, the public causes for the greater good, and the generous funding of the Forensics Institute are overshadowed by needless (and, to my mind, mindless) speculation about her personal life, which is more appropriate fare for gossip columnists and the tabloid rags that take a positive delight in showing that even the rich and famous have feet of clay.

None of that matters to me, and none of that should matter to you, either. I feel Patricia Cornwell is entitled to make her own mistakes and learn from them, as she obviously has; but unlike you and me, she's opened up her wallet and contributed a fortune for what she believes in—most notably funding the forensics center, which benefits everyone.

That, to me, is the principal difference between Cornwell as a bestselling author and her contemporaries. Scarpetta is an extension of Cornwell, and in real life, Cornwell fights the good fight because it's her philosophy of life.

With 70 million books sold to date and a net worth estimated at $60 million (according to www.telegraph.co.uk), Patricia Cornwell can afford the luxury of writing not for money but for the joy of writing and growing as a writer.

In her forties, Patricia Cornwell has many more stories to tell, dozens of books yet to be published. Looking back, it seems obvious that a talented writer was in the works; looking ahead, it seems equally obvious that Cornwell's unique brand of storytelling will continue to build an audience of admiring readers who, deep down, are rooting for Scarpetta and what she believes in, and rooting for Cornwell—the little engine that could—as well.

CORNWELL WRITES A NEW CHAPTER IN HER OWN LIFE

I have not cut my Virginia ties but simply found it better for me to live closer to New York.

—CORNWELL, IN A FAXED RESPONSE TO
A Q&A FROM THE *Times-Dispatch*

Nine years ago Patricia Cornwell moved from Charlotte, North Carolina, to Richmond, Virginia. Then married to Charles Cornwell, who left his job as an English professor at Davidson College behind to pursue a career in the seminary, Patricia Cornwell faced an uncertain future: no job, a new city, and a shaky marriage.

In December 2001, Patricia Cornwell left Richmond behind and moved to Greenwich, Connecticut, near New York City. Cornwell fans looking for Cornwell's Richmond will still find reminders—her former office at the Belgrade Shopping Center, now up for sale; one of her Southside homes sold and the other rented out to Gary Gilmore, the former Virginia governor.

What, though, does this mean, if anything, in terms of Cornwell's fiction? Frankly, it's too early to tell. It may signal a new storyline for Kay Scarpetta, who will move beyond the confines of working cases within the Commonwealth of Virginia as its chief medical examiner, to working on national and international cases, which could provide a much needed change of scenery.

Since 2003 saw the publication of a nonfiction book about Jack the Ripper, with Scarpetta novels scheduled for subsequent years, it's too early to tell just what Cornwell has in mind, which probably suits her just fine. Intensely private—insofar as is possible for a celebrity constantly in the limelight—Cornwell is reluctant to give interviews, nor can we expect much information forthcoming from Susan Petersen Kennedy, her publisher at Putnam, who knows the first rule in publishing Cornwell: Privacy is paramount.

Though we can only speculate as to what life has in store for Cornwell personally, we know what is in store professionally: In 2003, the first of four new Scarpetta novels will be published, which is the principal reason Cornwell's fans remain true to her. (The Judy Hammer/Andy Brazil novels, though bestsellers, received mixed reviews. (Her most recent, *Isle of Dogs,* has garnered an average rating of one star out of a possible five on amazon.com. Nearly 275 readers have chimed in, most disenchanted with the novel and the series from which it springs. Cornwell, they opine, is barking up the wrong tree with her latest tale, which falls short of, say, the latest Carl Hiassen or John Kennedy Toole's comic novel, *A Confederacy of Dunces,* which won a Pulitzer for Best Novel.)

Under pressure to produce a detailed, extensively researched, nonfiction book about Jack the Ripper for the fall of 2002, Cornwell is holed up in Greenwich, Connecticut, barring the door to all inquiries. As she told the *Times-Dispatch* in a faxed response to their questions, "I am not giving interviews at this time due to endless Ripper requests and my need for solitude as I write the Ripper nonfiction book."

The book, Cornwell admits, is more than just another nonfiction book to her credit—her credibility is at stake. As a writer who is known for conducting exhaustive research on her books, she's spent, by her own estimate, approximately $4 million on this book project.

She can afford the cash, but what of her credibility if it takes a direct hit in the wake of the book's publication? It's Cornwell in one corner . . . and Ripperologists eager to take a slash at her theory—of which she's 100 percent convinced—that Jack the Ripper was, in fact, a well-known Impressionist painter, Walter Richard Sickert.

My guess is that the book itself will generate significant controversy—at this late date, though there are nearly a dozen suspects, no one can say for certain who the killer was—and, in the process, generate significant sales.

Personally and professionally, Cornwell is writing a new page to a life that, in itself, would make fascinating reading, for Cornwell's life is a story best told by herself: her occasional nonfiction piece, poignant and self-reflective, stands in the first rank of her work; and isn't it time for her to set the record straight?

Until that time, her fans will see her only when a brief window of opportunity opens up after the publication of each new book— a few television appearances, a few in-print interviews, and a handful of book signings, usually on the East Coast. And when that door closes, she returns to her private world, cocooned in privacy, to dream up more stories about murder and mayhem, about injustice and justice, about power and the abuse of power, and most memorably, Dr. Kay Scarpetta's ongoing battle against evil in what sometimes appears to be an uncaring world, and in doing so shows us a world not as it is but as it could be, summed up in her personal credo, her working philosophy: "Enlightenment. Do no harm. Leave the world better than you found it."

That, I think, will be Cornwell's enduring legacy.

APPENDICES

Appendix A: A Technical Key to the World of Kay Scarpetta

SO YOU WANT TO BE A MEDICAL DETECTIVE
by the National Association of Medical Examiners

Note: In order to understand, and appreciate, Dr. Kay Scarpetta, it's important to understand the terminology of her profession. For instance, do you know the differences between a coroner and a medical examiner? And what role does a pathologist play? Or, for that matter, a forensic pathologist?

The National Association of Medical Examiners clarifies these terms on its Web site and has graciously granted permission for their words to be reproduced here.

What is a coroner?
A coroner is a public official, appointed or elected, in a particular geographic jurisdiction, whose official duty is to make inquiry into deaths in certain categories. The office of coroner or "crowner" dates back to medieval days when the crowner was responsible for looking into deaths to be sure death duties were

paid to the king. The coroner's primary duty in contemporary times is to make inquiry into the death and complete the certificate of death. The coroner assigns a cause and manner of death and lists them on the certificate of death. The cause of death refers to the disease, injury or poison that caused the death. The coroner also decides if a death occurred under natural circumstances or was due to accident, homicide, suicide or undetermined means or circumstances.

Coroners are called upon to decide if a death was due to foul play. Depending upon the jurisdiction and the law defining the coroner's duties, the coroner may or may not be trained in the medical sciences. The coroner may employ physicians, pathologists, or forensic pathologists to perform autopsies when there appears to be a question of manner of death that autopsy can elucidate. In some jurisdictions, the coroner is a physician, but in many localities, the coroner is not required to be a physician nor be trained in medicine. In the absence of medical expertise, the non-physician coroner may have difficulty in sorting out subtle non-violent and violent causes of death.

What is a medical examiner?

A medical examiner is a physician, hence, the title medical examiner. When acting in an official capacity, the physician medical examiner is charged, within a particular jurisdiction, with the investigation and examination of persons dying a sudden, unexpected or violent death. The role of a medical examiner differs from that of the non-physician coroner in that the medical examiner is expected to bring medical expertise to the evaluation of the medical history and physical examination of the deceased. The physician medical examiner usually is not required to be a specialist in death investigation or pathology and may practice any branch of medicine. Most systems employing physicians as part time medical examiners encourage them to take advantage of medical training for medical examiners to increase their level of medical expertise as applied to death investigation. The National Association of Medical Examiners and the American Academy of Forensic Sciences are two organizations that offer specialized training.

What is a pathologist?

A pathologist is a physician trained in the medical specialty of pathology. Pathology is the branch of medicine that deals with the diagnosis of disease and causes of death by means of laboratory examination of body fluids (clinical pathology), cell samples (cytology), and tissues (pathologic anatomy). The autopsy is the procedure utilized to study the dead. It is primarily a systematic external and internal examination for the purposes of diagnosing disease and determining the presence or absence of injury. In modern times chemical analysis of body fluids for medical information as well as analysis for drugs and poisons should be part of any autopsy on a dead body coming under the jurisdiction of the medical examiner or coroner.

What is a forensic pathologist?

The forensic pathologist is a subspecialist in pathology whose area of special competence is the examination of persons who die sudden, unexpected or violent deaths. The forensic pathologist is an expert in determining cause and manner of death. The forensic pathologist is specially trained: to perform autopsies to determine the presence or absence of disease, injury or poisoning; to evaluate historical and law-enforcement investigative information relating to manner of death; to collect medical evidence, such as trace evidence and secretions, to document sexual assault; and to reconstruct how a person received injuries. Forensic pathologists are trained in multiple nonmedical sciences as well as traditional medicine. Other areas of science that the forensic pathologist must have a working knowledge of the applicability of are toxicology, firearms examination (wound ballistics), trace evidence, forensic serology and DNA technology. The forensic pathologist acts as the case coordinator for the medical and forensic scientific assessment of a given death, making sure that the appropriate procedures and evidence collection techniques are applied to the body. When forensic pathologists are employed as death investigators they bring their expertise to bear upon the interpretation of the scene of death, in the assessment of the consistency of witnesses' statements with injuries, and the interpretation of injury patterns or patterned injuries. In jurisdictions where there are medical examiner systems, forensic pathologists are usually employed to perform autopsies to determine cause of death.

Specifically what does a forensic pathologist do?

As a physician who specializes in the investigation of sudden, unexpected and violent deaths the forensic pathologist attempts to determine the identification of the deceased, the time of death, the manner of death (natural, accident, suicide or homicide), the cause of death and if the death was by injury, the nature of the instrument used to cause the death.

First, the forensic pathologist gathers a history as to how the death occurred and often obtains the past medical history of the deceased as well. Next, the forensic pathologist examines the body externally and then internally taking biopsies of tissues to further examine under the microscope for disease not visible to the naked eye. This postmortem examination is known as an autopsy.

During the course of the autopsy, various laboratory tests may be undertaken, including X-rays, retention of body fluids such as blood and urine for toxicologic analysis and cultures of body fluids and organs for evidence of infection.

When all of the information including the history, the results of the autopsy and the laboratory tests are completed, the forensic pathologist correlates all the information and draws conclusions as to the cause and manner of death. A report is then prepared summarizing these findings. The forensic pathologist can expect to be subpoenaed to testify before courts and other tribunals about the pathologic findings and conclusions. Coroners, medical examiners and pathologist[s] provide copies of their official reports to parties, such as insurers or public agencies, having a legitimate interest in the cause and manner of death of citizens.

How does the forensic pathologist use the history, external physical examination, autopsy and laboratory studies to determine the cause and manner of death?

The history is the beginning of the investigation and is of utmost importance in making the determination of cause of death. The scene investigation may disclose drugs or toxins which may be related to the cause of death. Some poisonous agents are not detected on a routine drug screen; therefore, the pathologist must have knowledge of medications and toxins in order to request the specific analytical tests needed to detect

them. An example would include the "sniffing" of aerosol pro-
pellants, a risky activity which has been frequently reported in
teenagers. Sniffing of propellant substances can cause sudden
death by precipitating lethal cardiac arrhythmias. A special
analysis (gas chromatography by head space analysis) is required
to detect the chemicals in the blood. In other cases there may be
sufficient natural disease to account for death but the individual
may in fact have died of a drug overdose or other subtle cause.
In the case of drowning and suffocation the autopsy findings
may not be specific and police investigation may be critical to
the understanding of the death. Data developed by coroners,
medical examiners and pathologists is studied by medical epi-
demiologists and health and safety agencies to develop strategies
to prevent disease and injury, thereby saving lives. The data
developed about motor vehicle injuries and fire deaths led to
legislation requiring seat belts in vehicles and smoke detectors in
building construction.

In the examination of skeletonized or severely decomposed
remains, the forensic pathologist needs a working knowledge of
multiple methods of identification including forensic anthropology in order to establish identity. If sufficient skeletal parts
remain, the pathologist may be able to determine the age, race and
sex of the individual and sometimes estimate the length of time
since death. Occasionally, specific markings on the bones may
enable the pathologist to come to a conclusion as to the cause of
death.

*What is the importance of performing an autopsy in someone in whom
the cause of death is "obvious"?*

The importance of examining people in whom the cause of
death appears obvious is several fold. In the case of shootings or

other fatal assaults the forensic pathologist, during the course of the examination, may recover bullets or other important trace evidence. In the case of motor vehicle occupants, it is important to determine who was driving and to assess driver factors, vehicle factors or environmental factors that might have caused or contributed to the crash. Forensic autopsies may identify inherited diseases that constitute a risk for next of kin. Examples include certain types of heart disease (premature atherosclerosis, hypertrophic cardiomyopathy) and certain kinds of kidney disease (adult polycystic kidney disease). Notifying the family would be an important service to the living. In individuals who have undergone medical treatment after collapse or injury it is important to share the findings with the treating physicians for educational purposes.

How does an autopsy authorized by the next of kin on a patient dying in the hospital of a natural disease differ from an autopsy authorized by law as part of a medicolegal investigation?

The hospital autopsy is often performed on individuals in whom the disease causing death is known. The purpose of the autopsy is to determine the extent of the disease and/or the effects of therapy and the presence of any undiagnosed disease of interest or that might have contributed to death.

The next of kin must give permission for the autopsy and may limit the extent of the dissection (for example the chest and abdomen only, excluding the head).

A medicolegal (forensic) autopsy is ordered by the coroner or medical examiner as authorized by law with the statutory purpose of establishing the cause of death and answer other medicolegal questions. The next of kin do not authorize and may not limit the extent of the autopsy. Common questions include the identity of the deceased person, the time of injury and death and the presence of medical evidence (for example bullets, hair, fibers, semen). Observations made at autopsy elucidate how and by what weapon lethal injury was inflicted. During the course of the forensic autopsy, blood and other body fluids are routinely obtained in order to check for alcohol and other drugs. The forensic autopsy should be complete (including the head, chest, abdomen and other parts of the body as indicated).

What is clinical forensic pathology?

Because of their expertise in interpreting methods of injury, many forensic pathologists also examine, upon request, living patients including individuals who have been sexually assaulted (rape) and children who have been injured to assist in determining if child abuse or neglect has occurred. The forensic pathologist also examines patients to determine whether the pattern of injuries is consistent with accidental or intentionally inflicted injuries. During these examinations a forensic pathologist may collect evidence for analysis. Examination of living patients is customarily performed on behalf of law-enforcement agencies needing the same information on the living as required on dead victims of injury.

Where do forensic pathologists work?

Forensic pathologists are employed by states, counties, groups of counties, or cities, as well as by medical schools, the military services, and the federal government. In some settings such as medium sized and smaller counties the forensic pathologist may work for a private group or hospital which contracts with the county to perform forensic autopsies.

How does one become a forensic pathologist?

1) After high school the future forensic pathologist attends college for 4 years and receives a bachelor's degree.

2) After undergraduate school the aspiring forensic pathologist spends 4 years in medical school, earning an M.D. or D.O. degree.

3) After medical school there are several routes by which one may become a forensic pathologist. One may spend 5 years training in anatomic and clinical pathology followed by 1 year of residency or fellowship in forensic pathology. A second option is to train for 4 years in anatomic pathology and train for 1 year in forensic pathology. The residency training in forensic pathology involves practical (on-the-job) experience supervised by trained forensic pathologists. The forensic pathology resident actually performs autopsies and participates in death investigation. To become certified, one then must pass an examination given by the American Board of Pathology certifying special competence in forensic pathology.

Forensic pathologists practice medicine in the finest tradition of preventive medicine and public health by making the study of the dead benefit the living.

In the Morgue: Tools of the Trade

If Mopec™ is a familiar name, then you'd feel right at home, so to speak, in the morgue. Mopec is a manufacturer that supplies morgues worldwide. Their stark catalog consists of 352 pages of "morgue, pathology and histology products" laid out in a practical manner, tabbed on the right margin with subheads that include:

dissection, autopsy accessories, histology supplies, fume handling, grossing workstations (rather appropriate, I'd say), autopsy sinks and tables, necropsy equipment, dissecting tables, morgue refrigerators, walk-in morgue refrigerators, stainless steel cabinets, cadaver handling, and cadaver storage racks.

The design and durability of the equipment attest to the design and durability of the human body. There's a stark beauty to the equipment, no frills, all business. Here are a few samples:

- Dissection: It takes saw, forceps, scissors, knives, shears, mallets, hammers, chisels, probes, knives, and skull breakers to do a proper job.
- Autopsy accessories: There's a device called, appropriately, "SawBones," which is advertised as "your best consultant when you need a safe and easy way to remove a slice of bone for histologic examination."

Cornwell fans will no doubt recognize one of Mopec's products, the Stryker Autopsy Saw, which "has long been a reliable instrument for the pathology laboratory. The high-speed oscillating action quickly cuts through bone without harming soft tissue. Used for removing the cranial cap, making linear cuts, or taking small bone specimens. Durable and easy to handle."

Other autopsy accessories include dissecting boards, disaster pouches, body bags, transport bags (antimicrobial-treated and electronically heat-sealed "bag-in-a-bag" vinyl inner liner), and autopsy scales, lights, and disinfectants that destroy "a wide range of pathogenic bacteria, viruses and fungi."

As you'd expect, the variety of carts, tables, and sinks are extensive, designed for every possible contingency. For instance, a wall-mounted sink, seven feet long, "provides all of the features normally found in a typical pedestal type autopsy table without the space requirements. This style autopsy sink also eliminates the physical strain of moving the body since the autopsy is performed directly on the cart that it is stored on. The autopsy cart overhangs the station on the right side and drains directly into the sink. Adjacent to the sink is a dissecting area which is comprised of removable and interchangeable grid plates. The dissecting area has grid plates which are elevated above a sloped surface, and drain directly into the sink. The wall mounting allows for quick cleanup of your work area. The autopsy sink is delivered fully plumbed and wired ready for installation."

Necropsy tables, designed for animals, are available in different sizes depending on the size of the animal. The large necropsy table has a heavy-duty stainless steel top, a hydraulic scissor lift and hydraulic pump unit, and can hold a maximum of two thousand pounds and "raises animal to ergonomic position."

Morgue refrigerators are available in every possible configuration: end opening, side opening, roll-in, a roll-in/end opening combination, and massive walk-in units.

An end-opening morgue refrigerator opens with doors sized 27 × 21 inches. "A telescoping mechanism fully supports the body tray containing the cadaver. When the door is open and the end of the telescoping mechanism is fully extended approximately 6'6", the body and tray are in full head to toe view. The cadaver can be removed by itself or in conjunction with the body tray."

There's even such a thing as a "cadaver fork lift," adjustable from sixty-four to one hundred inches, capable of lifting fifteen hundred pounds. (Have you ever tried to lift a dead deer?)

The catalog itself is straightforward, no nonsense, matter-of-fact in its approach and presentation of products—sober and somber, as you'd expect; in fact, given their body of work, their customers wouldn't have it any other way.

Abbreviations in the Kay Scarpetta Novels
compiled by Birger Nielsen

Birger Nielsen, who is a big fan of Cornwell's fiction, lives in Denmark; like many foreign readers, he discovered that in order to understand the novels, he had to understand the acronyms used. To aid foreign readers, Nielsen constructed a basic listing of the acronyms in her work. (Nielsen's extensive Web site on Cornwell can be found at http://hjem.get2net.dk/bnielsen/cornwell.html.)

- AB0: Blood-type system with four types: A, B, AB, and 0
- ACLU: American Civil Liberties Union
- ACTMAD: American Coalition of Tough Mothers Against Drugs
- ADA: Blood-type system
- AFIP: Armed Forces Institute of Pathology
- AFIS: Automated Fingerprint Identification System
- AG: Attorney General
- AIDS: Acquired Immunodeficiency Syndrome
- AK: Blood-type system
- AmEx: American Express
- AOL: America Online (Internet service provider)
- AP: Associated Press
- ASAP: As soon as possible
- ATF: Bureau of Alcohol, Tobacco and Firearms
- AT&T: American Telephone & Telegraph Company
- AWOL: Absent without leave
- BB gun: Air rifle (uses shotgun pellet-size BB)
- BC: Buoyancy control (vest)
- BDU: Battle dress uniform

- BL-4: Bio level 4—highest protection level against biological hazards
- BLT: Bacon, lettuce, and tomato, i.e., a sandwich
- BMW: (car made by) Bayerische Motor Werke
- BO: Body odor
- BOLO: Be on the lookout
- BP: Blood pressure
- BWI: Baltimore-Washington International airport
- B&E: Breaking and entering
- CA: The Commonwealth's Attorney
- CAIN: Crime Artificial Intelligence Network
- CASKU: Children Abduction Serial Killer Unit
- CB: Citizen band (receiver/transmitter)
- CCH: Computerized criminal history
- CCRE: Central criminal records exchange
- CDC: Centers for Disease Control and Prevention
- CD-ROM: Compact disc—read-only memory
- CEO: Chief executive officer
- CIA: Central Intelligence Agency
- CIA: (FBI) Criminal investigative agents
- CID: Criminal Investigative Division
- CME-1: Chief medical examiner's initial report of investigation
- CNN: Cable Net News
- CO: Carbon monoxide
- CP: Cathodic protectors
- CP&L: Commonwealth Power & Light

- CPR: Cardiopulmonary resuscitation
- CRT: Cathode ray tube; computer screen
- DBA: Database administrator
- D.C.: District of Columbia (also sometimes indicating Washington, D.C.)
- DEA: Drug Enforcement Administration
- DJ: Disk jockey
- DMV: Department of Motor Vehicles
- DNA: Deoxyribonucleic acid
- DOA: Dead on arrival
- DOB: Date of birth
- DOS: Disk operating system, a PC operating system
- DP: Data processing
- DRMS: Defense Reutilization Marketing Service
- DT: Delirium tremens
- DUI: Driving under the influence
- EAP: Erythrocyte acid phosphatase, blood-type system with six types: A, B, BA, CB, CA, C
- ECT: Electroconvulsive treatment
- EOT: End of tour
- EPA: Environmental Protection Agency
- ER: Emergency room
- ERF: Engineering research facility
- EsD: Blood-type system
- ESPN: TV network (sports)
- FAA: Federal Aviation Administration
- FBI: Federal Bureau of Investigation
- FEMA: Federal Emergency Management Agency

- FIP: Fingerprint image processor
- FMP: Fingerprint matching processor
- FOP: Fraternal Order of Police
- GE: General Electric
- GIF: Graphics interchange format (file)
- GPS: Global positioning system (navigator)
- GQ: *Gentlemen's Quarterly* (a magazine)
- GRC: General rifling characteristics (register)
- GRE: Graduate Record Examinations
- HALT: Homicide Assessment and Lead Tracking system
- HEPA: Highly efficient particulate air filter
- HHSD: Health & Human Services Department
- HIV: Human immunodeficiency virus
- HLA: Human leukocyte antigen
- HMMWV: High-mobility multipurpose wheeled vehicle
- HQ: Headquarters
- HRT: Hostage Rescue Team (FBI)
- HRX: A higher resolution (416 × 277 color pixels; view: 106 degrees) eye phone from VPL (computer company)
- I-64: Interstate highway number 64 (passes through Richmond and Hampton Roads)
- I-95: Interstate highway number 95
- IBM: International Business Machines, a computer company
- ICU: Intensive Care Unit
- ID: Identification (Unit)
- IOC: Interception of communications statute
- I.Q.: Intelligence quotient
- IRA: Irish Republican Army

- IRS: Internal Revenue Services
- IV: Intravenous
- IVF: In vitro fertilization
- KTW: Brand name of Teflon-coated ammunition
- LAD: Left anterior descending artery
- LAN: Local area network
- LSD: Lysergic acid diethylamide
- MAC-V: Military Assistance Command—Vietnam
- MCV: Medical College of Virginia
- M.D.: Medical doctor
- ME: Medical examiner
- MIT: Massachusetts Institute of Technology
- MMPI: Minnesota Multiphasic Personality Inventory
- MO: Modus operandi
- Monticello: The home of Thomas Jefferson
- MP: Military police
- MRI: Magnetic resonance imaging
- MSUD: Maple syrup urinary disorder
- MTV: Music television—A TV channel
- NAACP: National Association for the Advancement of Colored People
- NAVSEA: Naval Sea Systems Command
- NCIC: National Crime Information Center
- NCIS: Naval Criminal Investigative Service
- NCR: National Cash Register, a computer company
- NOW: National Organization for Women
- NVSE: Naval Sea Systems Command
- NYPD: New York Police Department

- O&C: Oregon & California Railroad
- OCME: Office of the Chief Medical Examiner
- OPR: Office of Professional Responsibility (FBI)
- PA: Public announcement (system)
- PADI: Professional Association of Dive Instructors (certification)
- PBS: Public Broadcasting System, a TV station
- PC: Personal computer
- PCP: PhenylCyclohexylPiperidine (angel dust)
- PCR: Polymerase chain reaction
- PD: Police department
- PEP: Blood-type system (PhosphoEnolPyruvate)
- PERK: Physical Evidence Recovery Kit
- PGM: Blood-type system (enzyme phosphoglyceromutas)
- pH: power hydrogen—acidity/alkalinity measure (0 = acid, 14 = caustic)
- Ph.D.: Doctor of Philosophy, academic grade
- PIN: Personal identification number
- PMC: Ammunition manufacturer
- PX: Post exchange
- QE2: The *Queen Elizabeth II* passenger ship
- QMC: Quartermaster Corps
- RAM: Random access memory (i.e., normal computer memory)
- RIA: RadioImmunoAssays
- RSVP: *Respondez, s'il vous plait*: please respond.
- RV: Recreational vehicle (i.e., mobile home)
- SAC: Special agent in charge

- SBI: State Bureau of Investigation
- SEAL: Sea Air Land (navy command)
- SEM: Scanning electron microscopy
- SID: State identification number
- SIDS: Sudden infant death syndrome
- SIGMET: SIGnificant METeorological information
- SOB: Son-of-a-bitch
- SOP: Standard operating procedure
- SPCA: Society for the Prevention of Cruelty to Animals
- SQL: Structured query language
- STAT: Latin: statim = immediately. An instant test with a degree of accuracy that might be improved with a test that requires more time
- SWAT: Special weapons and tactics (team)
- TEM: Transmission electron microscope
- THC: TetraHydroCannabinol (the active ingredient in marijuana)
- TU: Tenprint update
- UFO: Unidentified flying object
- UNICEF: United Nations Children's Fund
- UPS: United Parcel Service
- USAMRIID: U.S. Army Medical Research Institute of Infectious Diseases
- UT: University of Tennessee
- UV: Ultraviolet (radiation)
- UVA: University of Virginia
- VCR: Videocassette recorder
- VICAP: Violent Criminal Apprehension Program

- VIN:Vehicle identification number

- VIP:Very important person

- VMC: University of Virginia Medical College

- VPL: Computer company; inventor of the dataglove

- VS:Vital statistics

- VZV:Varicella-Zoster virus

- Wadcutter: Flat-nosed bullet (good for making a perfectly round hole in a target)

10 Codes

Cornwell's novels, celebrated for their authenticity, are peppered with "10 codes." Used by public safety dispatchers, these codes are in essence a verbal shorthand to minimize confusion—especially valuable in emergency situations when time is of the essence and communication clarity is paramount.

Ready for a 10-63?

The following generic list is used, with some variations, through-out the United States and is an easy way to decode "dispatcher speak" when they are cited by characters in Cornwell's fiction.

That's a 10-24!

10-0 use caution

10-1 cannot receive you

10-2 receive you OK

10-3 stop transmitting

10-4 OK, I acknowledge, etc.

10-5 relay this transmission

10-6 responding from a distance

10-7 out of service

10-8 available for incidents

10-9 repeat your transmission

10-10 off-duty

10-11 animal incident

10-12 stand-by, hold transmission

10-13 weather/road report

10-14 prowler report

10-15 en route with arrest

10-16 domestic problem

10-17 out of service for fuel

10-18 out of service for repairs

10-19 returning to ____

10-20 what's your location? my location is ____

10-21 telephone ____

10-22 cancel assignment, disregard

10-23 stand-by, hold transmission

10-24 assignment completed

10-25 meet the person

10-26 person clear of warrants

10-27 driver's license info

10-28 vehicle registration info

10-29 warrant check for person

10-30 improper radio use

10-31 crime in progress

10-32 subject with gun

10-33 alarm sounding, emergency

10-34 riot

10-35 what is the time?, major crime alert

10-36 can you copy confidential info?

10-37 suspicious vehicle

10-38 stop suspicious vehicle

10-39 urgent—use lights and siren

10-40 silent response

10-41 beginning tour of duty

10-42 welfare check, ending tour of duty

10-43 information

10-44 permission to leave for

10-45 dead animal at ___

10-46 assist motorist

10-47 emergency road repair

10-48 traffic signal repair

10-49 traffic light out at ____

10-50 accident

10-51 tow truck needed

10-52 ambulance needed

10-53 road blocked at ____

10-54 animals on highway

10-55 security check

10-57 hit-and-run accident

10-58 direct traffic

10-59 escort

10-60 squad in vicinity, lock-out

10-61 personnel in area

10-62 reply to message

10-63 clear to copy info?

10-64 message for delivery

10-65 net message assignment

10-66 net message cancellation

10-67 person calling for help

10-68 dispatch message

10-69 message received

10-70 prowler, fire alarm

10-71 gun involved, advise nature of fire

10-72 shooting, fire progress report

10-73 smoke report

10-74 negative

10-75 in contact with ____

10-76 enroute

10-77 ETA

10-78 need assistance

10-79 bomb threat, coroner's case

10-80 bomb has exploded

10-81 Breathalyzer report

10-82 reserve lodging

10-83 work school crossing at

10-84 if meeting ____, advise ETA

10-85 delay due to ____

10-86 officer on-duty

10-87 pickup

10-88 present phone number of ____

10-89 bomb threat

10-90 bank alarm at ____

10-91 pick up prisoner

10-92 improperly parked vehicle

10-93 blockage

10-94 drag racing

10-95 prisoner/subject in custody

10-96 psych patient

10-97 check signal

10-98 prison/jail break

10-99 wanted/stolen record

11-24 abandoned vehicle

11-25 road obstruction

11-94 pedestrian stop

11-95 vehicle stop

11-96 suspicious vehicle

11-97 security check on officer

11-98 meet at ____

11-99 officer needs help

Appendix B: Scarpetta's Home Turf: Virginia

Visiting Virginia

Just as Maine is inextricably linked to Stephen King, South Florida to Carl Hiassen, the Deep South to Larry Brown and John

Grisham, New Orleans to Anne Rice, and Washington, D.C., to Tom Clancy, Richmond was put on the literary map by Patricia Cornwell, who, as she's put it in several interviews, doesn't make anything up. Although she has recently moved to Connecticut, it doesn't change the fact that Virginia—notably Richmond—has served double duty as the stomping grounds for not only Cornwell but also her fictional creation Kay Scarpetta.

In Cornwell's novels, the geography of Richmond can literally be plotted on a city map, which makes visiting the area all the more fun for Cornwell fans. For anyone with more than a casual interest in Cornwell, a trip to Richmond is a must. Fortunately, Richmond is conveniently accessible by air at the Richmond airport—frequently mentioned in the Scarpetta novels—and easily accessible by car as well, since two major interstates intersect in the city: I-95 and I-64.

The best way to explore Richmond is by car and on foot, with the help of a recent guidebook and a recent map. (I recommend the *Insiders' Guide* series, which is written by locals, and the maps issued by ADC, which include a traditional fold-out map and a detailed book map.) While you're in Richmond, drive south toward Williamsburg and Hampton Roads, since both have served as backdrops for several Scarpetta novels and many sights will be familiar to her readers.

Richmond was, personally and professionally, home turf for Patricia Cornwell from 1983 until the end of 2002. She used to live in an exclusive subdivision in town and was one of the town's most visible philanthropists and celebrities, infusing into her books an intimate knowledge of the city to form the geographical background for her books.

There are no official Cornwell tours of Richmond, so your best bet is to get a good city map and go off on your own.

The following list of interesting sights featured in Cornwell's work, arranged alphabetically, is by no means all-inclusive, but it's a good starting point for any fan who wants to see Cornwell's fiction come to life.

1. **Biotech II, Biotechnology Research Park (*Unnatural Exposure, The Last Precinct*).** A leading center of its kind, located on the east campus of Virginia Commonwealth University off Leigh Street.

2. **EyeSpy (*The Body Farm*).** Located in the Springfield Mall off I-95, this retail store is a treasure trove for wannabe double agents, secret agents, or anyone who wants to be a junior G-Man.

3. **HeloAir (*The Last Precinct*).** Located near the Richmond airport, this is the company that hangars Cornwell's helicopter. (No, you can't lease it for a flight, but the cheapest, and best, way to see Richmond from air is to ride with the traffic reporters in the morning or evening.)

4. **Hollywood Cemetery (*Southern Cross*).** Located south of the downtown expressway, on Cherry Street, this is the final resting place of many historical figures, including Jefferson Davis, the president of the Confederate States, which figures prominently in this novel.

5. **John Marshall Courthouse (*Cruel and Unusual*).** Located southeast of the Coliseum, it is adjacent to the Federal Building and the Department of Social Services. This is where Kay Scarpetta is put on the stand in *Cruel and Unusual*.

6. **Lockgreen (*The Last Precinct*).** Located near Williams Island north of the James River, this subdivision is south of Cary Street. This is Scarpetta's current residence.

7. **MCV (*The Body Farm, From Potter's Field*).** Medical College of Virginia. Both Kay Scarpetta (*From Potter's*

Field) and her niece, Lucy (*The Body Farm*), were treated at this hospital.

8. **Monument Avenue (*Cause of Death*).** Located in the historic Fan District, where you will find million-dollar mansions and renovated, turn-of-the-century town houses. A trendy place to live for the upwardly mobile Richmonder.

9. **Office of the Chief Medical Examiner (OCME).** Located at 400 East Jackson Street, this is at the center of Cornwell's Scarpetta novels. This is also where, in the real world, Dr. Marcella Fierro, a mentor and good friend of Cornwell's, works as the CME.

10. **Regency Mall (*The Last Precinct*).** South of exit 181 off I-64, Regency Square Shopping Center is one of the big malls in town. In *The Last Precinct,* Scarpetta meets her niece, Lucy, in front of Waldenbooks, and also stops at Sea Dream Leather.

11. **Richmond International Airport.** Located off I-64, on Airport Drive, RIA is the major airport in the area, served by several major carriers, including USAir. Both in her fiction and in the real world, RIA crops up frequently.

12. **Richmond Police Department.** This is located between the Virginia Biology Center and the John Marshall Courts Building in the downtown area. The authenticity of Cornwell's fictional Peter Marino and police operations is drawn in part from the stint Cornwell served as a volunteer police officer.

13. **Richmond Port (*Black Notice, The Last Precinct*).** Flanking the James River, the Port of Richmond terminal is located off Deepwater Terminal Road. In *Black Notice,* the body of Thomas is found in a cargo container at this port.

14. **Richmond skyline.** Mentioned several times throughout the Scarpetta novels, the skyline is distinctive and impressive from any perspective, on the ground or in the air.

15. *Richmond Times-Dispatch.* The local newspaper is mentioned throughout Cornwell's novels. As you'd expect, it has covered Cornwell's comings and goings. Worth a subscription for Cornwell fans who want to get a real "feel" for the city.

16. **Science Museum of Virginia.** Located near Broad Street West where it intersects with Boulevard, this is where Cornwell fans can become sleuths and solve a crime at the museum's latest exhibit, funded by Cornwell. (The exhibit was opened to the public on the same day she held a signing for *The Last Precinct*.)

17. **The Jefferson Hotel (*The Last Precinct*).** Richmond's newest, newly minted millionaire, Scarpetta's niece, Lucy Farinelli, stayed at this stately hotel (in *The Last Precinct*). My recommendation is to take advantage of their "Discover Richmond Package" for $250, which includes one night's accommodation in a deluxe room, a breakfast for two, valet parking, and "Discover Richmond" tickets, plus all taxes.

18. **Windsor Farms (*The Last Precinct*).** An affluent subdivision, this is Scarpetta's current residence and, in fact, was Patricia Cornwell's former residence.

19. **Virginia Center for the Book.** If you ever attend a Cornwell book signing in Richmond, you'll likely see a table set up by the Virginia Center for the Book to promote the organization. Its mission is simple: "To promote reading, books, and the literary heritage of the Commonwealth." Located at The Library of Virginia (800

East Broad Street, Richmond, Virginia 23219-8000), the Virginia Center for the Book sells at Cornwell's signings and by mail a color poster showing "Scarpetta's Richmond," available for ten dollars plus shipping. (The map, though outdated, is still a great item for Cornwell fans— something unusual to put on the wall, near your bookshelf of Cornwell's novels.)

Hampton Roads. The *Greater Hampton Roads* "Street Map Book," includes points north up to Middlesex County and points south to the Virginia–North Carolina border. Most of the population in southeast Virginia live in the Greater Hampton Roads area, which locals simply call Hampton Roads.

A further distinction: If you catch the news, you'll hear references to the Peninsula and to the Southside. The Peninsula refers to Hampton, Poquoson, Newport News, York County, with some coverage of the James City County and Williamsburg; Southside refers to Norfolk, Portsmouth, Suffolk, Chesapeake, and Virginia Beach, with some coverage of Surry County, Isle of Wight County (which includes Smithfield), Southampton County, and Franklin, as well.

Predictably, most of the geographical background in Cornwell's novels is comprised of Richmond, Williamsburg, and North Carolina—all places with which she's intimately familiar. The Peninsula, on the other hand, is simply not a place—judging from her fiction—where she's spent much time; Southside, however, seems to be more familiar stomping grounds.

On the Peninsula.

1. **The Newport News Williamsburg International Airport (*All That Remains*).** In terms of passenger traffic and in size, it's eclipsed by its neighboring airports: Norfolk

International and Richmond International; however, because of Air Tran and USAir, passenger trips are up and the parking lot has been expanded to handle the overflow.

Benton Wesley flies into this airport because of its proximity to a current case involving killings within a fifty-mile radius of Williamsburg.

2. **Yorktown (*All That Remains*).** Part of the historic triangle—the other two "legs" are Williamsburg and Jamestown—Yorktown makes its appearance throughout the novel: It's the home of the dog handlers who are called in to help solve the case; in York River State Park, the bodies of Phillips and Roberts are found; and the bodies of another pair of lovers are also found within county boundaries. (Most of the novel is set in nearby Williamsburg.)

3. **The U.S. Navy's dead fleet (*Cause of Death*).** En route via helicopter to the nuclear power plant in Surry, Scarpetta and company fly over the "dead fleet" of decommissioned ships anchored in the James River off Fort Eustis, an army post (home to its Transportation School).

Southside.

1. **Norfolk Office of the Chief Medical Examiner (*Cruel and Unusual*).** One of four state medical examiners offices, it is located at 830 Southampton Avenue in Norfolk, which is responsible for the Tidewater District.

Dr. Wright, the local medical examiner, makes his appearance in *Cruel and Unusual*.

2. **Sentara Norfolk General Hospital (*Unnatural Exposure*).** Located near the waterfront, this is one of the major hospitals in the area. (It's also where *Nightingale,* the medical evacuation helicopter, is stationed.)

In *Unnatural Exposure,* Dr. Crowder makes an appearance at this hospital.

3. **Sandbridge (*Cause of Death*).** A narrow strip of land with the North Bay on its west side and the Atlantic Ocean on its right, Sandbridge is part of Virginia Beach. Dotted for miles with expensive waterfront homes, Sandbridge is the home of Dr. Philip Mant, the deputy chief medical examiner for the Tidewater District. As *Cause of Death* opens, Scarpetta is at his house, filling in on the job because of his family emergencies.

Williamsburg.

For me part of Cornwell's appeal as a writer is her familiarity with southeast Virginia, which I've called home for some years now. In Cornwell's most recent Scarpetta novel, southeast Virginia plays a pivotal part.

In *The Last Precinct,* nearby Jamestown gets a nod, but in Cornwell's forthcoming novel, *Isle of Dogs,* the historic settlement will take center stage.

As a resident of Williamsburg, I strongly recommend a trip to visit the historic triangle—Williamsburg, Jamestown, and Yorktown—and as a Cornwell fan, I'd like to point out where her world of fiction and the real world intersect.

1. **The Silversmith's Shop (*All That Remains*)** is located on the Duke of Gloucester Street toward its eastern end. At that shop, Kay Scarpetta bought a "hand-wrought sterling silver pineapple charm and a handsome chain." (The pineapple is the symbol of Colonial Williamsburg.)

2. **The Apothecary Shop (*All That Remains*),** as Cornwell termed it in *All That Remains,* is in fact called the Pasteur &

Galt Apothecary Shop. Located a short distance east of the Silversmith Shop, it has a sign showing a mortar and pestle with the symbol of a caduceus. In this shop, Kay Scarpetta bought soaps for herself, shaving cream, and potpourri.

3. **The Trellis (*All That Remains*).** Located on the Duke of Gloucester Street, this restaurant is in the Merchant Square area, the favorite place in town for tourists to shop. After shopping at the Silversmith Shop and the Apothecary Shop, Scarpetta met Abby Turnbull, a Richmond journalist, to discuss the case at hand. (*Note to the wise:* Make reservations early, especially for Saturday nights when the tourist trade is especially heavy; the best seats are in the cozy room fronting the Duke of Gloucester Street, where you can watch the tourists go by.)

    For the souvenir minded, get *The Trellis Cookbook,* or *Death by Chocolate,* featuring the recipes of chef Marsalis Desaulniers.

4. **Carriage houses (*All that Remains*).** The preferred places to stay in town, if you have the money, are available through the central booking office, Colonial Williamsburg Lodging, which manages the hotels and guest houses. Although the premiere lodging can be found at the Williamsburg Inn, which is where visiting dignitaries stay, a cozier lodging experience can be had at the guest houses, which are Scarpetta's preferred lodging.

5. **Hot apple cider (*All That Remains*).** Throughout the Colonial Williamsburg area, stands are set up to serve beverages, including hot apple cider—a real treat on a cool evening. (If you prefer to have your beverage inside, head to the Bakery on the Duke of Gloucester Street, where you can enjoy a wide selection of breads and pastries, as well.)

6. **Merchant's Square (*All That Remains*).** For locals and tourists alike, this is the main shopping area in town (the outlet mall northwest of the city is almost as popular). My recommended list of stores to check out include: the Nancy Thomas Gallery, the Henry Street Chocolatier, the Peanut Shop of Williamsburg, Wythe Candies, The Christmas Shop, and The Toymaker of Williamsburg. After hitting those stores, you'll certainly want to get a bite to eat, so try either Berret's Seafood Restaurant & Raw Bar or The Trellis.

7. **The Marshall-Wythe School of Law (*All That Remains*).** This well-regarded law school is located next to the National Center for State Courts on South Henry Street. The late Jill Harrington, a graduate of this school, worked for a small firm in town. (Harrington, along with Elizabeth Mott, were murdered; this was the case Scarpetta was discussing with Abby Turnbull at The Trellis.)

8. **Police headquarters (*Body of Evidence*).** Located at the intersection of Lafayette Street and Boundary Street, police HQ is across the street from the fire department and adjacent to the parking garage and post office.

9. **Culpeper's Williamsburg Tavern (*Body of Evidence*).** There's no tavern with that name in town. It may be modeled after the taverns in the Historic District: Josiah Chownings Tavern, King's Arms Tavern, or the Market Square Tavern. Alternatively, it may be modeled after one of the small taverns located near the College of William & Mary. (Your guess is as good as mine.)

10. **Camp Peary, called "the Farm" (*All That Remains*).** This figures largely in the plot of the book, though to say more than that would be to give away too much. Located off Interstate 64 at exit 238, Camp Peary is the one place in the Williamsburg area that I would strongly recommend

you avoid. On the ADC *Greater Hampton Roads* map, it's labeled "Department of Defense, Armed Forces Experimental Training Activity," which means, in plain English, the CIA.

If you consult the Commonwealth of Virginia 2000 Aeronautical Chart, you'll note that airspace over Camp Peary is restricted.

Tourists who accidentally take the wrong turn and head toward Camp Peary instead of Williamsburg are in for a surprise: An armed military guard will stop your vehicle and immediately turn you around.

Camp Peary is the main CIA training facility, with its own airstrip. According to the local newspaper, the *Daily Press*: "The Farm . . . has a long if mostly low-key history. . . . Classes taught at Peary are said to include lock picking, demolition and wiretapping, though spokesmen for the 10,000-acre base, located in York County along the York River, have long remained mum on what goes on there. Over the years Camp Peary has achieved an urban legend status. There've been claims that foreign agents have trained there never knowing they were in the United States and that the military equipment from the former Soviet Union has been tested there."

11. **The Colonial Parkway (*All That Remains*).** The most scenic drive in the area, the Colonial National Historical Parkway begins on its south end in Jamestown, winding its way east past Sandy Bay, Back River, and the James River; it then heads north through the heart of Williamsburg and heads east flanking the York River until it terminates in Yorktown near the waterfront.

To this day the infamous Colonial Parkway murders have remained unsolved. In *All That Remains,* a blue van belonging to Mike Martin, a homicide victim, is found abandoned along the Colonial Parkway.

12. **Cutler Grove (*Body of Evidence*).** Because this figures prominently in the novel, I'll simply point you in the direction of the novel. For those curious enough to seek out this place, be forewarned: There is no such place with that name in Williamsburg. There is, however, a similar-sounding plantation in Williamsburg, Carter's Grove, located on the James River, just south of Busch Gardens on Route 60, Pocahontas Trail. Now part of Colonial Williamsburg, Carter's Grove is well worth a side trip.

13. **Jamestown (*The Last Precinct*).** Jamestown Settlement and Jamestown proper, located within the boundaries of the Colonial National Historical Park flanking the James River, are mentioned in *The Last Precinct,* but it's a locale that will take center stage in Cornwell's forthcoming novel, *Isle of Dogs.* Offstage and outside the pages of her novels, Cornwell celebrated Thanksgiving 2000 in Jamestown, with her guests Dan Ackroyd, his wife Donna Dixon, and others. (They flew in on two helicopters.)

Further Afield in the Commonwealth of Virginia. Since she is the Commonwealth of Virginia's chief medical examiner, Dr. Kay Scarpetta's work has literally taken her all over the map of Virginia. Here are a few of those places, some off the beaten path.

1. **Virginia farmland (*Cruel and Unusual*).** If you fly over Virginia, you will get a sense of how much of the state is rural, especially points west and south of Richmond. Though Virginia is best known for its tobacco crops, cotton and corn are also favorites.

2. **Quantico, Virginia (*The Body Farm*).** Located south of D.C., off Interstate 95, this is a Marine Corps training base that also serves as home to the FBI training academy. An obvious, frequent reference in many of Cornwell's books, the FBI training academy is familiar turf to Scarpetta, her niece, Lucy (a former FBI agent who custom-designed a computer system for the Bureau), and Pete Marino.

3. **Fort Lee, Virginia (*From Potter's Field*).** Located south of Richmond and northeast of Petersburg, this is the home of the U.S. Army's Quartermaster Corps. Its mission is simple: To provide the soldier in the field everything he needs, from "beans to bullets," as the army likes to say.

   In *From Potter's Field,* the Quartermaster Museum holds over twenty-six thousand artifacts, one of which proves useful in helping Scarpetta in her current case.

4. **Virginia Diner, in Wakefield, Virginia (*Unnatural Exposure*).** While working a case, Scarpetta stops here to meet a local law-enforcement official. Located southeast of Petersburg on Route 460, the diner is justly famous for its peanut dishes, which is not surprising since Virginia is the peanut capital of the world.

   In a nutshell, here's what you need to know about the diner: If you like down-home cooking, make the trip to Wakefield and be prepared to loosen your belt afterward. (If you fly in to Wakefield's airport, you can call the diner and a car will be dispatched to pick you up—it's only a mile away, so it's a quick trip.)

   From its Web site (Virginia_diner.com): "The Virginia Diner has been a refuge for folks who like down-home cooking ever since Mrs. D'Earcy Davis served hot biscuits and vegetable soup to hungry customers way back in 1929. In those days the little diner was a refurbished Sussex, Surry, and Southampton Railroad car. As business grew, so did the restaurant, with dining room after dining room added on to accommodate a growing list of satisfied customers.

Today the Virginia Diner has been replicated and the old railroad car has become a legend, but its quaint atmosphere has been faithfully preserved and still reflects throughout the restaurant.

Antique peanut vendor roasters and buckets of free peanuts for munching continue to greet guests at the front door along with the irresistible aroma of freshly prepared dishes just like Grandma Galloway used to make. Traditional southern hospitality and efficient service blend with an atmosphere of red-and-white tablecloths, Bentwood chairs, and antique cast-iron toys. All are reminiscent of those early days when the Diner began to serve customers peanuts fresh from local fields and prepared in its kitchen instead of after-dinner mints. Today this peanut business has grown into a national and international gourmet mail-order business, and the Virginia Diner is rightfully known as "the Peanut Capital of the World."

5. **Atlantic Waste Landfill, Reeves Road, off 460 East (*Unnatural Exposure*).** I haven't been here, nor do I know if this place actually exists, but if it doesn't, there's plenty like it throughout Virginia, because the landfill business is big business, in dollars and in actual volume. New York City gets our tourist business and in return we get mountains of garbage that, like NYC ex-mayor Giuliani's justifications for using the Commonwealth as a dumping ground and toxic waste dump, stink to high heaven.

6. **Tangier Island (*Unnatural Exposure*).** Situated almost halfway between Virginia's mainland and her eastern shore, Tangier Island is accessible only by private plane or by ferry.

The plot of *Unnatural Exposure* requires a town that can easily be quarantined. Given that requirement, Tangier Island would be a good choice because of limited access. (If necessary, the Coast Guard could institute a blockade.)

Tangier Island is a great place to get away, far from the madding crowds: very few cars—most people use bicycles, ride golf carts, or travel on foot—and enough small B and Bs and restaurants to handle the tourist trade. (Its year-round population is approximately seven hundred people.)

7. **University of Virginia; Charlottesville, Virginia (*Cause of Death*).** Scarpetta and Marino visit the campus's high energy physics lab. While there, Scarpetta wants to have lunch with her niece, Lucy, who is taking a class in nuclear design "for fun." Approximately sixty-eight miles from Richmond, UVA was founded in 1819 by Thomas Jefferson.

Patricia Cornwell: Proud Virginian

Patricia Cornwell's commitment to Virginia goes far beyond featuring it in her fiction. She's a fixture in the local community and a patron of many Richmond-area charities. In general, she seems to have tried to use her financial resources to make the world a better place. Nowhere is this more obvious than at the Virginia Institute of Forensic Science and Medicine, which Cornwell helped become a reality with a generous contribution. The following article illustrates her deep commitment to both her community and to the fictional world of crime fighting and forensic investigation she has created in her work.

> ## Don't Miss: Science Sleuth Theater, the Science Museum of Virginia
>
> As all Kay Scarpetta fans know, dead bodies speak volumes.
>
> Fortunately for the Cornwell fan fascinated by forensics but squeamish at heart, the Science Sleuth Theater is a fun and entertaining way to spend some time and solve the crime. Located on the second floor, to the right as you get off the elevator, the Science Sleuth Theater is located in the Bioscape section—rather appropriate, as the other exhibits flesh out the body of knowledge about human physiology on display. Unlike most theaters in which you are merely a passive observer, in this one you are an active participant.
>
> At its starting point, a television flashes a news bulletin about a crime committed in Richmond. By making your way around the various stations you then piece together the puzzle to solve the crime. You will definitely need the provided map/scorecard to negotiate this maze of stations and clues, but don't dally because there's a criminal loose in Richmond and it's up to you to solve the crime so he can do the time.

FORENSIC INSTITUTE A REALITY
By Michael Hardy, *Times-Dispatch* Staff Writer

It's a high-tech institute with a real-world purpose.

"We're going to take bad people off the streets and do it fast," best-selling crime novelist Patricia Cornwell declared yesterday at the formal announcement of the new Virginia Institute of Forensic Science and Medicine.

Thanks to Cornwell's gift of $1.5 million, the institute has become a reality, housed in the Virginia forensic science building near the Richmond Coliseum. The joint state-private venture is a first-of-its-kind center providing practical and academic training in sophisticated medical techniques to fight crime.

It will offer a one-year program leading to certification as a forensic scientist, and the institute's students will include biologists, toxicologists and pharmacologists.

The first class is made up of six students in DNA examining, two in toxicology and two Patricia Cornwell fellows in forensic pathology.

Dr. Marcella Fierro, the state's chief medical examiner and the inspiration for heroine Kay Scarpetta in Cornwell's blockbuster fiction, said the center is "a dream come true because Patricia Cornwell shared a vision with us."

"This institute will make something very good come out of the very bad things we see" in autopsies or investigations involving people killed or otherwise maimed," she said. "It will help justice and promote peace among all Virginians."

In an interview, Fierro, Cornwell's friend and mentor, said the gift will underwrite core functions of the institute. She expects other substantial funds to come from the state and federal governments and private sources.

Its influence will extend beyond Virginia, helping the war against violent predators by training medical experts, several participants said yesterday. The announcement was attended by about 150 political, medical and government leaders.

The institute's training experts are expected to reduce the staggering backlog of crime investigations in forensic laboratories, both in Virginia and across the nation, caused by a dearth of scientists and pathologists.

"It's a small beginning," said Dr. Paul B. Ferrara, the institute's other co-director, "but as it expands, it is going to be a major player in forensic science not only in Virginia but across the world."

U.S. Sen. Orrin G. Hatch (R-Utah), chairman of the Senate Judiciary Committee and a presidential hopeful, told the group, "This will help every state and the federal government" to catch criminals and bring them to justice.

Hatch, a longtime friend of Cornwell and a member of the center's board of directors, pointed out that hundreds of millions of dollars in federal funds will be available to states next year to finance medical and other research and training for criminal justice.

Gov. Jim Gilmore, who is expected to include a generous state grant for the center in his next two-year budget, also praised the project. It has been predicted that the state would at least match Cornwell's donation in the center's first year of operation.

"We're here today to inaugurate a partnership, one that reinforces Virginia's position as a national and innovative criminal justice leader," said Gilmore, a former chief prosecutor in Henrico County and state attorney general.

"We are extremely proud to be able to be in partnership with Patricia Cornwell to create it," he said.

The crime novelist has credited the Republican chief executive for helping move Ferrar's dream of a training institute to a reality.

In addition to Hatch, Cornwell, Fierro and Ferrar, Gilmore named four others to the institute's 11-member board of directors. He will fill out its membership later this summer. James Kouten is executive director of the institute.

The new board members, introduced by Gilmore yesterday, are Joseph Benedetti, director of the Virginia Department of Criminal Justice Services; Linda Fairstein, who heads the sex crimes protection unit in the Manhattan district attorney's office; Dr. Anne Peterson, acting commissioner of the Virginia Department of Health; and Larry Sabato, a much-quoted political commentator who heads the Center for Governmental Studies at the University of Virginia.

Resources for Visiting Virginia

The Insiders' Guide to Greater Richmond, published annually by Falcon Publishing; trade paperback. As stated in the preface: "If you're a newcomer or a visitor, we hope this book will help you discover our city with the ease and confidence of a longtime resident."

Currently in its seventh edition, this $14.95 trade paperback is 356 pages. Authoritatively written by Paula Neely and Ryan Croxton, it's the best single-source guidebook in print.

Contents include: Richmond history, getting around Richmond, the Civil War, neighborhoods, government, school and child care, colleges and universities, shopping, restaurants, nightlife, accommodations, campgrounds, golf, sports, medical care, hospitals, worship, real estate, commercial real estate, retirement, historical preservation, monuments, the arts, attractions and other fun things to do, annual events, kid stuff, daytrips, media, service directory, index of advertisers, a general index, and a directory for the maps.

An excellent, portable edition that will surely be well-thumbed if you want to visit the city, this is far and away the best book of its kind.

Patricia Cornwell: A Reader's Checklist and Reference Guide ($4.95, trade paperback, 47 pages). This is part of the CheckerBee Publishing series. This slender volume lives up to its namesake—it is a checklist, but nothing more. This book opens with a brief biography, but its bulk consists of a listing of each book and a synopsis, with a fill-in-the-blank facing page for you to record whatever notes you wish after reading the book.

Considering its cost and limited usefulness, I don't recommend this except for completists.

ADC Metro Richmond (published annually by ADC The Map People®); a book map, 10 × 14 inches, in full color; extensively indexed, 76 pages. The fifteenth edition, published in 2000, is $11.95 and worth every penny. You *cannot* adequately navigate Richmond without this resource!

If you want to get around Richmond, you'll need either a good street map or, better yet, this exhaustive book-map.

A first-rate publication, this oversized book provides an overview of the area, then detailed segments from the overview, with a very detailed street index for easy reference.

ADC also has a very good fold-out map (39" × 27") of the city, with a street index. This is pocket-size, since it folds down to 4 × 9 inches. At $3.50, it's a bargain.

Greater Hampton Roads (ADC, spiral-bound, oversized paperback; first edition; $36.95; 300 pages).

As a longtime resident of this area, let me clear up some points regarding geography.

First, out-of-towners usually call this whole area "Tidewater." Locals don't term it such, since to us "Tidewater" means points northeast, the area encompassed by the Chesapeake Bay.

The Greater Hampton Roads area includes ten cities and five counties (all detailed in this book-map).

North of the York River: Middlesex County, Gloucester County, and Matthews County; north of the James River but south of the York River, James City County, Williamsburg, York County, Newport News, Poquoson, and Hampton; and south of the James River, Surrey County, Smithfield, Isle of Wight County, Southhampton County, Franklin, Suffolk, Portsmouth, Norfolk, Chesapeake, Virginia Beach, Gates County (North Carolina), Camden County (North Carolina), and Currituck County (North Carolina).

When we talk about "Southside," we're referring (mostly) to Norfolk, Virginia Beach, Portsmouth, Suffolk, and Chesapeake.

When we talk about the "Peninsula," we're referring (mostly) to Hampton, Newport News, Poquoson, and the surrounding area.

As you can well imagine, it takes three hundred pages to adequately chronicle every major and minor road in the Greater Hampton Roads area. Fortunately, the map is current, fully indexed, and in full color for easy viewing.

Since Cornwell writes frequently about the Greater Hampton Roads, this book map is an excellent companion (as is its Richmond counterpart) for anyone wanting to get a "feel" for Cornwell country, which to my mind ranges from Richmond to the Greater Hampton Roads.

Richmond (Rand McNally). There are two laminated maps of Richmond; McNally's is larger, and therefore less portable, but the print is larger and more legible. Measuring 9 × 12.5 inches when folded, it measures eight letter-sized panels when unfolded— 24.5 × 36 inches.

I like laminated maps because they can be marked upon with grease pencils and nonpermanent marking pens. This makes it easy to mark where you want to go and navigate, which is much more difficult with a nonlaminated map.

Appendix C: A Guide to Collecting Patricia Cornwell

A Price Guide to Patricia Cornwell's Books

In the days before the Internet, used/rare book dealers were the principal source for out-of-print books. Today, of course, the picture has dramatically changed: Online auction sites like ebay.com and amazon.com cut out the middleman, the book dealer, which might appear to be advantageous to the buyer, but *caveat emptor!* Forgeries are not uncommon and in descriptions of books, editions and condition are not uniform.

Do you pay more if you are buying from an established used/rare book dealer? Sometimes. But you can usually buy with confidence, knowing that the dealer will know the specifics of the various editions, with an expertise that a part-time bookseller may lack.

For the novice collector looking to acquire Cornwell's books, the following guidelines will prove helpful. As to the valuations, I researched them online and, because of the fluidity of the marketplace, have indicated a price range in lieu of a fixed price.

In Thomas Lee's *20th Century First Edition Fiction: A Price and Identification Guide* (Book Emporium Press, Rockville, Maryland), he lists the most common defects that devalue a book's worth.

Regarding the dust jacket: This is the most fragile part of a book, and its absence greatly devalues a book's worth. Intended principally as an advertising vehicle for the publisher, the dust jacket is usually printed on heavy stock, since it is designed to take some wear and tear from book browsers in stores; even still, the jacket is fragile and is easily creased, chipped, or torn.

1. **Clipped price.** This is sometimes the fate of a book that is given as a gift; the giver doesn't want the recipient to

know the amount of the gift, and so clips the price, usually printed on the corner.

As a book collector, you should make it clear that if anyone gives you a book, he or she should not clip the price or write a personal inscription in the book. (Suggest that the person write such a note on a gift card from Hallmark instead.)

The only time a clipped price is justified is when the publisher intentionally clips it, as was done with the first edition, second state, of Stephen King's *Salem's Lot*.

Be sure to inspect both flaps of the jacket to ensure the dust jacket is intact.

2. **Tears.** As I've said before, a dust jacket is printed on heavy stock, but it's not printed on Tyvek, which is a paper stock so durable that it can't be torn—scissors must be used! Until the day comes when printers use Tyvek or its equivalent, we must be careful in handling jackets because they are very easily torn.

Visually inspect the edges of the jacket to ensure there are no tears whatsoever.

3. **Creasing.** A more common affliction, an unintentional fold in the paper, a crease, cannot be removed! Usually this afflicts a corner, but with older books, this problem is more pronounced, especially if a jacket is mailed separately from the book. (The only way to safely mail a dust jacket is to use a sturdy, reinforced mailing tube; shipping a flat sheet of paper measuring 10 × 22 inches is problematic, regardless of carrier.)

It's best to keep the jacket on the book and, if possible, I recommend you install a Gaylord cover or a Brodart cover that will protect the jacket itself.

4. Chipping. This is more of a problem with older books; small chips, usually on the edges, can soon become big chips or tears. Again, the best insurance against this kind of ongoing deterioration is installing a protective acetate dust jacket cover (Gaylord or Brodart).

5. Trimmed. For whatever reasons, you will actually find dust jackets that have been trimmed! The owner, at some point, has decided for whatever reasons that he thinks the trim size is too large, and so he uses a pair of scissors and merrily starts cutting away!

Because dust jackets are designed to protect the book, they are printed in a size that envelopes the book itself, so there's no rational reason for trimming the jacket.

6. Tape. Usually this is the first aid for a tear in the jacket; but because tape will yellow in time, the cure is worse than the problem in the long term. I'm sure archivists and restorers use special tape that is nonacidic, but even then, it's only done to repair a book.

If there's a tear in the book, it's best to leave it is as, rather than try to fix it with adhesive tape.

7. Adhesive price sticker affixed. This is usually a sin of commission by the bookstore—a sin that makes no sense, since all books have prices clearly printed on the dust jacket or book cover.

Unfortunately, to combat theft, the stickers are devilishly designed to be nonremovable or time-consuming in removal—sufficiently daunting so that a book thief wouldn't have enough time to remove it without being observed.

While I sympathize with retail stores concerned about shrinkage, I believe strongly that no books should be thus marred! (Retailers apparently feel this is their right; car dealers love to put decals on a new car or, worse, drill holes to install a plastic plate emblazoned with their name and address as a form of advertising!)

Even when the sticker is removed, it leaves a sticky residue that is difficult to remove without damaging the book.

The worst offender is Rizzoli Bookstore, an upscale chain that charges full retail, so there's no point in putting on a price sticker!

8. **Plastic antitheft device installed.** Make no mistake— this is the devil's work, my friends. A small piece of plastic (usually a quarter inch by an inch) is *permanently affixed* to the jacket with Superglue! The book must then be demagnetized at the checkout register, neutralizing the chip; otherwise, the in-store sensors, positioned near the store's entrance doors, will detect it and set off a store-wide alarm that will cause "swarming." (In an episode of the television show *Seinfeld,* George Costanza attempts to steal a book, and Jerry Seinfeld, who is properly appalled, takes matters into his own hands by yelling "Swarm! swarm!" and store security descend on the hapless Costanza, who is shocked that his friend Jerry would rat him out. Hey, Jerry, way to go!)

Obviously, you should check the dust jacket on the back side to ensure a chip is not installed, which is where these fiendish devices can be found.

9. **Written markings.** This is more of a problem with used books, for two reasons:

First, for whatever reasons, there is a special kind of book owner who feels compelled to write his name in his copy of a book, usually in ink! Needless to say, the only person who should sign the book is the author. All others need not apply.

Second, used books may bear a price on the endpaper, written in pencil. The presumption is that you can then erase that price, which is true if the marking is done with a soft lead pencil and a clean, nonabrasive eraser is used to remove the entry. (These erasers are not the ones found on the end of a pencil, which are hard rubber; if dirty, the hard rubber erasers will simply smear whatever residue is on its tip onto the book—so inspect the eraser tip first! Buy, instead, a soft gum eraser, the kind Pentel sells under the name "Clic Eraser.")

10. **Stamped markings.** This is usually the owner's name stamped on the front inside cover. Enough said.

11. **Adhesive labels.** This usually takes the form of book-plates or, less often, a bookseller who puts his address in the book itself. (I was at a convention and bought from a specialty dealer a first edition of Joe Haldeman's *The Forever War,* to which the dealer affixed a metallic label that proudly proclaimed his name, store address, and telephone number. When it came time to sell it, however, this now valuable book sold for less because the dealer had put his unmistakable stamp on every book he sold. (Alas, tar and feathering has fallen out of practice.)

Unfortunately, these cannot be removed without permanent damage.

12. **Excessive wear.** This is usually more of a problem with used books, but of late, it's a problem with new books as well: If you order a book without inspecting it first, which is obviously the case if it is bought from a mail-order dealer or from an Internet dealer, the book may be shopworn because it has encountered "churn" in a retail store first.

Books are returnable, which means that the copy you buy isn't necessarily direct from the publisher to you. Your copy may have sat in a retail store, where it's been pawed over and put back on the shelf, then sent back to the store's warehouse, and then reshipped to you as if it were a brand-new copy.

Your best insurance is to not buy from on-line booksellers like amazon.com or bn.com (barnesandnoble.com), and rely instead on a specialty bookseller that buys direct and visually inspects books before shipping. (I know it's cheaper to buy from amazon.com, but they don't cater to collectors, unlike specialty booksellers.)

Regarding the book itself:

1. **Water staining.** This is probably the single most damaging thing that can afflict a book. Because books absorb moisture like sponges, water stains will cause permanent damage.

   The best way to ensure this does not happen is to store the book in a dry, low-humidity environment.

   I've had my basement flooded twice, with disastrous results. Read and heed.

2. **Embossing.** The same fool who thinks that it makes sense to write his name in a book thinks it's even cooler to physically mutilate the book by using a hand embosser, a seal, usually with the legend "This book is from the library of——." The fool then literally embosses a page from the book, which causes permanent damage.

   Not surprisingly, this same fool is the one who usually demands top dollar for his book when he's ready to sell, usually on the grounds that it's "rare." (As if condition has nothing to do with pricing! Talk to any specialty bookseller, who will have numerous stories of valuable books that have been defaced, embossed, and otherwise damaged by an owner who is surprised when his copy is devalued for resale purposes. You reap what you sow.)

3. **Creased pages.** Bookmarkers were invented for a reason, but there are people who simply prefer to turn down a corner of a book to mark its place. Go figure.

   Sometimes the creasing occurs in the binding process, but more often, this is owner-inflicted.

4. **Torn or ripped pages.** This is usually an accidental occurrence, but it obviously affects the condition of the book. Booksellers (and buyers) prefer books "as new" or, if that's not possible, in "good" condition.

5. **Removed pages.** Again, this is usually accidental, but it's a problem with improperly bound books.

   More of a problem with magazines, removed pages are nonetheless something that show up as a defect with improperly bound books.

6. **Bumped corners.** There's a law of nature that if a book is dropped, it will fall and hit the ground on one of its corners, irreparably damaging the book.

   I once bought a shrink-wrapped copy of an art book at Barnes and Noble, and had to return it, because I neglected to see that one corner was visibly bumped— so hard, in fact, that *all* the pages in the book were affected!

7. **Remainder marks.** These are physical markings that the publisher has made on the top or bottom edge of a book to indicate it was sold to a retailer as an overstock.

   Because books are returnable, the publisher must protect himself from someone buying overstock, then returning them for full credit (or cash); thus, the books are marked on one edge: an indelible Magic Marker, spray painting, or a stamped logo of the publishing house itself are the most common methods.

All of these, unfortunately, permanently deface the book.

8. **Marked pages.** This is rare, but it does happen. I bought a copy of a book in which the previous owner obviously disagreed, and at length, with what the author wrote because the owner had written in the margins his responses, engaging in a one-way discourse with the author, so to speak.

Obviously, before buying any book, a quick scan of the pages will detect this abominable practice. (Hell hath no fury like an unpublished writer who feels compelled to write in someone else's book instead of writing his own.)

9. **Discoloration of pages.** Booksellers make a distinction here—if due only to the inevitable aging of acid-based paper stock, then it is usually not a major defect; however, if it was inadvertent, as in the case of an acidic piece of paper laid in that has browned the book itself, then it is a major defect. (Books printed on acid-free stock usually don't suffer from this affliction, but older books, printed in the days when permanence was not a concern, may inevitably have pages that brown with age—foxing, as it's called in the book trade.)

10. **Spine defects.** If a book is improperly stored, its spine may crack, slant, or become loose. Books are designed to be stored upright and be easily removed. (Obviously, shelved books that are literally wedged in compress the spine; books that are laid as bridges in loose stacks will bend; and books that are laid at a slant will also warp.)

Books are sturdy but not indestructible! (Except, perhaps, Madonna's metal-covered *Sex* or the Whitney
Museum's *My Pretty Pony.*)

The books listed below are alphabetical and assumed to be first
editions in at least good condition. Prices were determined by
researching current offerings on the Internet for which I discarded
the lowest and highest prices—thereby eliminating the under-
priced and overpriced books—and listed the price range. Therefore, the prices should be considered as a general guide. For actual
book value, please contact a reputable secondhand book dealer
(e.g., The Mysterious Bookshop).

I have limited the selection of Cornwell's books to ARCs
(advance reading copies), first editions published in the United
States, and first editions published in the UK. I have not covered
the large print editions or the audio/CD editions.

The first list includes Cornwell's novels; the second list includes
all other books.

The ARCs are in trade paperback; all other books are in trade
hardback with dust jackets.

Where applicable, I've made pertinent notes on the collectibility
of the book in question.

1. ***All That Remains***
   a. Advance reading copy, signed, $55.
   b. First edition, signed, $50–95.
   c. First edition, signed on a signature card, laid in, $27.
   d. First edition, signed on the author's bookplate, $55.
   e. First edition, inscribed, $75.
   f. First edition, UK, signed, $125–175.

g. First edition, with owner's inscription, $40. (*Note:* As you can see, having the owner put his name in the book *devalues* its worth.)

2. *Black Notice*

a. First edition, signed, $42.50–45.

b. First edition, UK, signed, $93.75.

c. Limited edition of 200 copies, with slipcase (no dust jacket issued by publisher), $149.

3. *The Body Farm*

a. Advance reading copy, signed, $25–65.

b. First edition, $30–45.

c. First edition, signed, $45–65.

d. First edition, UK, signed, $65.

4. *Body of Evidence*

a. First edition, signed, $110.

b. First edition, inscribed, $95.

c. First edition, signed by owner, $65.

5. *Cause of Death*

a. First edition, signed, $50–60.

b. Limited edition, 185 copies, with slipcase, $135–150.

6. *Cruel and Unusual*

a. Advance reading copy, $45.

b. First edition, $35.

c. First edition, signed, $65–90.

7. *From Potter's Field*

a. First edition, $23.

b. First edition, signed, $50–65.

c. First edition, UK, $50.

8. *Hornet's Nest*

   a. First edition, signed, $45–60.

9. *Isle of Dogs*

   a. First edition, signed, $45–60.

10. *The Last Precinct*

   a. First edition. *Note:* Currently in print and available at retail, $26.95.

   b. First edition, signed, $40.

   c. Limited edition, 175 copies, with slipcase, $175–200.

11. *Point of Origin*

   a. First edition, signed, $40–45.

   b. Limited edition, 500 copies, with slipcase, $150–185.

12. *Postmortem: A Kay Scarpetta Mystery* (*Note:* This is her first published novel, her first Scarpetta book, and the cornerstone of any serious Cornwell collection.)

   a. First edition, $925.

   b. First edition, signed, $950.

13. *Southern Cross*

   a. First edition, signed, $50–95.

14. *Unnatural Exposure*

   a. First edition, signed, $40–55.

   b. Limited edition, 175 copies, with slipcase, $175–200.

Cornwell's "Collector's Corner" from Her Official Web Site

On Cornwell's official Web site, in a section called "Collector's Corner," she offers a line of tie-in products, including apparel, books, and posters—all for a good cause: *All* the money goes to charity. Keep in mind that all sales are final, however. (*Note:* Because her Web site is currently under construction, I can't predict what, if any, merchandise will be for sale when it goes back up, but this is what's been available in the past and what a savvy collector might find by poking around in other marketplace sources or talking to other collectors.)

1. *T-shirts:* **$15 each**

   a. The Cornwell T-shirt, with her crest in color.

   b. *The Last Precinct* T-shirt.

   c. *Black Notice* T-shirt.

   d. *Southern Cross* T-shirt.

   e. The Cornwell Signature 2000 T-shirt.

2. *Other shirts*

   a. Polo shirt, with crest, $35.

   b. Denim shirt, with crest, $45.

3. *"Baseball" caps:* **$15 each**

   a. Cornwell cap, with crest.

   b. A high-profile cap, with crest.

   c. *The Last Precinct* cap.

   d. *Southern Cross* cap.

4. *Books*

   a. *Life's Little Fable,* $11.99, signed by Cornwell.

   b. *Ruth, a Portrait* (the UK edition, published by Hodder & Stoughton), $30.

5. *Miscellaneous*

   a. "The Patricia Cornwell Poster 2000." Color poster of Cornwell in lab gear at the Richmond morgue; 16 × 23.5 inches, with her facsimile signature, $10.

      (*Note:* Two other posters are in print but not available from Cornwell's office: sixteen hundred copies of a color poster promoting the Virginia Literary Foundation were distributed free of charge to libraries statewide; the poster shows Cornwell holding a copy of Helprin's *A Soldier of the Great War.* Also, the Richmond Red Cross sells a Scarpetta map of Richmond, usually at her local book signings; the poster is also available via mail from the Virginia Center for the Book.)

As a collector and fan, a great way to meet your favorite author and get a book or a memento signed with a personal touch is to attend one of Patricia Cornwell's promotional book signings. Check her Web site or talk to your local bookseller to find out when she'll be appearing near you.

The Science of a Cornwell Book Signing

The black helicopter with its distinctive red, yellow, and lime green markings approached the Science Museum of Virginia and immediately attracted the attention of hundreds of Cornwell fans, who shielded their eyes to look up at Cornwell's private helicopter, a Bell JetRanger, circling, and then descending slowly to land on the grounds.

Orange cones were placed around the chopper and Cornwell disembarked, heading inside, surrounded by Richmond police and her entourage.

The line of Cornwell fans stretched out to Broad Street, which faces the museum itself. Most of them were casually dressed on what turned out to be an unseasonably warm late October afternoon—a stark contrast to Cornwell's entourage, fashionably dressed in what appeared to be custom-made clothing in black from head to toe. (Predictably, most of them could be seen hovering near and around Cornwell, similarly garbed, seated at a table where stacks of *The Last Precinct* commanded her attention.)

Two hours were allotted for the signing, which appeared to be just enough time for her to greet each person individually, sign her name with a black Sharpie pen, and then recompose herself for the next brief encounter.

As with her previous hometown signings, Cornwell coordinated with the Red Cross to assist in a blood drive: Donate a pint and you go to the head of the line—a real inducement, since the line was long.

Taking advantage of an estimated two thousand people who came out to celebrate the museum's grand reopening—a $21.5 million renovation—the carnival-like atmosphere included attractions both in and outside the museum.

On the front lawn, various rides and attractions commanded the attention of children. For Cornwell fans, the Virginia Center for the Book offered for $10 a color poster showing "Scarpetta's Richmond," and from Cornwell Enterprises, two tables were set up near the front entrance to the museum, offering copies of Cornwell's biography of Ruth Bell Graham, *Children's Fable,* a color poster of Scarpetta in the morgue with facsimile signature, and two new pieces of apparel: *The Last Precinct* cap and *The Last Precinct* T-shirt.

And in case you got hungry or thirsty, a food vendor had set up near the entrance, serving cold sub sandwiches, canned soft drinks, bottled water, and various juices at modest prices.

The colorful balloons, banners, and decorations outside the museum could also be seen inside as well. Fortunately, despite the crushing crowds, museum volunteers in distinctive uniforms made it easy to navigate the three levels of exhibits, including a new exhibit in the Bioscape section, "Science Sleuth Theater," a forensics exhibit funded by Cornwell, who gave it a trial run the day before during its inauguration, accompanied by Dr. Marcella Fierro and Roxane Gilmore, the Virginia governor's wife.

Predictably, the demand for free tickets to attend a lecture/Q&A sponsored by the Forensics Institute, initially funded by Cornwell, was so great that by early morning, all had been given out.

For a Cornwell fan, though, it was enough to see the author arrive in grand style in her own helicopter, get two books signed, share a few private moments with her, and then tour the museum itself.

A Book Signing in Boston
by Kevin Quigley

To promote *The Last Precinct,* Cornwell gave two public talks—one in Boston and one in San Francisco. In other cities particularly nearer to home, she supported them with book signings.

Kevin Quigley, an aspiring novelist, put on his reporter's hat and headed out to the First Chapel Church in Cambridge, Massachusetts, where Cornwell's only New England appearance on her book tour predictably drew a large crowd.

Patricia Cornwell brushes past me in the hallway of the First Chapel Church in Cambridge, Massachusetts. A striking, diminutive woman, she seems all business. A horde of publicity people escort her into a quiet place where she can flat-sign copies of her latest novel, *The Last Precinct.* "I won't have time to do it afterwards," she says, as she's swept into the small back room.

One glance at the church proper, and you know her prediction is correct: There's quite a crowd packed into the pews, eager fans clutching copies of *The Last Precinct* and other Cornwell novels. After the discussion period, these folks will line up for a chance to get their Kay Scarpettas signed—and get a close-up look at their favorite author.

Ms. Cornwell is ushered to the podium at the front of the church in a fanfare of applause and praise. From where I am sitting— eight pews back, on the right—she seems like a well-dressed preacher prepared to give a sermon. To her reverent cadre of Bay State fans, that's exactly what they'll hear: Before the scheduled question-and-answer portion of the night, Ms. Cornwell has decided to tell us some stories. Nothing so grand, maybe, as that of Noah and his Ark, or of Adam and Eve, or of the creation of the world—tales most suited to this venue. No, Patricia Corn- well doesn't need such fire and brimstone to keep these revelers enrapt. All she needs to do to entertain this crowd is talk about the world of crime . . . and the slightly more dangerous world of writ- ing fiction.

At once, she engages the crowd with her humor—something you may not expect from such a stern-looking woman. Her slight southern drawl rolls over the crowd in waves—once she gets a rhythm, she can't seem to stop. In talking about her last Kay Scar- petta novel, *Black Notice,* Cornwell reveals that she expected it to be the last in that series, a realization that "put [her] in a bad mood." The journey to *The Last Precinct,* then, was long and ardu- ous. Cornwell laments that Kay Scarpetta simply refused to fit into anything new, that she was stubborn and wanted to do things her way. Throughout the night, Cornwell will discuss her character as if she were a real person, something her readers undoubtedly love. For the fans, Kay Scarpetta has become real. Speaking about her character as if she were a living, breathing human being, Patricia Cornwell becomes not only the creator, but also a fan. Instead of speaking down to her readers and listeners, she speaks right to them—and her audience loves her for it.

The talk segues neatly into the question-and-answer portion of the night. One spectator asks if Kay Scarpetta will ever be happy. Cornwell grins, answering that "happiness would be boring to read about." Then she hints that an upcoming novel will bring a big surprise for Kay Scarpetta. "You'll be in for a jolt," she says, with a glint in her eye, and the people around me nearly froth in anticipation.

Another reader asks if Cornwell plans on continuing the *Hornet's Nest* series, and even before the question is out, the author is nodding. A third book—titled *Isle of Dogs*—will be in stores within the next year. In fact, the setting for the novel—Jamestown, Virginia—was to be the locale of the next Kay Scarpetta book, but it was one of the scenarios in which Scarpetta refused to fit. Instead of discarding all the research that went into the new book, Cornwell simply moved Kay Scarpetta out and moved the *Hornet's Nest* cast in. The end result is a book where "I'm not only telling the story, I'm telling the history of America." Don't shake your heads in James Michener–inspired boredom yet: Cornwell promises that *Isle of Dogs* will be as entertaining as the rest of her novels.

Over the next hour, Cornwell discusses her writing history (her teachers always read her short stories aloud in class), her methods of research ("If you really want to learn something, make yourself useful"), and her writing process (she doesn't write every day, preferring to spend quite a lot of her time researching, just to get the facts right). "Writing is not a job," she tells the audience, "it's a relationship." Therefore, she does not allot herself an hour or two a day to write, she simply does it when the spirit moves her. The idea of setting time limits appalls her. "I work for the book; it doesn't work for me."

In response to an audience question, Cornwell talks about her beginnings as a police reporter and shares some rather grisly tales of her stint in an autopsy room. Autopsies, she tells us, are "not about gore—they're about making the dead speak." This credo is applied to her novels, as well; unraveling the mystery of an untimely death. But, interestingly, Cornwell doesn't like to call her books mysteries. "Calling it a mystery," she says, comparing it to the old Agatha Christie novels, "trivializes death." Discussing these past cases seems to put a tremble into Cornwell's voice: It is clear that the type of violent crime she writes about outrages her. This is the same outrage that fuels Kay Scarpetta, and it is this outrage that brings Patricia Cornwell's novels of crime down to the human level.

Soon the question-and-answer period is over, and people begin to line up at the signing table, holding out copies of *The Last Precinct* for Patricia Cornwell to sign. I took in the sheer size of the line and it brought back one thing Ms. Cornwell had said earlier that evening: When discussing her frustration at not being able to write the new Scarpetta, Cornwell says at one point, she had to take a deep breath and say, "I refuse to let the success of what I've accomplished take away from the joy of it." Judging by this line of readers, and the thunderous applause that closed her final answer, the joy of Patricia Cornwell seems to want to stick.

INDEX